NEW
BIBLE ATLAS

Contributing editors:

J.J.Bimson, BA., PH.D., Librarian and Lecturer in
Old Testament and Hebrew at Trinity College, Bristol.

J.P. Kane, Ph.D., Dip.Ed., Lecturer in Hellenistic
Greek in the University of Manchester.

Consulting editors:

J.H. Paterson, M.A., formerly Emeritus Professor of
Geography in the University of Leicester.

D.J.Wiseman, O.B.E., M.A., D.Lit., F.B.A., F.K.C., F.S.A,
Emeritus Professor of Assyriology in the University of London.

Organizing editor:

D.R.W. Wood, M.A., formerly Managing Editor, Inter-Varsity Press.

INTER-VARSITY PRESS, LEICESTER, ENGLAND

INTERVARSITY PRESS, DOWNERS GROVE, ILLINOIS

INTER-VARSITY PRESS
38 De Montford Street, Leicester LE1 7GP, England
E-mail: ivp@uccf.org.uk
Website: www.ivpbooks.com

Published and sold in the USA and Canada by
INTERVARSITY PRESS, USA
5206 Main Street, PO Box 1400, Downers Grove, Illinois 60515, USA.

First published 1985
Reprinted 1986, 1990, 1992, 1996, 1997, 1999, 2003, 2005

UK   IVP ISBN 0-85110-953-5
USA ISBN 0-8308-1443-4

British Library Cataloguing in Publication Data

A catalogue record for this book is
available from the British Library

US Library of Congress Catalog Card Number 84-52722

Designed and typeset in 10pt Palatino by
Swanston Publishing Limited, Derby, England

Printed and bound in Great Britain by CPI Bath

*InterVarsity Press, U.S.A., is the book publishing division of the InterVarsity Christian
Fellowship, a student movement active on campus at hundreds of universities, colleges and
schools of nursing in the United States of America, and a member movement of the
International Fellowship of Evangelical Students. For information about local and regional
activities, write Public Relations Dept., InterVarsity Christian Fellowship,
6400 Schroeder Rd., P.O. Box 7895, Madison, WI 53707-7895.*

*Inter-Varsity Press is the publishing division of the Universities and Colleges Christian
Fellowship (formerly the Inter-Varsity Fellowship), a student movement linking Christian
Unions in Universities and colleges throughout Great Britain and a member movement of
the International Fellowship of Evangelical Students. For information about local and
national activities write to UCCF, 38 De Montfort Street, Leicester LE1 7GP.
E-mail us at e-mail@uccf.org.uk, or visit the UCCF website at www.uccf.org.uk*

Contents

Abbreviations

BIBLICAL BOOKS

Books of the Old Testament:

Gn.	Genesis	Song	Song of Solomon
Ex.	Exodus	Is.	Isaiah
Lv.	Leviticus	Je.	Jeremiah
Nu.	Numbers	La.	Lamentations
Dt.	Deuteronomy	Ezk.	Ezekiel
Jos.	Joshua	Dn.	Daniel
Jdg.	Judges	Ho.	Hosea
Ru.	Ruth	Joel	Joel
1, 2 Sa.	1 & 2 Samuel	Am.	Amos
1, 2 Ki.	1 & 2 Kings	Ob.	Obadiah
1, 2 Ch.	1 & 2 Chronicles	Jon.	Jonah
Ezr.	Ezra	Mi.	Micah
Ne.	Nehemiah	Na.	Nahum
Est.	Esther	Hab.	Habakkuk
Jb.	Job	Zp.	Zephaniah
Ps.(Pss.)	Psalms	Hg.	Haggai
Pr.	Proverbs	Zc.	Zechariah
Ec.	Ecclesiastes	Mal.	Malachi

Books of the Apocrypha featured in the Atlas
1, 2 Macc. 1 & 2 Maccabees

Books of the New Testament

Mt.	Matthew	1, 2 Thes.	1 & 2 Thessalonians
Mk.	Mark		
Lk.	Luke	1, 2 Tim.	1 & 2 Timothy
Jn.	John	Tit.	Titus
Acts	Acts	Phm.	Philemon
Rom.	Romans	Heb.	Hebrews
1, 2 Cor.	1 & 2 Corinthians	Jas.	James
Gal.	Galatians	1, 2 Pet.	1 & 2 Peter
Eph.	Ephesians	1, 2, 3 Jn.	1, 2 & 3 John
Phil.	Philippians	Jude	Jude
Col.	Colossians	Rev.	Revelation

This list of Old and New Testament abbreviations is given
for completeness, but not all the Bible books are
mentioned in the Atlas.

GENERAL ABBREVIATIONS
In addition to the commonly understood abbreviations
such as *i.e.*, *e.g.*, BC and AD the following are used
throughtout:

ACA	Sir Moses Finley, *Atlas of Classical Archaeology*, 1977
Ant.	Josephus, *Antiquities of the Jews*
AV	Authorized Version of the Bible (King James' Version)
C	Centigrade
c.	*circa* (Lat.), about, approximately
cf.	*confer* (Lat.), compare
ch(s)	chapter(s)
cm	centimetre(s)
E	East, eastern
F	Fahrenheit
f.(ff.)	and the following
ft	foot, feet

Gk.	Greek
Heb.	Hebrew
in(s)	inches
Jos.	Josephus
Kh.	Khirbet (in place-names indicating ruin mound)
km(s)	kilometre(s)
L.	lake
Lat.	Latin
m	metre(s)
MS(S)	manuscript(s)
Mt	mount, mountain
N	North, northern
NEB	New English Bible
NIV	New International Version of the Bible
NT	New Testament
OT	Old Testament
pap. Zen.	Zeno papyri
passim	(Lat.) appears frequently
pl.	plate
R.	river
RSV	Revised Standard Version of the Bible
S	South, southern
V.	valley
W	West, western
W.	wadi (river valley, seasonally dry)
War	Josephus, *Jewish Wars*

TRANSLITERATION
The following systems have been adopted:

Hebrew

א	= '	ד	= d	י	= y	ס	= s	ר	= r
ב	= b	ה	= h	כ	= k	ע	= '	שׂ	= ś
ב	= b	ו	= w	ך	= k	פ	= p	שׁ	= š
ג	= g	ז	= z	ל	= l	פ	= p̄	ת	= t
ג	= ḡ	ח	= ḥ	מ	= m	צ	= ṣ	ת	= ṯ
ד	= d	ט	= ṭ	נ	= n	ק	= q		

Long Vowels		Short Vowels		Very Short Vowels	
(ה)ָ = â	ָ = ā	ַ = a	ֳ = °
ֵ = ê	ֶ = ē	ֶ = e	ֳ = °
ִ = î	ִ = i	ֲ = ° (if vocal)
וֹ = ô	ֹ = ō	ָ = o	ֳ = °
וּ = û	ֻ = u		

Greek

α	= a	ι	= i	ρ	= r	ῥ	= rh
β	= b	κ	= k	σ, ς	= s	'	= h
γ	= g	λ	= l	τ	= t	γξ	= nx
δ	= d	μ	= m	υ	= y	γγ	= ng
ε	= e	ν	= n	φ	= ph	αυ	= au
ζ	= z	ξ	= x	χ	= ch	ευ	= eu
η	= ē	ο	= o	ψ	= ps	ου	= ou
θ	= th	π	= p	ω	= ō	υι	= yi

Arabic

ا	= '	خ	= ḫ	ش	= š	غ	= ġ	ن	= n
ب	= b	د	= d	ص	= ṣ	ف	= f	ه	= h
ت	= t	ذ	= ḏ	ض	= ḍ	ق	= k	و	= w
ث	= t	ر	= r	ط	= ṭ	ك	= k	ي	= y
ج	= ǧ	ز	= z	ظ	= z	ل	= l	ة	= t
ح	= ḥ	س	= s	ع	= '	م	= m		

Preface

The Bible is unique in setting out its message from God to mankind in a definite geographical and historical setting. It therefore includes very many references to lands and peoples, places and features, ranging from Persia in the east to Rome and Spain in the west; from Ethiopia and Egypt in the south to the parts of Asia Minor (ancient Anatolia, modern Turkey), where early Christian churches flourished, in the north. At the centre is the region of Syro-Palestine, the Holy Land, and its neighbouring countries where the Bible story unfolded. The reader who wants to understand these many references fully will need to use a biblical atlas.

This Atlas aims to provide the Bible reader, student and teacher with maps and plans, photographs and text, arranged for the most part chronologically. The opening section on the Holy Land includes a contour map, geological and climatic information and a satellite photograph showing the sea-level contour. This thorough approach, using modern methods of representation, serves to remind us that the events recorded in the Bible occurred in real places, with real rocks underfoot and real rain falling.

This faithfulness to reality is accentuated by the inclusion of a selection of colour photographs, but we are conscious that these have their own limitations. They are each confined to a single scene. They lack the range and breadth of maps and cannot, on their own, represent the essence of a region. We have been at pains therefore to make this an atlas – a book of maps – in the full sense, believing that the intelligent reader will want more than a set of tourist views of the Palestine scenery.

Brief summaries of biblical history are given to help those who do not have ready access to more detailed discussion of the history of the peoples of this area, whose life, work and faith have for long influenced western civilization.

It has become customary in recent popular Bible atlases to include illustrations drawn from archaeology. This emphasis has not been neglected in the *New Bible Atlas*, but to do justice to the numerous discoveries made in many lands and countries would require detailed explanation and illustrations beyond the scope of this book. For these the reader is referred to such works as *The Illustrated Bible Dictionary* (three volumes, IVP, 1980) with its wealth of coloured photographs, or the text edition, *New Bible Dictionary*, second edition (IVP, 1982). This Atlas springs from the research first undertaken for those books, though much of the content is totally new.

The index will help to locate Bible place-names and their modern equivalents.

We acknowledge gratefully the work undertaken by the Contributing Editors, Dr John Bimson of Trinity College, Bristol and Dr John Kane of the University of Manchester, and not least by Derek Wood and the staff of the Inter-Varsity Press and the designers, Swanston Graphics Limited of Derby.

May this Atlas help many in their understanding of God's Word as they live in a world often far different from that of those who first received it.

J.H.P.
D.J.W.

How to use this Atlas

Arrangement
The division of the Atlas into six parts follows a logical sequence.

Part One is, broadly speaking, geographical. After a general introduction map to the Bible lands (pages 6–7) the focus is on the Holy Land, describing the nature of the terrain, climate and vegetation.

Parts Two and Three are arranged historically, based on the biblical record from the Old and New Testaments respectively, and are chiefly concerned with the Holy Land.

Part Four features the major empires and peoples which play a part on the biblical scene.

Part Five concerns the historical development and crucial significance of Jerusalem, the Holy City, and Part Six provides a brief view of the Holy Land as it is today.

Place-names
Names of regions, provinces, kingdoms, *etc.*, are printed in large roman capitals, *e.g.* BABYLONIA

Tribes and ethnic groups: usually large italic capitals, *e.g. AMORITES*

Towns and villages: lower case roman, *e.g.* Jerusalem

Geographical features such as mountains, rivers, lakes, seas, *etc.*: lower case italic, *e.g. Great Sea*

Modern place-names: as above but in brackets, *e.g.* (*Mediterranean Sea*)

Absolute consistency has not been possible but, in general, where the modern name is clearly derived from the ancient (*e.g.* Creta = Crete, Italia = Italy) or where it would be pedantic to place modern names in brackets (*e.g.* Egypt, Jerusalem) brackets have been omitted. In a few other cases, where nearly all the place-names are modern, the principle has been abandoned for the sake of simplicity. On pages 6–7 modern national states are shown in grey.

Where a site was known by two or more alternative names they are divided by an oblique stroke, *e.g.* Ezion-geber/Elath.

The word 'or' indicates uncertainty about the name or the location, as does a question mark.

The Lands of the Bible

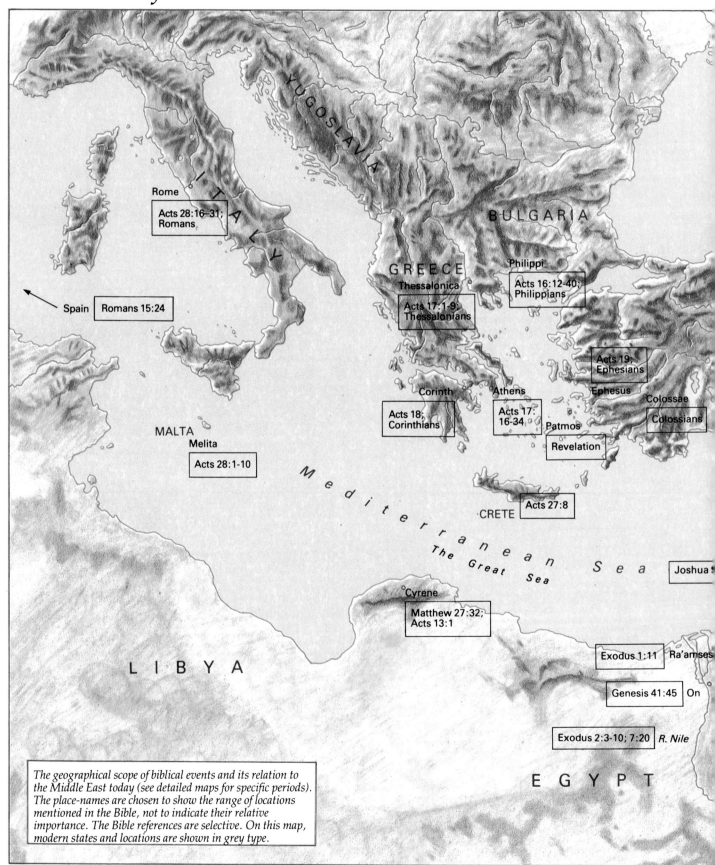

Rome
Acts 28:16–31;
Romans

ITALY

YUGOSLAVIA

BULGARIA

GREECE

Philippi
Acts 16:12-40;
Philippians

Thessalonica
Acts 17:1-9;
Thessalonians

Spain | Romans 15:24

Acts 19;
Ephesians

Ephesus

Colossae
Colossians

Corinth
Acts 18;
Corinthians

Athens
Acts 17:
16-34

Patmos
Revelation

MALTA

Melita
Acts 28:1-10

Mediterranean Sea

The Great Sea

CRETE Acts 27:8

Joshua

Cyrene
Matthew 27:32;
Acts 13:1

L I B Y A

Exodus 1:11 Ra'amses

Genesis 41:45 On

Exodus 2:3-10; 7:20 *R. Nile*

E G Y P T

The geographical scope of biblical events and its relation to
the Middle East today (see detailed maps for specific periods).
The place-names are chosen to show the range of locations
mentioned in the Bible, not to indicate their relative
importance. The Bible references are selective. On this map,
modern states and locations are shown in grey type.

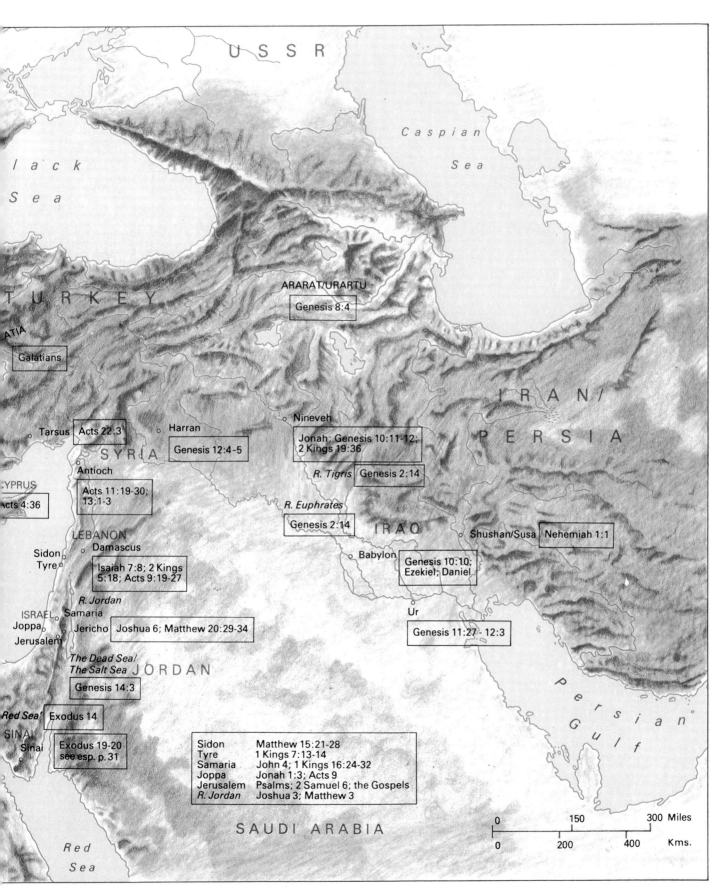

USSR

*Caspian
Sea*

*lack
Sea*

ARARAT/URARTU

Genesis 8:4

TURKEY

ATIA

Galatians

Tarsus Acts 22:3   Harran

Nineveh

Genesis 12:4-5

Jonah; Genesis 10:11-12;
2 Kings 19:36

IRAN/

SYRIA

R. Tigris Genesis 2:14

Antioch

PERSIA

Acts 11:19-30;
13:1-3

CYPRUS

R. Euphrates

cts 4:36

Genesis 2:14   IRAQ

LEBANON
    Damascus

Shushan/Susa Nehemiah 1:1

Sidon
Tyre

Isaiah 7:8; 2 Kings
5:18; Acts 9:19-27

Babylon

Genesis 10:10;
Ezekiel; Daniel

R. Jordan

ISRAEL Samaria
Joppa
Jerusalem Jericho Joshua 6; Matthew 20:29-34

Ur

Genesis 11:27 - 12:3

*The Dead Sea/
The Salt Sea* JORDAN

Genesis 14:3

Red Sea Exodus 14

SINAI

Sinai

Exodus 19-20
see esp. p. 31

*P
e
r
s
i
a
n*

*G
u
l
f*

Sidon	Matthew 15:21-28
Tyre	1 Kings 7:13-14
Samaria	John 4; 1 Kings 16:24-32
Joppa	Jonah 1:3; Acts 9
Jerusalem	Psalms; 2 Samuel 6; the Gospels
R. Jordan	Joshua 3; Matthew 3

SAUDI ARABIA

*Red
Sea*

| 0 | | 150 | | 300 Miles |

| 0 | | 200 | | 400 | Kms. |

Physical description

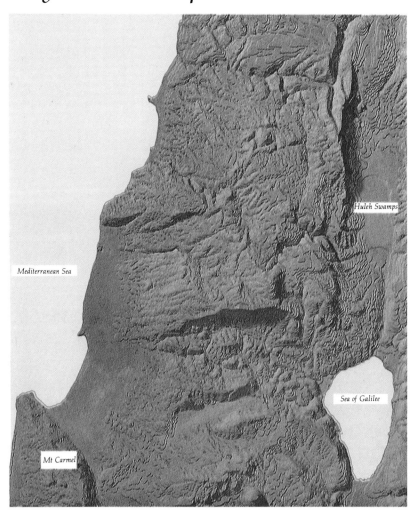

Mediterranean Sea

Huleh Swamps

Sea of Galilee

Mt Carmel

Physical structure and relief can be represented in various ways, such as the three shown on pages 8 and 9. They are:

Relief model
The photograph (left) shows a model of N central Palestine. It is made of plaster from a fretwood mould and built up on the basis of the 100ft (*c.* 30m) contours surveyed by the British in the 1870s. The Plain of Megiddo is at the S edge of the map, and the Sea of Galilee and Mt Carmel are easily recognizable. This method of representing relief exaggerates the vertical, making the landscape appear more dramatic than it would appear on a photograph.

Cross-section
The line of section used here (below) is indicated on the map on page 9, and the most prominent feature is the deep rift valley which contains the River Jordan and the Dead Sea. See also pages 11 and 21.

Relief map
The Holy Land (right) belongs physically to the shorelands of the Mediterranean, with a gentle rise inland from the coast to the mountains of Judaea, and then a precipitous plunge eastwards into the deepest gash on the earth's surface (the Dead Sea).
   With this map compare the satellite photograph on pages 12 and 13.

Right: The Holy Land: physical.

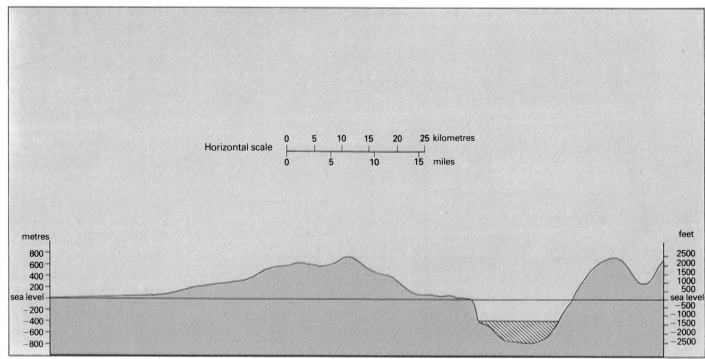

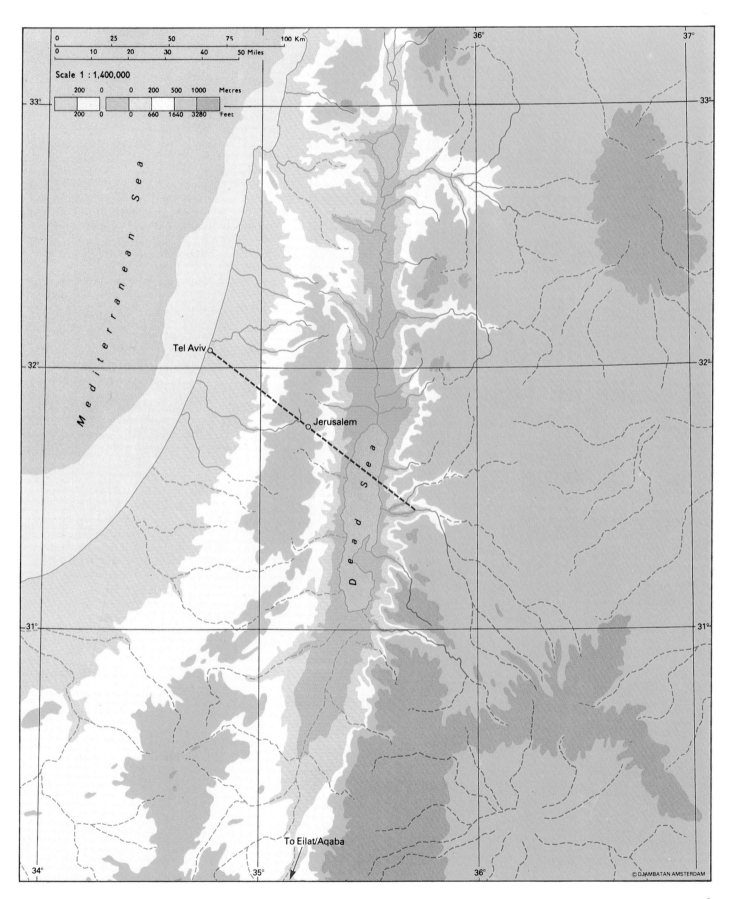

Scale 1 : 1,400,000

Mediterranean Sea

Tel Aviv

Jerusalem

Dead Sea

To Eilat/Aqaba

© DJAMBATAN AMSTERDAM

Physical regions

The Holy Land has traditionally been divided into five regions: the coastal plains, the central hills, the Rift Valley, the plateaux of Transjordan, and the desert.

The coastal plains stretch for a distance of about 200 km (*c*. 125 miles) from the borders of Lebanon to Gaza, interrupted by Mt Carmel. To the N of the latter, the plain of Asher runs to the ancient Ladder of Tyre, where the Galilean hills crowd close to the coast. To the SE of it, the valley of Jezreel and plain of Esdraelon have been areas of major significance. Some 20 km (*c*. 13 miles) at their widest, they formed the main route from Egypt to Damascus. Along it were situated the strategic centres of Megiddo, Jezreel and Bethshan, famous in Israel's wars (Jdg. 5; 6:33; 1 Sa. 29:1; 31:12) and the apocalyptic site of the future (Rev. 16:16). S of Carmel is the plain of Sharon, with its five great Philistine strongholds: Ekron, Ashdod, Ashkelon, Gath and Gaza, merging E into the hill lands of the Shephelah, a buffer between Israel and Philistia. These hills witnessed the early struggles of Israel from the times of the Judges to David. Notable among them are the valleys of Aijalon (Jos. 10:10-15; 1 Sa. 14:31), Sorek (Jdg. 16) and Elah (1 Sa. 17:1-2).

The central hills

The Central Hills run some 300 km (*c*. 188 miles) from N Galilee to Sinai, and are made up of interlocking hills and plateaux. In the S, Judah has gently undulating folds except in the E, where the deeply dissected chalk falls steeply to the Rift Valley. This Judaean plateau runs N into the hill country of Ephraim, but to the N again the hills of Samaria decrease gently to an average of just over 300 m (*c*. 985 ft) in the central basin. Together with other fertile basin lands, Samaria was exposed early to outside influences, and its faith corrupted. N of the plain of Esdraelon lies Galilee, divided into S or lower Galilee, which has a similar landscape to that of Samaria, and N or upper Galilee, where the mountains reach to a height of over 900 m (*c*. 2,955 ft).

Rift Valley, plateaux and desert

Slicing across Palestine for over 100 km (*c*. 63 miles), the Jordan follows the great Rift Valley from its source at Mt Hermon, through the Huleh and Galilee basins, to the Dead Sea. S of here commences the Arabah, stretching 160 km (*c*. 100 miles) to the Gulf of Aqabah, a desert dominated by the great wall of the Transjordan tableland. W stretches the desolate, hilly relief of the central Negeb. E over the edge of the Transjordan plateaux extend a series of regions well known in Bible times: the tableland of Bashan; Gilead, situated in a huge oval dome 55 km by 40 km (*c*. 34 miles by 25 miles); the level steppes of Ammon and Moab and, S of the Zered Valley, the faulted and tilted block of Edom with its impregnable strongholds. Beyond, to the E and S, are the deserts, tablelands of rock and sand, blasted by the hot winds.

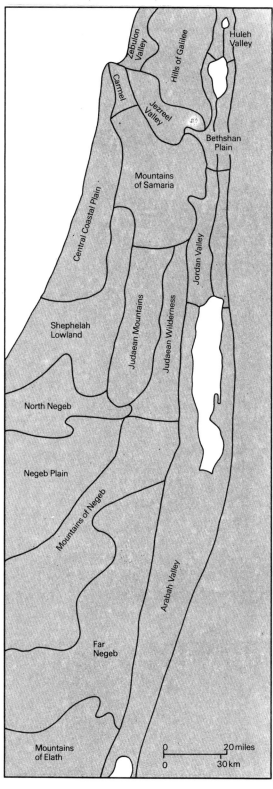

The Holy Land: physical regions.

Geological structure

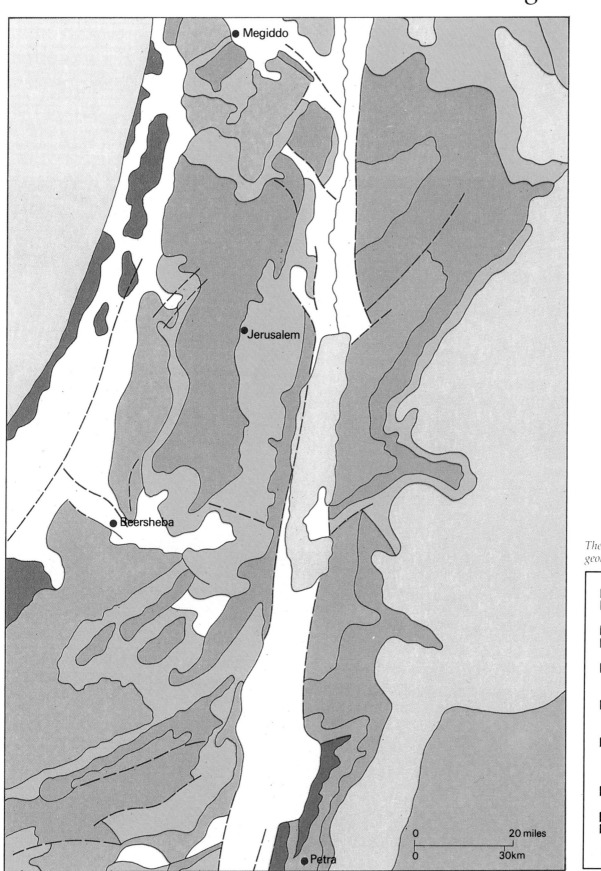

The Holy Land:
geological structure.

Alluvium
Quaternary
Red Sand
Basalt
Eocene
Limestone
Senonian Chert
(Upper
Cretaceous)
Senonian Chalk
(Middle
Cretaceous)
Cenomanian
Limestone
(Lower
Cretaceous)
Nubian
Sandstone
Granite
Dune sand
Principal
Faults

0   20 miles
0   30km

Satellite over-view

Satellite photographs of parts of the S Holy Land. The photographs whose scale is roughly 1:1 million, or 16 miles to 1 inch, are arranged on these pages with N to the left. They cover the Rift Valley from the lower Jordan, past the Dead Sea, to the Gulf of Aqabah, where the modern port of Elat corresponds to the biblical Ezion-geber.

False-colour techniques make irrigated farmlands appear in red: in this way, the extensive, aqueduct-based irrigation schemes instituted by the Israelis in the hills of Judaea are easily identified on the left-hand page, as are the oases of Jericho and the middle Jordan Valley.

Jerusalem and Amman, the region's principal cities,

appear as blueish patches below and above the left-hand (N) end of the Dead Sea. On the right-hand page, Petra is located almost in the centre, above (E of) the Rift Valley. At the top of this page, a maze of dry stream courses form white lines, converging from the mountains of Edom towards the desert basins, where their occasional flow of storm water quickly disappears. The dotted line indicates the sea-level contour.

The shape of the Dead Sea is familiar to all users of maps of the Holy Land. It is noticeable, however, that on maps produced since about 1970 the familiar shape has altered. This satellite photograph shows the S end of the

Sea differently from the maps in the body of the Atlas.

There are two explanations for this apparent discrepancy, both of them attributable to the large-scale development programmes of the modern Israeli state. The first is that the level of the Dead Sea has changed. Like all lakes in areas of inland drainage the level of the Dead Sea depends on a balance between inflow (in this case from the R. Jordan) and evaporation. The latter is likely to remain roughly constant from year to year. Inflow into the Dead Sea, however, has been considerably reduced by the diversion of Jordan water and its use for irrigating crops further N. Little of the water so diverted returns to the parent stream. Consequently, inflow has not kept pace with evaporation and the level of the Sea has fallen, altering its shoreline.

The second explanation is that, at the S end of the Dead Sea, where the flat floor of the Arabah continues the line of the Rift Valley, the Israelis have developed a series of evaporating pans, fed by canals from the Sea. From these pans they extract the salts contained in the water, especially those of potassium and sodium. It then becomes a question for the cartographer whether to represent these pans as a part of the Dead Sea or not.

Climate

In the Levant three climatic zones may be distinguished: a Mediterranean, a steppe and a desert zone, each with its distinct type of vegetation.

Mediterranean zone

Along the coast as far S as Gaza, the Mediterranean zone has mild winters (53·6°F, 12°C, mean monthly average for January at Gaza) compared with the severer conditions of the interior hills (Jerusalem 44·6°F, 7°C, in January). But summers are everywhere hot (Gaza 78·8°F, 26°C in July, Jerusalem 73·4°F, 23°C). The prolonged snow cover of the high Lebanon mountains (Je. 18:14) is exceptional, though snow is not infrequent in the Hauran. Elsewhere it is a rare phenomenon (2 Sa. 23:20). Less than one-fifteenth part of the annual rainfall occurs in the summer months from June to October; nearly all of it is concentrated in winter to reach a maximum in mid-winter. The total amount varies from about 35-40 cm (c. 14-16ins) on the coast to about 75 cm (c. 30 ins) on Mt Carmel and the Judaean, Galilean and Transjordan mountains.

Steppe and desert

In the Beersheba area to the S, and in parts of the Jordan valley and of the Transjordan plateau the climate is steppe, with only 20-30 cm (c. 8-10 ins) of rain, though temperature conditions are comparable to those of the Judaean hills. The deep trough of the Jordan has sub-tropical conditions with stifling summer heat; at Jericho mean daily maxima remain above 100°F (38°C) from June to September, with frequent records of 110-120°F (43-49°C). The winter, however, has enjoyable conditions of 65-68°F (18-20°C) (January mean daily maximum). In the Negeb, the S part of the Jordan valley, and the country E and S of the Transjordan steppe the climate is desert, with less than 20 cm (c. 8 ins) of rain a year.

Rainfall

The rainfall of Palestine is closely identified with the cool season: in Arabic, the same word refers to both winter and rain. During the preliminary period of mid-September to mid-October, misty sea air encountering hot, dry air from the land causes thunderstorms and irregular rainfall. The onset of effective rains normally begins in mid-October, but may sometimes be delayed until January. These are the 'former rains' which are eagerly awaited because they reduce the temperatures and produce bright, clear skies. The 'latter rains', by contrast, occur in April or early May, and represent the last showers of the rainy season (Am. 4:7).

Where rainfall is low, dew assumes great importance as a source of moisture. It is

beneficial to summer crops. In seeing it as a source of blessing, therefore, the ancients were not exaggerating (Gn. 27:28; Dt. 33:28). It permits dry-farming in the absence of rain, aids the vine harvest and freshens dry pasture in times of drought.

Has the climate changed?

It is often asked whether the climate of the Bible lands has changed since biblical times. Accepting that *fluctuations* can and do occur, there is no archaeological evidence for significant change. Near the Gulf of Aqabah, for example, excavated Roman gutters still fit the springs for which they were constructed. It is therefore necessary to seek other reasons why a land notable for milk, honey and splendid fruit crops (Nu. 13:27) had become, by the early 20th cent., a barren and treeless land of little or no agricultural value.

Rather than infer change of climate, it is simpler to assume that the people of Israel were responsible for initiating processes which were then continued and intensified over succeeding centuries. **1.** Because they never conquered and occupied the whole land assigned to them by God, the land became overcrowded, and overcrowding in dry lands usually brings with it soil erosion and loss of fertility. **2.** Because they lacked trust in God, they repeatedly became entangled in regional alliances, seeking the help of powerful neighbours for their own protection, and so became involved in wars. War brought invasion, devastation, the loss of tree cover (see *e.g.* Dt. 20:19; Je. 6:6), and frequent war resulted in desertification. In these lands of the Bible, the ecological balance is a delicate one: human carelessness is all too promptly followed by national disaster.

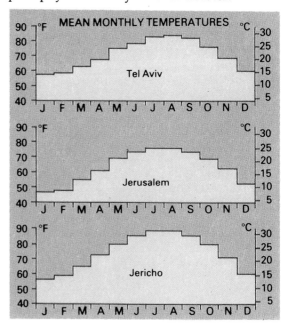

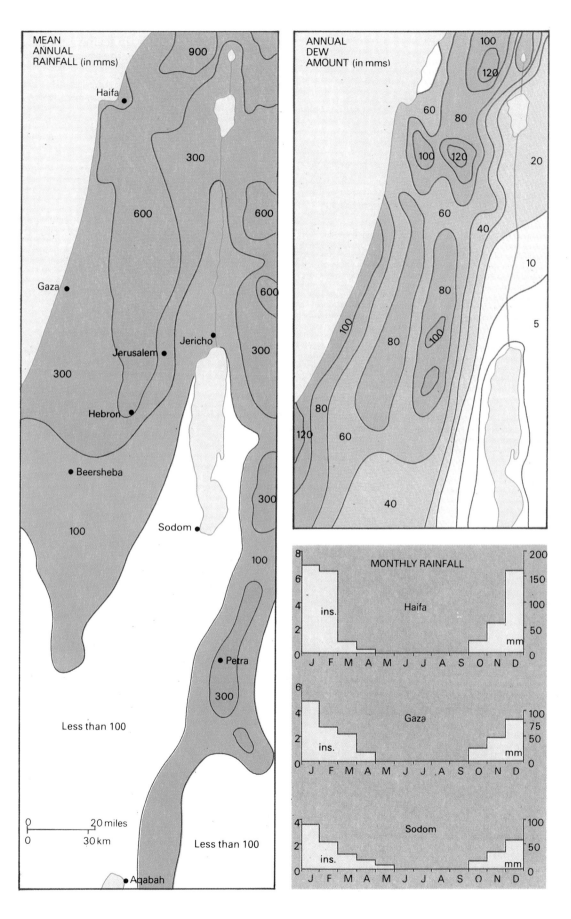

The Holy Land: aspects of the climate.

Principal water-courses

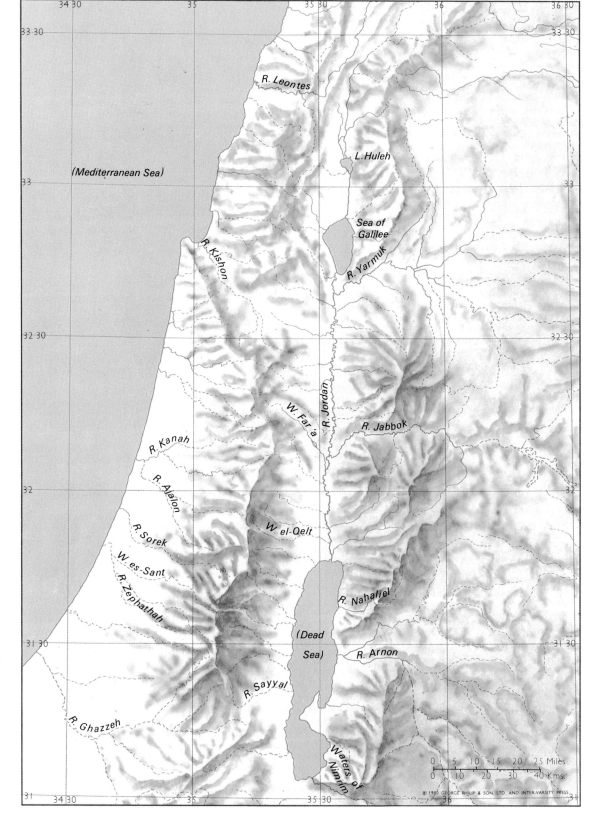

Apart from the Jordan, a few of its tributaries and four or five small coastal streams that are fed from springs, all the remaining rivers of Palestine are seasonal. Snow-fed streams account for their maximum volume in May-June (Jos. 3:15), but the majority dry up in the hot summer (1 Ki. 17:7; Jb. 24:19; Joel 1:20), notably in the Negeb (Ps. 126:4). The sudden spate caused by the autumn rains is graphically described in Judges 5:21 and Matthew 7:27. Thus 'the fountain of living waters' was the ideal of the Israelite settler.

The Holy Land: principal water-courses.

Vegetation

Because of contrasts of relief, from more than 1,000m (*c.* 3,283 ft) above sea-level near Hebron to 390 m (*c.* 1,281 ft) below sea-level at the Dead Sea, the flora of Palestine is very varied (about 3,000 vascular plants) for such a small area. A large proportion of them are annuals. Few districts have ever had dense forests, but over twenty types of tree are mentioned in the Bible, and remnant woodlands have been preserved on Mt Hermon and in Lebanon, which has always been noted for its cedars. Small forests of pine and oak still exist in Golan.

Oak forests long existed in Sharon, whose name means forest. But biblical prophecy as early as Isaiah's time foresaw the conversion of these forest areas — Sharon, northern Gilead and southern Galilee — into sheep pastures (Is.65:10). In other words, while there is no substantial evidence of *climatic* change in the Holy Land (see p.14), *vegetational* change, being largely man-made, has been widespread. The two principal elements of this change have been **1.** the removal of tree cover, for building; for constructing siege-works; for fuel, and **2.** the spread of pastoralism. Goats are notoriously destructive browsers, while sheep are selective in their grazing: both destroy vegetation unless strictly controlled. Under Mediterranean — let alone desert — conditions, pasture is seasonally short-lived, and stock should be moved to fresh grazing. Where this is not possible, loss of cover and erosion are inevitable.

Deterioration had gone so far before the establishment of the modern state of Israel in 1948 that most of the uncultivated land was a dreary expanse of *batha*, low scrub surrounding rocky outcrops. Towards the steppe and desert margins, vegetation thinned to a few shrubby elements — wormwood, broom, saltwort and such grasses as can survive in very dry conditions. Only along the banks of the Jordan is there a dense gallery forest of willow, poplar, tamarisk and oleander.

Since 1948, substantial areas have been afforested by the Israelis, partly to give new settlers an economic activity during the period of waiting for new plantations and orchards to reach fruit-bearing age. Pine, cypress, eucalyptus and acacia are among the types of tree introduced. Major areas of planting are the hills of the Gaza-Jerusalem corridor and N Galilee.

The second principal method of checking the decay of soil and vegetation is by *terracing*. Relics of old, abandoned terraces are plentiful, and a new programme of restoration and extension to these was initiated by the Israelis in the 1950s.

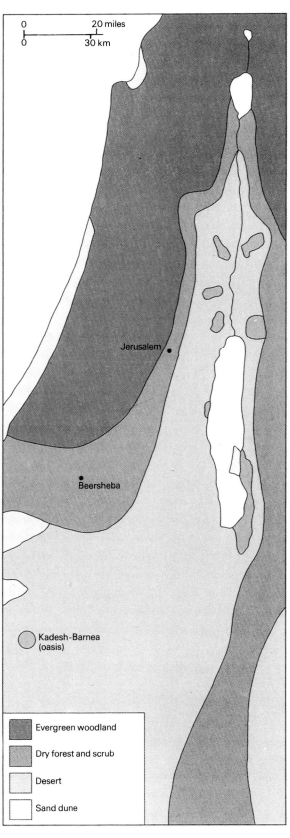

0   20 miles
0   30 km

Jerusalem •

• Beersheba

Kadesh-Barnea
(oasis)

Evergreen woodland

Dry forest and scrub

Desert

Sand dune

The Holy Land: natural vegetation regions.

The River Jordan

The River Jordan: aerial view of the river's flood plain, the
Zor. The river meanders through thickets of tamarisk and
thorn scrub called in the OT 'the jungle (NIV 'thickets') of
the Jordan' (Jer. 12:5).

The Jordan depression is a unique feature of physical geography. Geologically a rift valley, it is the deepest depression on the earth's land surface. Only a few miles from its source, the river is already nearly 200 m (*c.* 657 ft) below the Mediterranean, while at the N end of the Dead Sea it has plunged to 393 m (*c.* 1,280 ft) below sea-level. The name 'Jordan' (Hebrew *yardēn*) aptly means 'the descender'. The river is the largest perennial stream in Palestine, and its length of some 120 km (*c.* 75 miles) from former Lake Huleh to the Dead Sea is more than doubled by its meanders. Archaeological finds have revealed the valley to be one of the earliest centres of urban settlement in the world.

Lake Huleh

The headwaters of the Jordan rise below Mt Hermon (2,814 m, 9,236 ft). The river then shortly enters a depression some 5 by 15 km (*c.* 3 by 9 miles) formerly occupied by Lake Huleh (now drained and reclaimed for agriculture). At its S outlet from here, lava flows blocked the valley, forcing the river to cut through a series of gorges, in the course of which it falls over 200 m (*c.* 657 ft).

The Sea of Galilee

The Jordan then enters the Sea of Galilee, some 21 km (*c.* 13 miles) long and 13 km (*c.* 8 miles) wide, on whose shores and waters so much of the ministry of Christ took place. The river flows out on the S side into the 'Ghor', which extends for 105 km (*c.* 66 miles) to the Dead Sea. The river has cut its way into the floor of the trough to a depth of 50 m (*c.* 164 ft) in some places, and it is therefore possible to distinguish the Ghor, or broad valley feature, from the entrenched river plain, or Zor, pictured on page 18.

The Dead Sea

Several perennial streams join the Jordan in its passage through the Ghor, all of them flowing in from the E. In this section of the valley there are several fords (though the river was not bridged until Roman times), but between the Jordan-Jabbok confluence and the Dead Sea crossings are difficult. The miraculous crossing of the Israelites appears to have taken place opposite Jericho, while the waters were cut off at Adam (Tell ed-Damiyeh), some 25 km (*c.* 16 miles) to the north (Jos. 3:1-17; 4:1-24).

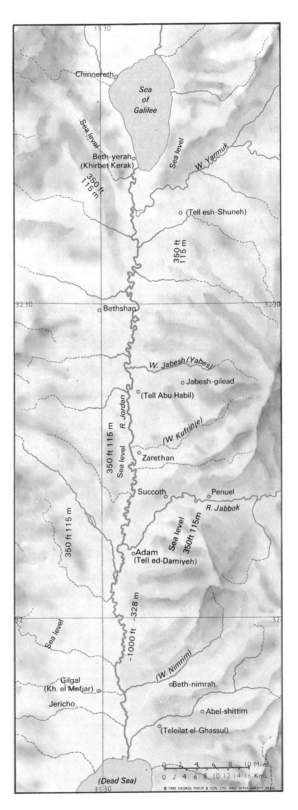

The Jordan valley.

The Dead Sea

The Dead Sea is referred to in the OT as the Salt Sea (Gn. 14:3; Nu. 34:3, 12; Dt. 3:17; Jos. 3:16; 12:3; 15:2, 5; 18:19), the Sea of the Arabah (Dt. 3:17; 4:49; Jos. 3:16; 12:3; 2 Ki. 14:25) and the Eastern Sea (Ezk. 47:18; Joel 2:20; Zc. 14:8). It occupies the deepest point of the great rift which extends from the N end of the Jordan Valley S to the East African lakes. Its surface is on average 395 m (c. 1,300 ft) below sea-level, the lowest point on the earth's surface, and at its deepest point the bed is about 433 m (c. 1,422 ft) lower still.

From the N shore where the Jordan enters, to the shallow S end where the sea merges into the salty Sebkha marsh, the distance is 77 km (c. 48 miles). N of the peninsula called the Lisan ('tongue') the width is 10-14 km (c. 6-9 miles). The Lisan itself extends to within 3 km (c. 2 miles) of the W shore. From here S the water is very shallow, and the narrow gap was fordable until the mid-19th century. Here in earlier times a Roman road joined the two shores, guarded at its W end by the fortress of Masada. Between the W shore and the Judaean hills is a narrow plain bordered on the W by low terraces. On one such terrace, by the NW shore, lie the ruins of Khirbet Qumran. On the E the sea is bordered by the sheer cliffs of Moab. S of the Dead Sea, the rift valley is dry, and from the Scorpion Cliffs to the Gulf of Aqabah is known as the Arabah (Dt. 1:1; 2:8; but in OT times the term was also applied to the valley N of the Dead Sea: Dt. 3:17; Jos. 11:2; 12:3). In addition to the Jordan, the sea is fed by other sources of fresh water on both the E and W shores, but concentrated chemical deposits ensure that the sea itself remains salty, since evaporation is the only means of escape.

The Dead Sea, looking E to the hills of Moab.

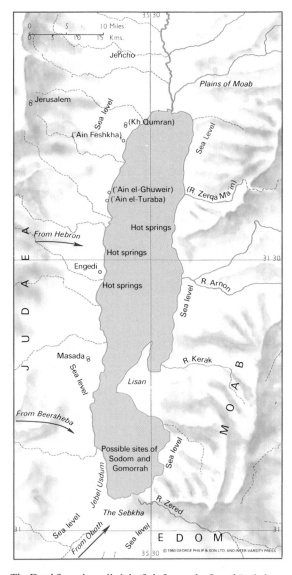

The Dead Sea, also called the Salt Sea or the Sea of Arabah.

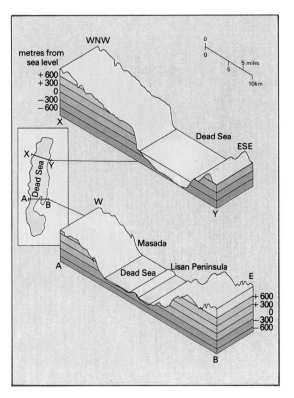

Sections through the Dead Sea at the N basin and at the Lisan peninsula in the S.

The Rift Valley which runs from Syria in the N, southwards to the Gulf of Aqabah and the Red ('Reed') Sea, is a remarkable feature, given its form by two parallel sets of faults. Between these the floor of the present valley has been let down to a probable depth of 5000 m (c. 16,500 ft), and then filled with later debris eroded from the surfaces on either side of the rift. These surfaces are largely composed of young materials, easily eroded by water or wind. In this geological cross-section of the rift, they are seen to rest uncomfortably on the much older Arabian sandstone.

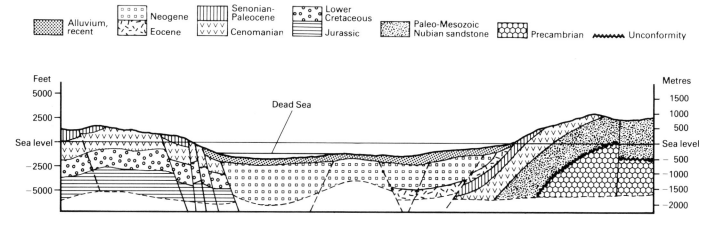

The Negeb

The Negeb or Negev (Hebrew *neḡeb*, dry) is the regional name applied to S Palestine, where rainfall is sparse and the true desert is approached. An indefinite region, it covers some 11,650 sq.km (*c.* 4,500 sq. miles). Its N boundary may be conveniently drawn along the Gaza-Beersheba road and then due E of Beersheba to the Dead Sea. On the S the region merges into the Desert of Sinai. When the state of Israel was established in 1948, the Negeb comprised some two-thirds of its area at that date. To Israel, it has since become a frontier of settlement.

About half of the Negeb receives less than 50mm (*c.* 2 ins) of precipitation annually. These areas possess little soil and are generally covered by desert debris (*hammada*). Elsewhere are areas of sand and, even where small pockets of soil exist, they are lacking in organic matter and extremely liable to erosion. The only favourable feature is found in the less arid areas, where there is a covering of *loess*, a light dust, very fertile when irrigated.

The strategic and economic importance of the Negeb has been significant. The 'Way of Shur' crossed it from central Sinai NE to Judaea (Gn. 16:7; 20:1; 25:18; Ex. 15:22; Nu. 33:8), a route followed by the Patriarchs (Gn. 24:62; 26:22), by Hadad the Edomite (1 Ki. 11:14, 17, 21-22), and probably the escape route used by Jeremiah (43:6-12) and later by Joseph and Mary (Mt. 2:13-15). The route was dictated by the zone of settled land where well-water is significant, hence the frequent references to its wells (*e.g.* Gn. 24:15-20; Jos. 15:18-19; Jdg. 1:14-15). Uzziah reinforced the defence of Jerusalem by establishing cultivation and defensive settlements in his exposed S flank of the N Negeb (2 Ch. 26:10). It seems clear from the history of the Near East that the Negeb was a convenient vacuum for resettlement whenever population pressure forced out migrants from the Fertile Crescent. Also significant was the location of copper ores in the E Negeb and its trade in the Arabah. Control of this industry explains the Amalekite and Edomite wars of Saul (1 Sa. 14:47f.) and the subsequent victories of David over the Edomites (1 Ki. 11:15f.). It also explains the creation by Solomon of the port of Ezion-geber, and, when it was silted up, the creation of a new port at Elath by Uzziah (1 Ki. 9:26; 22:48; 2 Ki. 14:22). The abiding hatred of the Edomites is explained by the struggles to control this trade (*cf.* Ezk. 25:12 and the book of Obadiah).

Between the fourth century BC and the beginning of the second century AD, when the Nabataeans finally disappeared, these Semitic people of S. Arabian origin created a brilliant civilization-based agriculture which in turn was made possible by wells or elaborate methods of collecting occasional rainwater. Larger-scale agriculture has necessarily had to wait upon the provision of water by aqueduct from N Palestine, so that irrigation can be practised. The first stage of the Negeb aqueduct was opened in 1955.

Deployed across the strategic trade routes

The Negeb (Negev): typical landscape in the dry S.

Lands east of the Jordan

between Arabia and the Fertile Crescent, they became rich on the spice and incense trade of Arabia, and other exotic goods from Somaliland and India.

The Negeb was also important in early Christian times. N. Glueck in *Rivers in the Desert*, has identified some 300 early Christian Byzantine sites in this area, dating from the fifth and sixth centuries AD. A comparison of this figure with the map on page 83 showing the spread of Christian congregations in the first three centuries is instructive.

The first attempts at re-colonization of the Negeb date from before World War II, but no substantial progress was made before 1948. Then a pioneer fringe was established along the less-arid N edge of the region but, even so, there have been many setbacks to progress. Mining has also been developed, first and foremost around the Dead Sea with its mineral repository, but also in the Negeb proper where mineral salts, gypsum and natural gas are found.

The Negeb (Negev).

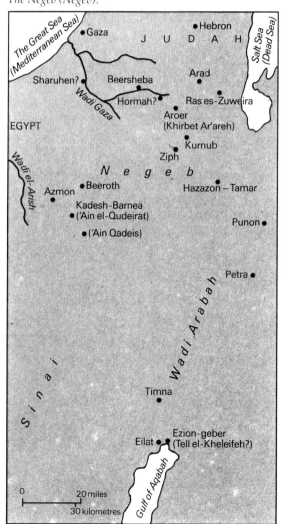

East of the Jordan line are the deserts of Syria and Arabia. But it is not always realized that between the river and the desert there is a narrow fertile belt, perhaps 30 km (16 miles) wide, running parallel with, and sometimes hidden behind, the savage, bare cliffs that overlook the Jordan and the Dead Sea. Here rainfall is, in many areas, no sparser than on the Judaean hills: the actual amount depends 1. on the height of the land beyond the Jordan, with the higher hills attracting most rainfall, and 2. access for rain-bearing winds from the Mediterranean. Lower Galilee, for example, permits easy access for these winds and ensures adequate rainfall to the hills of Bashan lying to the E.

The land rises generally from N to S, attaining nearly 1,730 m (5,680 ft) S of the Dead Sea. The N plateau is lower (450-600 m, or 1,500-2,000 ft), open, rolling and fertile, sufficiently so to have led the tribes of Reuben and Gad (Numbers 32; Joshua 1) to conclude that there was no advantage to be gained by crossing the Jordan into the Promised Land: they obtained permission from Moses and Joshua to settle on the E bank.

This fertile belt E of the Jordan was densely settled and prosperous in biblical times. The modern Jordanian capital of Amman is the former Rabbath Ammon, the 'city of waters' of 2 Samuel 12:27, later to become one of the prosperous cities of the Decapolis. The economy of the area varied – and still does – with soil, rainfall and terrain. D. Baly (*The Geography of the Bible*, London, 1957) makes a fourfold division from N to S, as follows: the farmers of Bashan (growing wheat and barley); the highlanders of Gilead (practising some forestry, producing the famous balm, and growing vines); the shepherds of Ammon and Moab (2 Kings 3:4, 'Mesha king of Moab was a sheep breeder'); and the traders of Edom, whose S mountains offered little support for stock or crops, and so drew them into commerce across the deserts to their S and E.

The settlements of the fertile edge were linked by the N–S line of the King's Highway. This line, however, was interrupted every few miles by the deep dissection of one of the Jordan's E bank tributaries cutting its way down from the plateau surface to the Rift Valley. In this way the area is sub-divided into identifiable sections – the plateau of Bashan, the wooded hills of Gilead and the mountains of Moab and Edom. Several of these names are recognizably those of kingdoms whose history impinged repeatedly on that of Israel. Their situation on the heights above the Rift Valley meant that none of them was an easy object of attack from the W, and only rarely could Israel hope to subdue Ammon, Moab or Edom. (For locations see page 87.)

Archaeological periods

Islamic AD 636 →

Byzantine AD 324 – 636

Roman 63 BC – AD 324

Hellenistic 330 – 63 BC

Iron Age 1200 – 330 BC
Sometimes known as
Israelite Period

Bronze Age 3150 – 1200 BC
Sometimes known as
Canaanite Period

Chalcolithic 4000 – 3150 BC

Stone Age → 4000 BC

Archaeological Periods	Sometimes known as	Approx. Period
Islamic		AD 636 –
Byzantine		AD 324 – 636
Roman III		AD 180 – 324
Roman II		AD 70 – 180
Roman I	Herodian	63 BC – AD 70
Hellenistic II	Hasmonaean/Maccabean	152 – 63 BC
Hellenistic I	Ptolemaic/Seleucid	330 – 152 BC
Babylonian/Persian	Late Iron (= LI)/Persian	587 – 330 BC
Iron Age III b		720 – 587 BC
Iron Age III a		800 – 720 BC
Iron Age II b	Middle Iron (= MI)	900 – 800 BC
Iron Age II a		1000 – 900 BC
Iron Age I b		1150 – 1000 BC
Iron Age (= IA) I a	Early Iron/Israelite (= EI)	1200 – 1150 BC
Late Bronze II b		1300 – 1200 BC
Late Bronze II a		1400 – 1300 BC
Late Bronze (= LBA) I	(Late Canaanite (= LC))	1550 – 1400 BC
Middle Bronze II c		1600 – 1550 BC
Middle Bronze II b		1750 – 1600 BC
Middle Bronze II a	(Middle Canaanite (= MC))	1950 – 1750 BC
Middle Bronze (= MBA) I	Early – Middle Bronze Age	2200 – 1950 BC
Early Bronze IV	Early Bronze Age III b	2350 – 2200 BC
Early Bronze III	(Early Canaanite III)	2650 – 2350 BC
Early Bronze II	(Early Canaanite II)	2850 – 2650 BC
Early Bronze (= EBA) I	(Early Canaanite (= EC) I)	3150 – 2850 BC
Chalcolithic	Ghassulian	4000 – 3150 BC
Neolithic (Pottery)		5000 – 4000 BC
Neolithic (Pre-Pottery	New Stone Age	7500 – 5000 BC
Mesolithic	Middle Stone Age/Natufian	10,000 – 7500 BC
Palaeolithic	Old Stone Age	– 10,000 BC

Earlier dates are approximate and in round figures. Later ones are those of
significant historical events known from written sources.

Tells (ruin mounds)

The sites of most biblical cities are marked by mounds known as tells (this being simply the Arabic term for a ruin mound). The true nature of these tells, which are a feature not only of Palestine but of all Near Eastern lands, was not properly understood until 1890 when W. M. Flinders Petrie began excavations at Tell el-Hesi (probably the site of OT Eglon, but believed by Petrie to be the site of Lachish). Previously, tells had been thought to be either natural formations, or, if artificial, simply platforms for towns or structures. At Tell el-Hesi, a stream bordering the mound had eroded part of it, exposing a section, so that even before excavation had begun Petrie could see that the mound consisted of numerous strata. It became apparent that a tell was actually the accumulated debris of a succession of ancient towns.

To understand the composition of a tell, it is necessary to understand the process of its formation. In the Ancient Near East, the common building material (as today in many places) was sun-dried mud-brick. While stone was used for foundations and for a few of the larger buildings, most structures were of mud-brick, and as a consequence were easily destroyed by fires, floods, earthquakes or attacking armies, or simply collapsed through poor maintenance. If most or all of a town were to be destroyed, the mud-brick of the ruins was not worth salvaging, so rebuilding would proceed by roughly levelling the ruins of the old buildings and erecting the new town on top of them. Over a period of thousands of years, towns or cities could be rebuilt many times, becoming large mounds 20-30 m (c. 66-99 ft) or more in height. The site of Hazor (Tell el-Qedah),

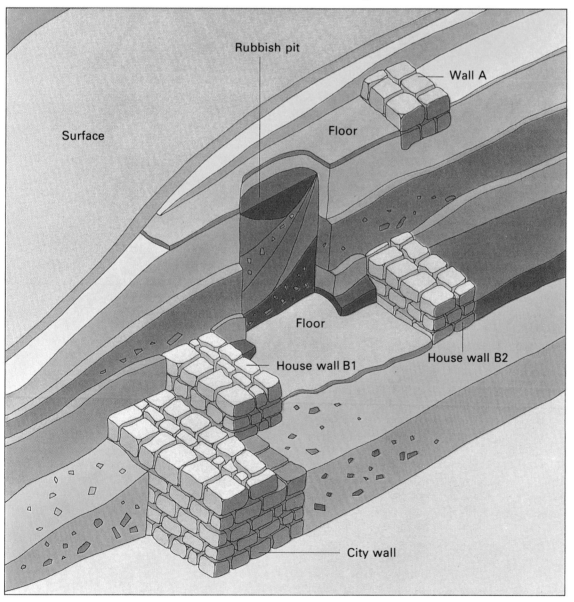

Left: section through part of a tell (ruin mound). The last building in use is represented by one wall (A) and a floor; the wall parallel to A has been destroyed by erosion at the edge of the mound. A rubbish pit cuts through the debris of an earlier house beneath (walls B1, B2), touching its floor. This house has been built partially over the remains of an older city wall.

Far left: classification of archaeological periods.

Tells (ruin mounds)

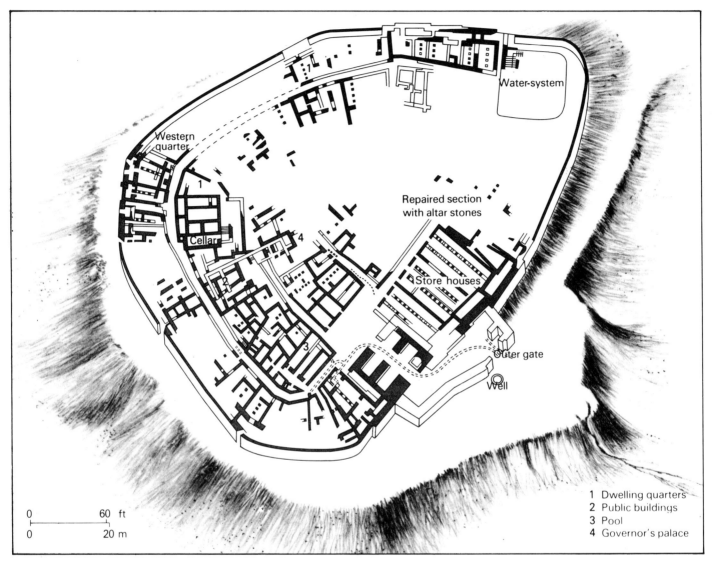

Above: plan of the Iron Age (Israelite) city represented by Strata V-II at Tel Beersheba (c. 950 – c. 700 BC).

Labels on image: Water-system; Western quarter; Cellar; Repaired section with altar stones; Store houses; Outer gate; Well

1 Dwelling quarters
2 Public buildings
3 Pool
4 Governor's palace

0 — 60 ft
0 — 20 m

Above right: aerial view of excavations on the mound of Tel Beersheba. The modern excavators' camp (top right) gives some idea of the small size of the Iron Age city.

for example, is a tell of some 21 strata, representing occupation from the 27th to the 2nd centuries BC.

Each stratum generally consists of not only the remains of the buildings — floors of hard earth and the foundations of walls covered by the collapsed mud-brick superstructure — but also, sandwiched between the floors and the remains of fallen walls and roofs, many of the everyday objects of the time. These might include tools and personal ornaments, but by far the most common material will be broken pottery vessels. When these are excavated and related to the chronology of changing pottery styles worked out for the whole of Syria-Palestine, they provide valuable dating criteria for the various strata.

The methods of tell excavation employed by Petrie were crude in comparison with those in

vogue today. Many refinements have been introduced during the intervening period by archaeologists such as G. Reisner (working at Samaria), W. F. Albright (at Tell Beit Mirsim), and Kathleen M. Kenyon (at Samaria and Jericho). Most refinements are aimed at more accurately distinguishing successive strata — by no means an easy task, since structures belonging to different strata can sometimes interlock in a confusing fashion. A trench for a foundation-wall, or a pit for the disposal of refuse, may have been cut into strata below that to which it belongs, and pottery fragments dropped into such cuttings will seem to be out of context unless the various features are correctly related to their own strata. Great expertise is therefore required, not only in excavating, but also in interpreting what is uncovered.

Below: schematic representation of a tell (ruin mound) showing methods of excavation and strata (levels) of occupation. In reality many of the periods shown here *would be represented at most tells by more than one stratum, while some periods would not be represented at all because of breaks in occupation.*

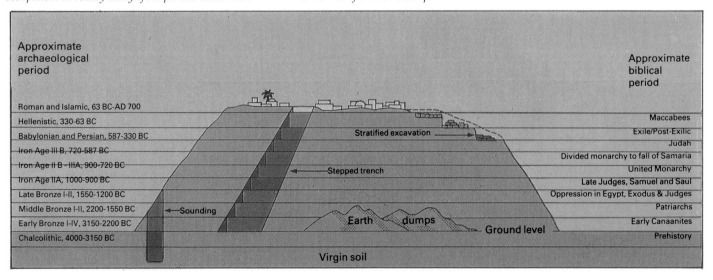

Approximate archaeological period		Approximate biblical period
Roman and Islamic, 63 BC-AD 700		
Hellenistic, 330-63 BC		Maccabees
Babylonian and Persian, 587-330 BC	Stratified excavation	Exile/Post-Exilic
		Judah
Iron Age III B, 720-587 BC		Divided monarchy to fall of Samaria
Iron Age II B - IIIA, 900-720 BC	Stepped trench	United Monarchy
Iron Age IIA, 1000-900 BC		Late Judges, Samuel and Saul
Late Bronze I-II, 1550-1200 BC		Oppression in Egypt, Exodus & Judges
Middle Bronze I-II, 2200-1550 BC	Sounding	Patriarchs
Early Bronze I-IV, 3150-2200 BC	Earth dumps	Early Canaanites
	Ground level	
Chalcolithic, 4000-3150 BC		Prehistory
	Virgin soil	

Abraham and the King's Highway

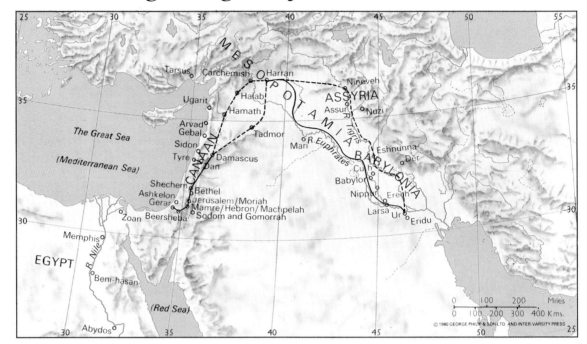

Possible routes for Abraham's journey from Ur to Canaan (Gn.11:31-12:6). Of the two possible routes to Harran, the southern (shown by solid line) is the more likely. It is uncertain which would have been the preferred route from Harran to Damascus.

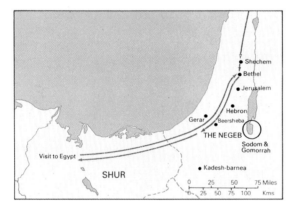

Abraham's movements as described in Gn.12:6-13:4.

Born in Ur in S Mesopotamia, Abraham travelled with a large family group to Harran in the NW (Gn.11:27-31). While most of the group settled there (= Paddan-aram in 28:2, *etc.*), Abraham obeyed God's call and moved on with his own family to Canaan (12:1-5).

After a visit to Egypt to avoid famine (12:10-20), his nephew Lot's decision to settle near Sodom involved him in that city's war with Chedorlaomer and his allies (ch.14).

Abraham's (and Isaac's) movements were thereafter focused in the S: the Negeb, the district of Gerar and around Hebron (18:1; 20:1-17; 21:22-34; 23:2-20; 24:62; 26:1-33).

Right: The route of the ancient 'King's Highway'. Although first mentioned in the OT in the time of Moses (Nu. 20:17 etc.) it was also in use between the 23rd and 20th cent. BC. It is therefore likely that Chedorlaomer and his allies approached Sodom and Gomorrah by this way (Gn. 14:5) and were pursued by Abraham (vv.14-15).

The time of the Patriarchs

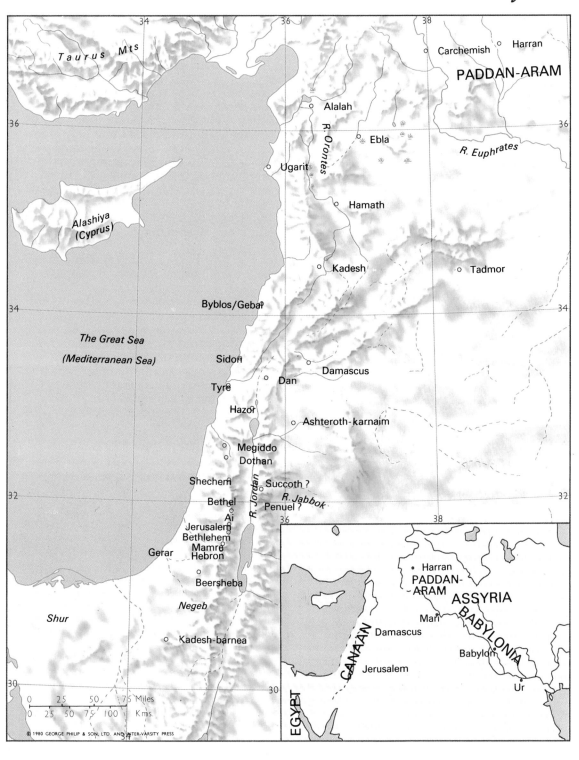

Map to illustrate the patriarchal narratives, where locations are known.

During the period covered by Gn.12-50 the patriarchs did not live in a cultural vacuum but had contact with Paddan-aram (NW Mesopotamia) where another branch of the family had settled (cf. 22:20-23; 24:10; 28:1-5), with the 'Philistines' of Gerar (20:1-18; 26:1-33) the Hittites at Hebron (23:1-16), Shechem (33:18-20), the 'cities of the valley' (13:12;

14:17-24), and Egypt (12:10-20; 39-50), where Jacob and his sons eventually settled.

Opinions vary as to a precise dating for the patriarchal age. Many writers have concluded that the Middle Bronze Age fits in well with the details of the narratives, giving dates between c.2000 BC and c.1500 BC.

Archaeological sites: Middle Bronze Age

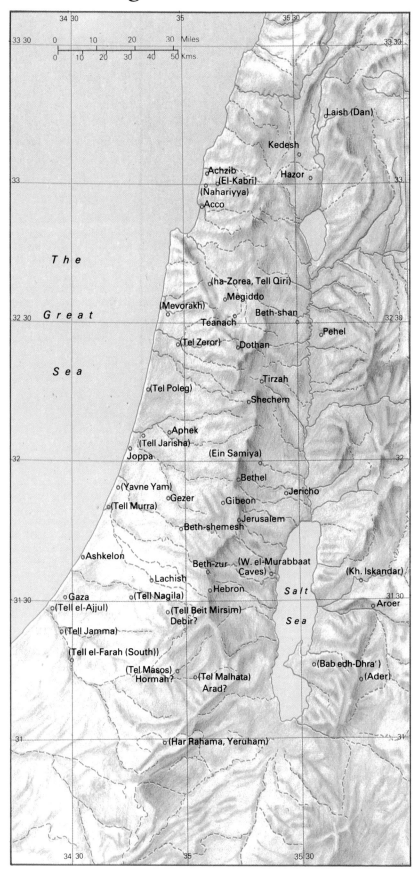

During the Early Bronze (EB) period in Palestine, many settlements developed into fortified cities of considerable size. However, the EB III phase ended *c*.2350 BC with the destruction of these urban centres, and the culture of EB IV-MB I was semi-nomadic. The Middle Bronze I (MB I) period (*c*.2200-1950 BC) was characterized by unwalled villages where occupation was often seasonal and only semi-sedentary. These agricultural settlements (too small and numerous to be featured on the adjacent map) occurred extensively in the central Negeb, stretching W along the biblical 'Way of Shur'. MB I may therefore provide the appropriate background to the sojournings of Abraham and Isaac in this region (Gn.20:1; 24:62; 25:11).

MB II (*c*.1950-1550 BC) was very different in character. It witnessed the revival of large centres in the central hill-country, *e.g.* at Hebron, Bethel, Shechem and Dothan. By the final phase of this period, MB IIc (1650/1600-1550 BC), this Canaanite culture had reached its zenith, many cities being large, densely populated and defended by monumental fortifications. An excellent example is Jericho, where well-preserved household artefacts from the MB tombs have shed light on daily life in this period. The elaborate defences were insufficient, however, to prevent the destruction of most of these major cities at the close of the MBA.

Above: a Middle Bronze Age pointed-base jug from Hazor (height c. 18cm).

Left: some important Middle Bronze Age excavated sites (c. 2200-1550 BC).

Moses and the Exodus

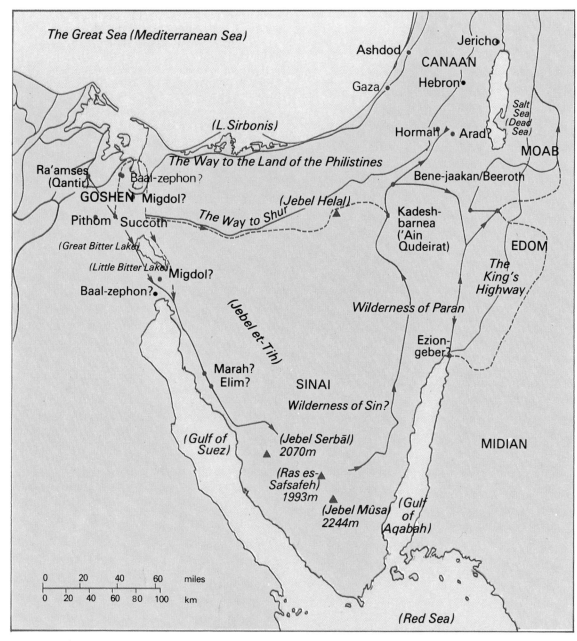

The Great Sea (Mediterranean Sea)

Jericho

Ashdod

CANAAN

Gaza

Hebron

(L. Sirbonis)

Salt
Sea
(Dead
Sea)

Hormah? • Arad?

The Way to the Land of the Philistines

MOAB

Ra'amses
(Qantir)

Baal-zephon?

Bene-jaakan/Beeroth

GOSHEN Migdol?

The Way to Shur

(Jebel Helal)

Pithom Succoth

Kadesh-
barnea
('Ain
Qudeirat)

EDOM

(Great Bitter Lake)

(Little Bitter Lake) Migdol?

Baal-zephon?

(Jebel et-Tih)

The
King's
Highway

Wilderness of Paran

Ezion-
geber?

Marah?
Elim?

SINAI

Wilderness of Sin?

(Gulf of
Suez)

(Jebel Serbāl)
2070m

MIDIAN

(Ras es-
Safsafeh)
1993m

(Jebel Mûsa)
2244m

(Gulf
of
Aqabah)

| 0 | 20 | 40 | 60 | miles |
| 0 | 20 | 40 | 60 | 80 | 100 | km |

(Red Sea)

Possible route of the Exodus and wilderness wanderings. Dotted lines indicate alternatives (see text for details).

Although Jacob and his sons settled in Egypt under a benevolent pharaoh (Gn.39-50), a later ruler pressed their descendants into hard slavery (Ex.1:8-14). When Moses was born, an edict ordering the death of all male Hebrew infants was in force, but the child was preserved and raised in Egyptian court circles (Ex.1:15-2:10).

After killing an Egyptian whom he saw beating a Hebrew (2:11-15), Moses fled to Midian where he settled for many years. He returned to Egypt after receiving the call from God to lead his people out of slavery (3:1-4:20).

Following the demonstration of God's power in the plagues (chs.7-12) the Israelites finally left Egypt 430 years after their ancestors

settled there (12:40-41; on the date of the Exodus see p.38). They left Ra'amses (in the modern district of Khata'na-Qantir) travelling SE to Succoth (12:37). Beyond Succoth the details of the route are debated. It is stated explicitly (13:17-18) that the Israelites did not take the direct coastal route from Egypt to Canaan ('the way of the land of the Philistines'), and this could be taken to imply that after leaving Succoth they continued moving towards the SE. Although 14:2 and 9 give precise details of where the Israelites encamped by the *yam sûp* ('sea of reeds'), they are of little use in locating the place because Migdol and Baal-zephon can each be identified with more than one site near Egypt's E border.

31

Moses and the Exodus

The term *yam sûp* was applied to both gulfs of the Red Sea (*cf.* Nu.33:10-11; 1 Ki.9:26) and by a logical extension to the marshy Bitter Lakes region N of the Gulf of Suez. The miraculous crossing of the sea (Ex.14:1-15:21) probably took place at one of the marshy lagoons in this latter region, somewhere between modern Ismailia and Suez. In view of the changes which have taken place in the topography of this whole area since ancient times, and the uncertainty surrounding the biblical place-names, it is impossible to be more precise.

A possible alternative interpretation of the details is that proposed by W. F. Albright. In this, the expression 'turn back' in 14:2 is taken to indicate a northward march from Succoth to Baal-zephon and the *yam sûp* becomes a S extension of Lake Menzaleh. Albright then assumes another turn S, and so his interpretation does not (like those of some other scholars) run contrary to 13:17.

The Israelites moved on into the wilderness of Shur, E of Egypt (15:22). There is considerable uncertainty surrounding the location of the various stopping-places listed between there and Mt Sinai/Horeb (15:23-16:1; 17:1; 19:1-2; *cf.* Nu.33:8-15). Even the location of Mt Sinai itself is not conclusively established. Although the mount of lawgiving is traditionally associated with the S Sinai peninsula (where three peaks vie for the title), that tradition cannot be traced back before the second century AD. While some scholars favour Jebel Helal in N Sinai, yet others suggest an unspecified peak E of the Gulf of Aqabah (on the basis of Ex.2:15; 3:1; *cf.* Dt.33:2; Jdg.5:4-5; Hab.3:3).

After the receiving of the law and the making of the covenant at Mt Sinai, the people moved on by stages to Kadesh-barnea (Ain Qudeirat) in the wilderness of Paran, S of Canaan (Nu.13:26; *cf.* Nu.20:1; 33:36, which place Kadesh in the wilderness of Zin; the boundaries of desert regions were doubtless ill-defined). Again, the locations of the stopping-places en route are uncertain, and it is debatable how the two itineraries listing them (Nu.10:33-11:3,34-35; 12:16; *cf.* 33:16ff.) should be interpreted and harmonized.

From Kadesh, Canaan should have been penetrated directly from the S, but the disobedience of the Israelites led to them wandering for a further forty years in the wilderness (Nu.13:17-14:45). Near the end of this period Aaron died at Mt Hor (Nu.20:22-29; 33:37-39; *cf.* Dt.10:6 which names the place as Moserah, presumably a more precise locality within the mountainous region referred to as Mt Hor). The exact location of this is unknown, but it was evidently not far from Kadesh.

There is an apparent contradiction between Dt.2:14, which places the departure from Kadesh near the beginning of the forty years of wandering, and Nu.33:37-38, where the death of Aaron at Mt Hor (the first stopping-place after Kadesh) is dated to the fortieth year. The solution is probably that Kadesh was a base to which Israel returned a number of times during that forty-year period.

Uncertainty also surrounds the route by which the Israelites then travelled through Transjordan to the plains of Moab (*cf.* Nu.21:4,10-20; 22:1; 33:41-49; Dt.2:1-3:29; Jdg.11:15-18). After victorious clashes with Sihon, king of the Amorites, and Og, king of Bashan (Nu.21:21-35), Israel encamped opposite Jericho (Nu.25:1; 33:48f.) on the threshold of the promised land. There Moses died and was buried (Dt.34).

'The threshold of the promised land.' The Judaean hills, viewed from the foothills of Moab.

The Conquest and settlement under Joshua

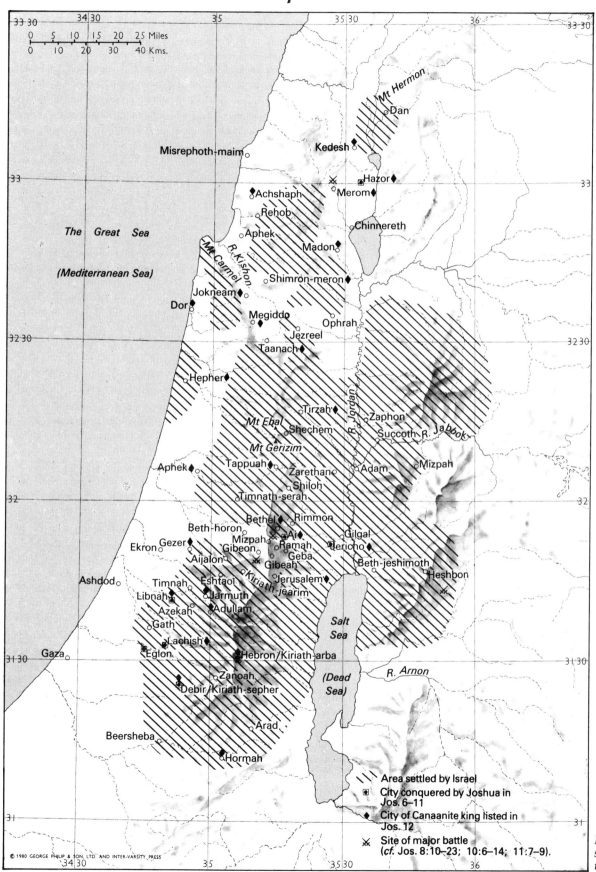

0   5   10   15   20   25 Miles
0   10   20   30   40 Kms.

33 30

34 30

35

35 30

36

33 30

Mt Hermon

Dan

Kedesh

Misrephoth-maim

33

Hazor

Merom

33

Achshaph

Rehob

The Great Sea

Aphek

Chinnereth

(Mediterranean Sea)

Madon

Mt Kishon

R. Kishon

Shimron-meron

Jokneam

Dor

Megiddo

Ophrah

Jezreel

32 30

Taanach

32 30

Hepher

Tirzah

Zaphon

Mt Ebal

Shechem

Succoth   R. Jabbok

Adam

Mizpah

Mt Gerizim

Aphek

Tappuah

Zarethan

Shiloh

Timnath-serah

32

32

Bethel   Rimmon

Beth-horon

Ai

Gilgal

Ekron   Gezer

Mizpah

Ramah

Jericho

Aijalon

Gibeon

Geba

Beth-jeshimoth

Ashdod

Gibeah

Jerusalem

Heshbon

Timnah

Eshtaol

Kiriath-jearim

Libnah   Jarmuth

Azekah   Adullam

Salt

Gath

Sea

Lachish

Gaza

Eglon   Hebron/Kiriath-arba

31 30

R. Arnon

31 30

Zanoah

(Dead

Debir/Kiriath-sepher

Sea)

Arad

Beersheba

Hormah

Area settled by Israel

City conquered by Joshua in
Jos. 6–11

City of Canaanite king listed in
Jos. 12

Site of major battle
(cf. Jos. 8:10–23; 10:6–14; 11:7–9).

© 1980 GEORGE PHILIP & SON, LTD. AND INTER-VARSITY PRESS

34 30

35

35 30

36

31

31

*Regions conquered and
settled by the Israelites
under Joshua.*

33

The Conquest and settlement under Joshua

Although there were some initial skirmishes with the Canaanites during Israel's wanderings to the S of Canaan (Nu.14:40-45; 21:1-3), the major Israelite offensive began from Shittim, in the plains of Moab opposite Jericho. From there, after succeeding Moses as leader of the people, Joshua sent spies across the Jordan to reconnoitre Jericho, the first fortress-city to be encountered by the Israelites on their W march (Jos.2). After the whole nation had crossed the Jordan, Joshua established a camp at Gilgal, where the practice of circumcision was renewed and a Passover celebrated (Jos.5). Gilgal was the base from which Joshua conducted all his campaigns in the S half of Canaan (9:6; 10:6-9,15,43).

The target of the first of these was Jericho. The city stood in the plain near the Jordan, and for Israel to press on into the highlands with a strong Canaanite fortress in their rear would have been military folly. After a week of ceremonial 'siege' the city's walls collapsed. Garstang's suggestion that a providentially-timed earthquake brought this about is still valid, though his interpretation of the archaeology of the site is not. After its collapse, the city was razed to the ground (6:24).

After Jericho, Joshua led the Israelites up into the central hill-country, where Ai was also taken and burned (7-8). Ai is conventionally identified with the mound at Et-Tell, though the archaeological evidence there does not accord with the biblical narrative (see p.38). Since Bethel lay close by Ai, it may have been at this time that Bethel too was conquered (Jos.12:16; Jdg.1:22-25).

After the fall of Ai, Joshua took the people N to Mt Ebal, near Shechem, where, in conformity with the instructions of Moses (Dt.27), he built an altar to God and led the people in a renewal of the covenant made at Mt Sinai (Jos.8:30-35).

To save their city from the fate suffered by Jericho and Ai, the people of Gibeon tricked the Israelites into making a treaty of peace (Jos.9). Gibeon lay only some 10 km (c. 6 miles) N of Jerusalem, and the king of Jerusalem, alarmed by its treaty with the Israelites, attacked Gibeon with the support of four other southern cities: Hebron, Jarmuth, Lachish and Eglon. Israel's treaty with the Gibeonites obliged Joshua to come to their aid, and thus Israel was swept into war with the coalition of five kings. During the miraculous 'long day' of Joshua 10, the coalition was routed at Beth-horon, and the five kings were later killed at Makkedah (location uncertain). The cities of Lachish, Eglon and Hebron were conquered in Joshua's subsequent campaign, along with Makkedah, Libnah and Debir (10:28-39).

With these victories, and the earlier skirmishes in the S, Joshua controlled the central hill-country as far N as Gibeon, and the Negeb to the S as far as Kadesh-barnea (10:41).

Joshua's troops next faced a coalition of several N kings under the leadership of Jabin king of Hazor, the largest city in Canaan during the Middle and Late Bronze Ages. Attacking the coalition suddenly at the Waters of Merom, Joshua's troops were once again victorious. Hazor itself was burned, and though its vassal-cities were spared this fate their kings were put to death (11:10-13).

Although the most important victories had been won, further battles occupied Joshua for a considerable time (11:18). Even when the land was allocated to the various tribes for settlement, large areas still remained unconquered (13:1-7). Not all the tribes completed the conquest of the territory allotted to them, and Judges 1:27-36 records that some settled their territory only by living alongside the Canaanites. The land allotted to Israel included the areas E of the Jordan which had been conquered earlier under Moses' leadership (Nu.21:21-35). During the period when territories were being allotted to the tribes, the Tabernacle was moved from Gilgal to a more central location at Shiloh (Jos.18:1).

Aerial view of Tell es-Sultan, OT Jericho.

Israel's tribal territories

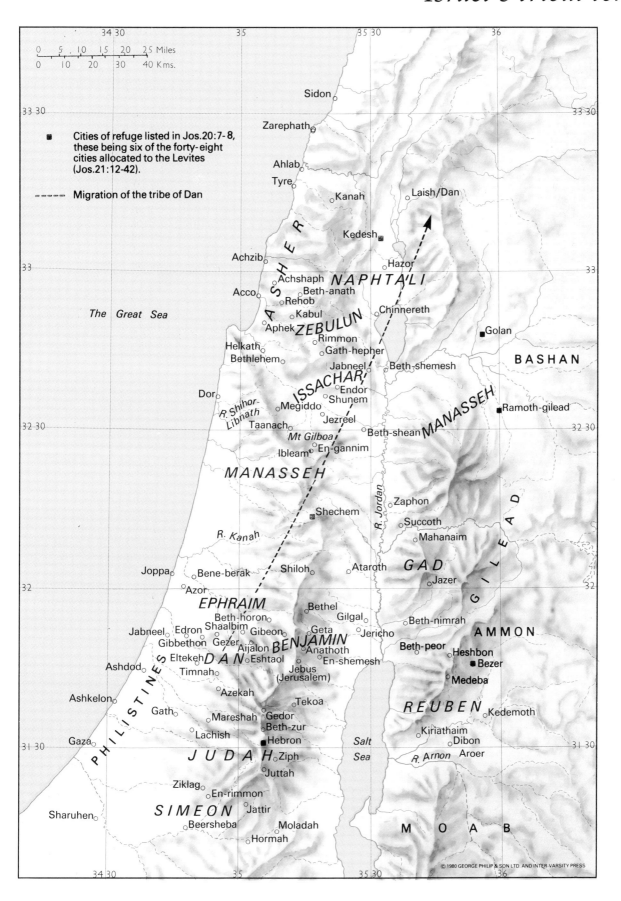

0 5 10 15 20 25 Miles
0 10 20 30 40 Kms.

■ Cities of refuge listed in Jos.20:7-8, these being six of the forty-eight cities allocated to the Levites (Jos.21:12-42).

- - - - - Migration of the tribe of Dan

The Great Sea

Sidon

Zarephath

Ahlab
Tyre

Kanah

Laish/Dan

Kedesh

Achzib

ASHER

NAPHTALI

Hazor

Achshaph
Acco
Beth-anath
Rehob
Kabul
ZEBULUN
Aphek
Rimmon

Chinnereth

Golan

BASHAN

Helkath
Bethlehem
Gath-hepher
Jabneel

Beth-shemesh

Dor

ISSACHAR
Endor
Shunem

R. Shihor-Libnath
Megiddo
Jezreel

MANASSEH

Ramoth-gilead

Taanach
Beth-shean
Mt Gilboa
Ibleam
En-gannim

MANASSEH

R. Jordan

Zaphon

Succoth

R. Kanah

Mahanaim

GILEAD

Joppa
Bene-berak
Shiloh
Ataroth
GAD
Jazer

Azor

EPHRAIM

Bethel
Gilgal
Beth-nimrah
AMMON

Beth-horon
Beth-peor
Heshbon
Bezer

Jabneel
Edron
Shaalbim
Gibeon
Geta
Jericho

Gibbethon
Gezer
Aijalon
BENJAMIN
Anathoth

Eltekeh
Eshtaol
En-shemesh

Ashdod
DAN
Jebus
(Jerusalem)
Medeba

Timnah

Ashkelon
Azekah
Tekoa

Gath
Mareshah
Gedor
REUBEN
Kedemoth

Gaza
Lachish
Beth-zur
Hebron
Kiriathaim

JUDAH
Ziph
Dibon

Juttah
Salt
Sea
Aroer
R. Arnon

Ziklag
En-rimmon

SIMEON
Jattir

Sharuhen
Beersheba

Moladah
MOAB

Hormah

PHILISTINES

© 1980 GEORGE PHILIP & SON LTD. AND INTER-VARSITY PRESS

35

The Judges

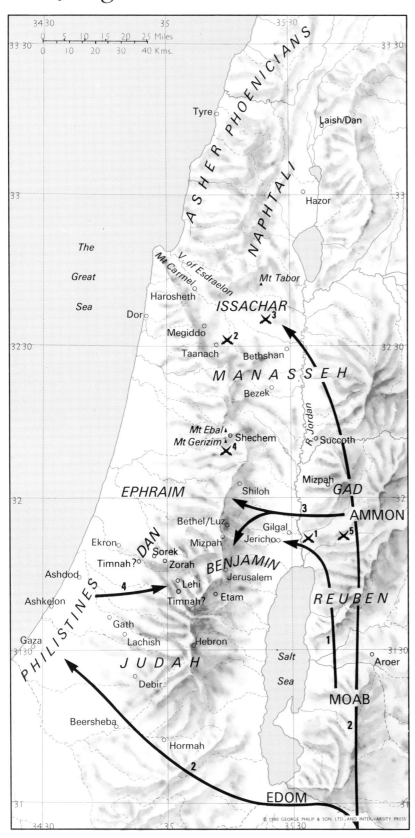

✕¹	Victory at the fords of the Jordan (Jdg.3:28-29).
✕²	Barak's victory over the forces of Jabin led by Sisera (Jdg.4:12-16; 5:19-21).
✕³	Gideon's victory over the Midianites by the hill of Moreh (Jdg.7:1,19-25).
✕⁴	Abimelech's battle with Shechem (Jdg.9:44-49).
✕⁵	Jepthah's victory over the Ammonites, achieved in a battle which ranged widely in the region S of Mizpah (Jdg.11:33).
1	Moabite invasion (Jdg.3:12-14).
2	Invasions of Midianites and Amalekites into the S (Jdg. 6:1–6) and into the valley of Jezreel (Jdg. 6:33).
3	Ammonite penetrations into Ephraim, Benjamin and Judah (Jdg.10:9).
4	Philistine raid into Judah (Jdg.15:9).

The period of the judges spanned the time between Joshua's death and Samuel. Most scholars would date the period *c.*1220-1050 BC, but an earlier date for the Exodus and Conquest (see pp.38-39) would push back the start of the period to *c.*1400 BC.

The book of Judges opens with an account of various attempts by individual tribes to conquer their allotted territories — some successful, some dismal failures. The successful conquests of Hebron (1:10), Debir (1:11-15) and Zephath-Hormah (1:17) seem to duplicate earlier events (Jos.10:36-39; *cf.* Nu.21:3). It may be that these towns revived as Canaanite centres and had to be captured a second time, or we may simply have here a retelling of the same events. (The attribution of the conquest of Hebron and Debir to Joshua in Joshua 10, rather than to the men of Judah and Caleb is not a serious discrepancy; *cf.* the way a victory by Jonathan is attributed to Saul, his superior, in 1 Sa.13:3-4.) On this reading of Judges 1, the words 'after the death of Joshua' in 1:1 must be understood as a general heading to the whole book, the events of chapter 1 occurring *before* Joshua's death, which is recounted in 2:6-9.

The failures recorded in Judges 1 were more significant for the subsequent history than the successes. The fact that Canaanites remained in several areas (especially in the N) meant that the Israelites settled alongside them (*cf.*1:29-33), and this led to many Israelites deserting the worship of God for the worship of the gods of Canaan. God punished this infidelity by

Major invasions and battles of the Judges period.

handing the tribes over to various enemies. When Israel turned to God for help, he raised up a leader ('judge' or 'governor') who delivered them. This pattern was repeated with depressing monotony.

Cushan-Rishathaim, king of Aram-Naharaim (*i.e.* NW Mesopotamia) extended his rule to Palestine and oppressed the Israelites for eight years. The deliverer on this occasion was Othniel, who had earlier acquired Debir (3:7-11; *cf.* 1:11-13).

Israel's next oppressor was Eglon, king of Moab, who crossed the Jordan along with bands of Ammonites and Amalekites and established a base at Jericho ('city of palms', 3:13). From there he dominated the Israelites, exacting tribute from them. He was assassinated by Ehud, a Benjaminite, who subsequently rallied the men of Ephraim to block the Moabites' retreat at the fords of the Jordan near Jericho.

Judges 4-5 records a twenty-year oppression by Jabin, 'king of Canaan, who ruled in Hazor', a namesake (descendant?) of the king defeated by Joshua. On the initiative of the prophetess Deborah, Barak gathered troops from Zebulun and Naphtali on Mt Tabor and marched from there to a place near Taanach by the river Kishon (4:13; 'the waters of Megiddo', 5:19). There he engaged the troops of Jabin, led by Sisera his commander. The river seems to have been running high (5:21), and may have made the adjacent plain too soft for Sisera's 900 chariots to be effective there. Barak's victory led eventually to the fall of Jabin (4:24). The list of tribes and districts which were expected to support Barak (5:14-18) suggests that Jabin's oppression affected only the N half of the country; the important tribe of Judah is not mentioned.

Israel's next oppressors were the Midianites, whose periodic invasions, along with Amalekites and other 'people of the east', made life intolerable. This was not an organized domination but a series of plundering raids by nomadic groups. The Midianite homeland lay E of the Gulf of Aqabah, while the Amalekites inhabited parts of the Sinai peninsula and S Canaan. Their initial raids were in the S (*cf.* 6:4) but subsequently they moved N through Transjordan from where they invaded the fertile Valley of Jezreel. It was against this invasion that Gideon led Israelite forces, and hence it was once again to the N tribes that the rallying-cry was given (6:35; 7:23). Following an initial victory at the Midianite camp, Gideon called upon the men of Ephraim to block the way of escape at the Jordan (7:24). However, two Midianite chieftains escaped with a considerable force. Gideon and his men therefore carried their assault into

Transjordan, and eventually routed the enemy completely (7:24-8:21).

The next period of oppression to be described is that of the E districts by the Ammonites, but 10:7 implies that it actually coincided with the Philistine oppression in the W, recounted in chapter 13. Other periods of oppression may also have been contemporary rather than consecutive, which makes the overall chronology of the period somewhat flexible and dependent ultimately on the date adopted for the Exodus and Conquest.

The Ammonite oppression chiefly affected the Israelites settled E of the Jordan in Gilead, but there were also attacks on Judah, Ephraim and Benjamin (10:8-9). The deliverer was a Gileadite, Jephthah, appointed commander by the elders of Gilead at Mizpah. He devastated the Ammonites as far S as Aroer (11:33). This was not the end of Gilead's troubles, however, for the men of Ephraim, offended that they were not allowed a share in the victory, crossed the Jordan to attack the Gileadites. Once again Jephthah's forces proved superior, and 42,000 Ephraimites died in the pointless war (12:6).

The Philistine oppression referred to in 10:7 provides the context for the life of Samson. Samson was from the tribe of Dan, which had already suffered from Amorite pressure (1:34). The migration of part of this tribe to the N (ch.18) may have already happened before the time of Samson.

The Philistines settled on the coastal plain *c.*1200 BC and soon dominated the W parts of Israel's territory. The area of Judah affected by Philistine rule seems to have accepted it (15:11) and even Samson did not regard them as enemies until a petty quarrel with them led to open aggression (chs.14-16). His exploits were acts of personal revenge, and he never accomplished national deliverance. That was left to Samuel, Saul and David.

The ruins of Hazor. In the distance can be seen the fertile plains of N Galilee.

Archaeological sites: Late Bronze Age

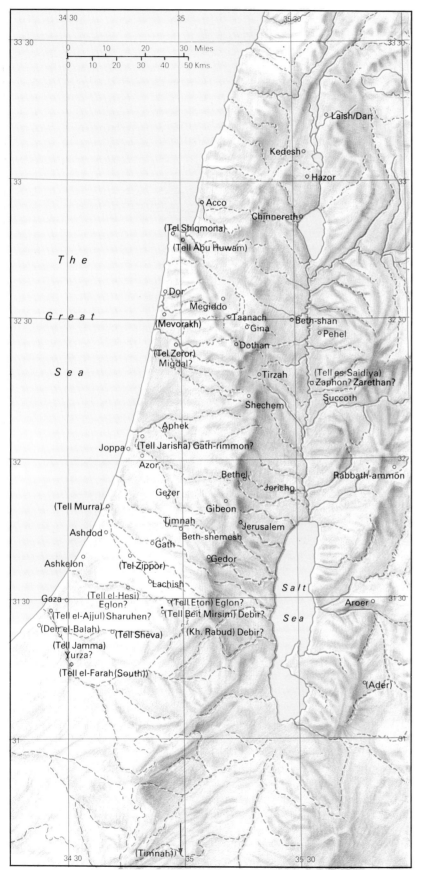

The transition from the Middle to Late Bronze Age in Palestine was marked by the destruction of many important cities and the subsequent abandonment of some sites for most of LBI.LBII (c. 1400-1200 BC) saw the final flourish of Canaanite culture before it was in turn destroyed and replaced by that of Iron Age I.

Among the LB towns destroyed at the end of the period are some listed among Israel's conquests : Lachish (Tell ed-Duweir), Eglon (Tell el-Hesi), Debir (Tell Beit Mirsim) and Hazor. Many scholars have therefore interpreted these destructions as the archaeological evidence for Israel's entry into Canaan, dating the event c.1230/20 BC. The relatively poor Iron Age I culture which followed has therefore been labelled 'Israelite'. This interpretation places the Exodus c.1270/60 BC.

This dating and interpretation of the Conquest, however, is not without difficulties. At the sites of other cities captured and destroyed by the Israelites, there is no evidence of occupation at the end of LB II. This is true at Jericho, Ai (if identified with Et-Tell) and Arad (whether Tel Malhata or Tel Arad). This may not be an insuperable problem however, since evidence of occupation at a particular period can sometimes be eroded away or simply not found in the limited excavations which time and money allow at most sites. On the other hand, the destructions mentioned above have to be seen in the context of others which were occurring in the same general period. The decades around 1200 BC were a time of widespread disturbance and change which affected cities not conquered by the Israelites. E.g. Jaffa and Aphek were both destroyed c.1240/30 BC; Tell Deir 'Alla in Transjordan was destroyed c.1200 BC; Tell Shera (Ziklag?) was destroyed c.1175 BC. It appears from the latest evidence that Lachish was also destroyed c.1175 BC rather than 1230/20 BC. Egyptian campaigns and an influx of 'Sea Peoples' (including the Philistines), which are known to have occurred in this period, may account for the destructions which ended the LB culture without associating those destructions with the arrival of the Israelites. In the absence of stronger evidence for Israel's involvement in the final LB destructions, the view that they mark Joshua's conquest must remain only a hypothesis.

An alternative view is possible, which rests on an earlier date for the Exodus and Conquest. Judges 11:26 and 1 Kings 6:1 imply a date for the Exodus in the mid-15th cent. BC,

Some important Late Bronze Age excavated sites (c.1550-1200 BC).

and thus a conquest some forty years later, towards the end of that century. On the present dating of the various phases of the Late Bronze Age there is no wave of destructions at that time (*i.e.* shortly before 1400 BC) which could signify the Israelite invasion. However, it is arguable that the destructions which ended the *Middle* Bronze Age can be redated from the currently accepted date of *c.*1550 BC to this later time (proportionally shortening the LBA). This would provide satisfactory archaeological evidence for occupation and destruction of all the identifiable cities listed in the Conquest narratives, with the exception of Ai if this is identified with Et-Tell. At Et-Tell there is evidence of neither MB nor LB occupation. Again there is the possibility that evidence has been destroyed or missed, but in this case it is also possible that Ai is to be located elsewhere.

On this latter view the LB culture must be seen not only as that of the Canaanites but also in some measure that of the Israelites. In view of the way many Israelites settled among the Canaanites and adopted their religious practices (*cf.* Jdg.1:27-33), it is feasible to assume that much of the material culture of Canaan was also adopted by the Israelites.

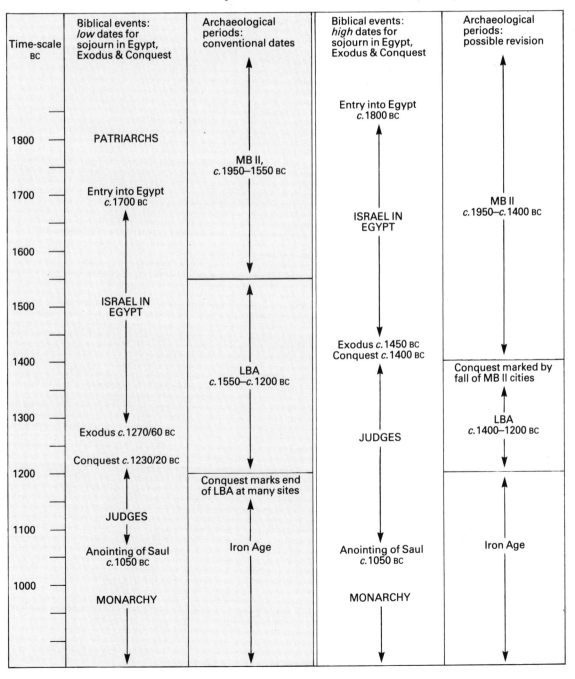

A summary of the alternative suggestions for dating biblical events and archaeological periods in the second millennium BC.

The founding of the Hebrew monarchy

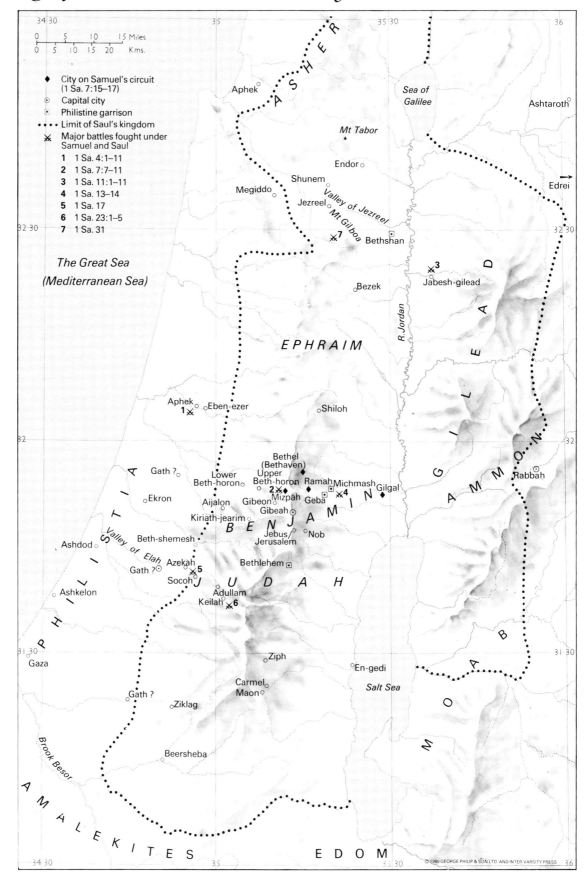

34 30

0   5   10   15 Miles
0   5 10 15 20 Kms.

♦ City on Samuel's circuit
   (1 Sa. 7:15–17)
⊙ Capital city
▣ Philistine garrison
••• Limit of Saul's kingdom
⨉ Major battles fought under
   Samuel and Saul
  1 1 Sa. 4:1–11
  2 1 Sa. 7:7–11
  3 1 Sa. 11:1–11
  4 1 Sa. 13–14
  5 1 Sa. 17
  6 1 Sa. 23:1–5
  7 1 Sa. 31

The Great Sea
(Mediterranean Sea)

A S H E R

Sea of Galilee

Ashtaroth

Aphek

Mt Tabor

Endor

Edrei

Shunem

Megiddo

Valley of Jezreel

Jezreel

Mt Gilboa

7⨉

Bethshan

G I L E A D

3⨉

Bezek

Jabesh-gilead

R. Jordan

E P H R A I M

Aphek

Eben-ezer

Shiloh

1⨉

A M M O N

Bethel
(Bethaven)
Upper
Lower   Beth-horon   Ramah   Michmash Gilgal
Beth-horon   **2**⨉ ♦ ♦   **4**⨉
Gath ?   Mizpah   Geba
Ekron   Gibeon

Rabbah

Aijalon   Gibeah

Kiriath-jearim

B E N J A M I N

Ashdod

Beth-shemesh

Jebus/
Jerusalem   Nob

P H I L I S T I A

Valley of Elah

Azekah   Bethlehem

Gath ?   **5**⨉
Socoh

Ashkelon   J U D A H

Adullam
Keilah **6**⨉

Gaza

Ziph

Zib

En-gedi

Salt Sea

Carmel
Maon

Gath ?   Ziklag

Beersheba

Brook Besor

A M A L E K I T E S   E D O M

M O A B

© 1980 GEORGE PHILIP & SON LTD. AND INTER-VARSITY PRESS

Although defeated under Samuel (1 Sa.7), the Philistines remained a threat; when in addition an invasion by Ammon seemed imminent, the people pressed Samuel for a king (ch.8; cf. 12:12). At first Saul was effective against the Ammonites, Philistines and Amalekites (chs.11-15), but by his tragic death at Gilboa the Philistine domination was re-established (ch.31).

Wars of David's reign

David the military leader

David had already made his mark as a military leader during the reign of Saul, scoring repeated victories over the Philistines (1 Sa.18:12-16, 24-27,30; 23:1-5). However, because of Saul's jealousy, David later fled to Philistine territory himself and served Achish, king of Gath, as a mercenary. His campaigns during this time were nevertheless directed against the enemies of Israel, notably the Amalekites (27:8; 30:1-20).

The capture of Jerusalem

After Saul's death in battle against the Philistines, the kingdom was torn by civil war; David became king over Judah in Hebron, while Saul's son Ish-bosheth ruled over the N tribes from Mahanaim in Gilead (2 Sa.2:1-10). There was war between the two factions until Ish-bosheth was assassinated (ch.4), after which the elders of the N tribes anointed David as their king (5:1-3). With the whole of Saul's former kingdom under his control, David captured Jerusalem from the Jebusites, creating there a new, strategically situated capital (5:6-10). David subsequently installed the ark there, thus making Jerusalem the religious centre as well (6:1-19).

The independent kingdom

David had become king of Judah as a Philistine vassal, but his new status as king of Israel amounted to a declaration of independence for the whole kingdom, and involved him immediately in war with the Philistines. David defeated them in the Valley of Rephaim (5:17-25), and subsequently subdued them altogether (8:1).

Wider conquests

To the E, David made the Moabites tribute-paying subjects (8:2) and conquered Edom with great brutality, establishing garrisons there (8:13-14; cf. 1 Ki.11:15-16). To the N, the Aramaean kingdoms of Zobah and Damascus were brought under his control (8:3-8), though Zobah and its vassal-states later rebelled, joining Ammon in an alliance against David. They were defeated, however, at Helam in Transjordan (10:6-19) and the Ammonite capital Rabbah was later captured (12:26-31).

Alliances

At an early stage David had the friendship of Hiram, king of the Phoenician city of Tyre (5:11), and after his defeat of Hadadezer of Zobah, King Toi (or Tou) of Hamath, who had himself been at war with Hadadezer, made an alliance with David (8:9-10).

Wars of David's reign.

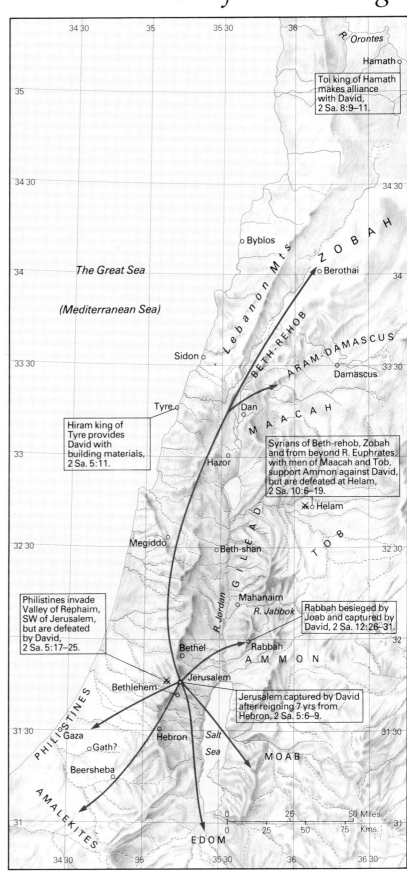

David's Kingdom

Legend:
- Israelite territory
- Conquered region under Israelite rule
- Region dominated by vassal treaty

The territory ruled by David.

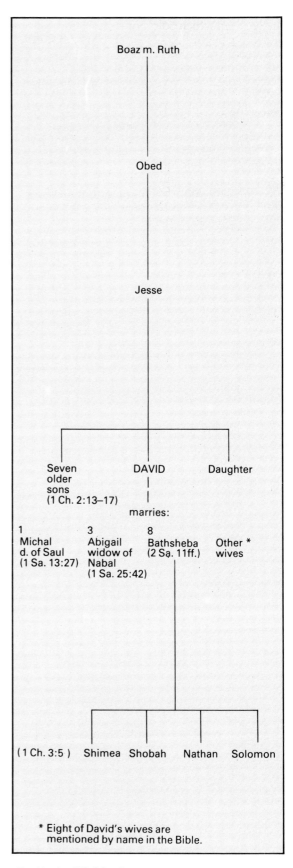

David: simplified family tree.

Boaz m. Ruth

Obed

Jesse

Seven older sons (1 Ch. 2:13–17) — DAVID — Daughter

marries:

1 Michal d. of Saul (1 Sa. 13:27)

3 Abigail widow of Nabal (1 Sa. 25:42)

8 Bathsheba (2 Sa. 11ff.)

Other * wives

(1 Ch. 3:5) Shimea Shobab Nathan Solomon

* Eight of David's wives are mentioned by name in the Bible.

As a result of his military and diplomatic successes, David transformed a small kingdom, threatened by its various neighbours, into an empire which stretched from the Gulf of Aqabah and the border of Egypt in the S to the Upper Euphrates in the N. His kingdom now had access to important trade-routes and thus its economic as well as its military security was ensured for as long as the empire held together. It was this promising state of affairs which David bequeathed to his son Solomon (*cf.* 1 Ki.4:21,24-25).

Solomon's Kingdom: administrative districts

The wisdom which Solomon requested from God at the beginning of his reign (1 Ki.3:4-14) was an apt choice, since the task facing him was a daunting one. The tribal confederacy which had existed from the time of the judges needed to be transformed if Israel was to maintain its empire. The new situation brought about by David required strong centralized government to sustain it and this Solomon determined to develop by administrative reform.

For the better administration of the kingdom's revenue, Solomon reorganized Israel into twelve tax districts which effectively replaced the traditional tribal boundaries

(1 Ki.4:7-19). Whether Judah comprised a thirteenth district in this system (*cf.* 4:19 in RSV; compare NIV, NEB, *etc.*) or was itself divided into a further twelve districts (a scheme which some see reflected in Jos.15:20-62) is debatable. What is explicit is that the twelve tax districts of *Israel* (as distinct from Judah) were responsible for providing for the royal court, each supplying food for one month of the year (4:7,27-28). The court's requirements for one day, as listed in 4:22-23, imply that this was a very burdensome obligation. If Judah was exempt from it, this may have contributed to the bitterness which eventually led to Israel's rebellion.

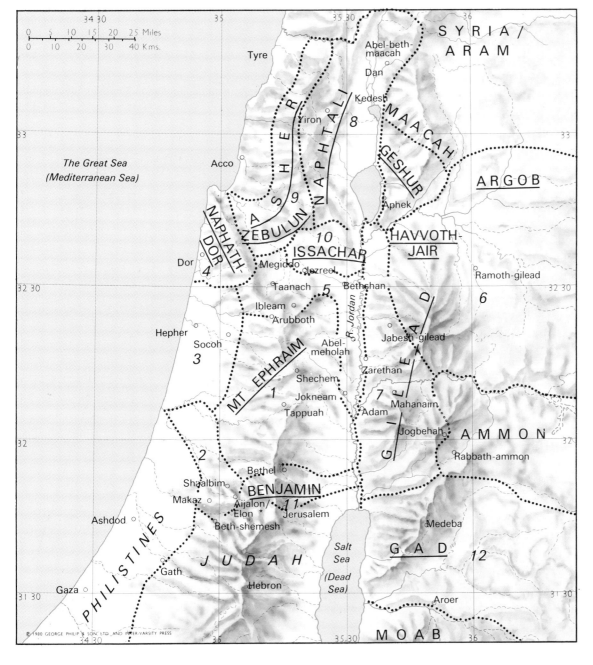

Solomon's administrative districts as described in 1 Ki. 4:7-19.

Solomon's Kingdom: trade routes and imports

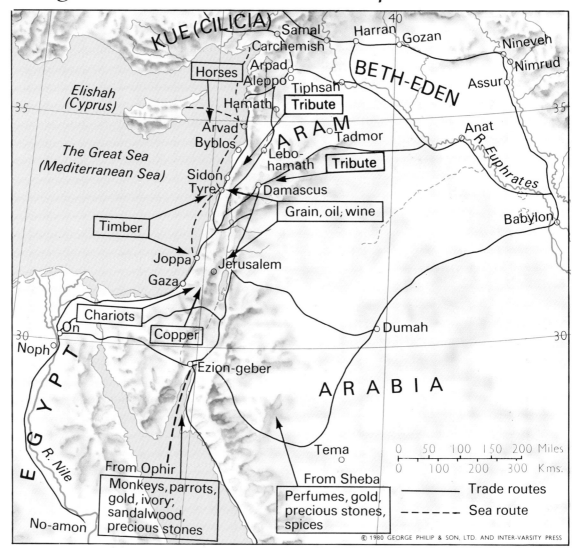

Trade routes in Solomon's time, showing principal imports and their sources.

On his accession to the throne, Solomon inherited a particularly favourable situation: international contacts, economic prosperity and freedom from war. In particular, the empire created by David occupied a significant position between Egypt and Asia, embracing major N-S trade routes.

Thus Solomon was able to monopolize the trade in horses and chariots between the Hittites, the Aramaeans and Egypt (1 Ki. 10:28-29); he was also in a position to demand revenue from the countries of Arabia whose trade in gold, precious stones and spices would not have survived without Solomon's co-operation (10:15; *cf.* the Queen of Sheba's gift, 10:10).

Hiram of Tyre supplied Solomon with Lebanese cedar and Phoenician craftsmen (1 Ki.5:1-10; 7:13-14), receiving grain and oil in return (5:11). He also supplied Solomon with sailors to aid him in his maritime ventures. From Ezion-geber, Solomon's fleet made voyages to Ophir (perhaps an Arabian locality or perhaps in NE Africa), bringing back almug wood (a type of hardwood), precious stones and great quantities of gold (9:26-28; 10:11). Solomon's 'ships of Tarshish' may have been the same Red Sea fleet, or they may have been a second fleet operating from a Mediterranean port. Their destination is not named, but their three-year voyages brought back gold, silver, ivory and exotic animals.

Although it was in some respects a golden age, for many of his subjects Solomon's rule was oppressive. The wealth was centralized and soaked up by the lavish court. Ambitious building projects (9:15-19) demanded more labour than could be raised from subject peoples, so that the policy (9:22) of not using Israelites in the corvée (system of conscripted labour) was abandoned to meet requirements (*cf.* 11:28; 12:4). Conditions for many Israelites were harsh enough to cause the secession of Israel from Judah on Solomon's death (ch.12).

The Kingdoms of Israel and Judah

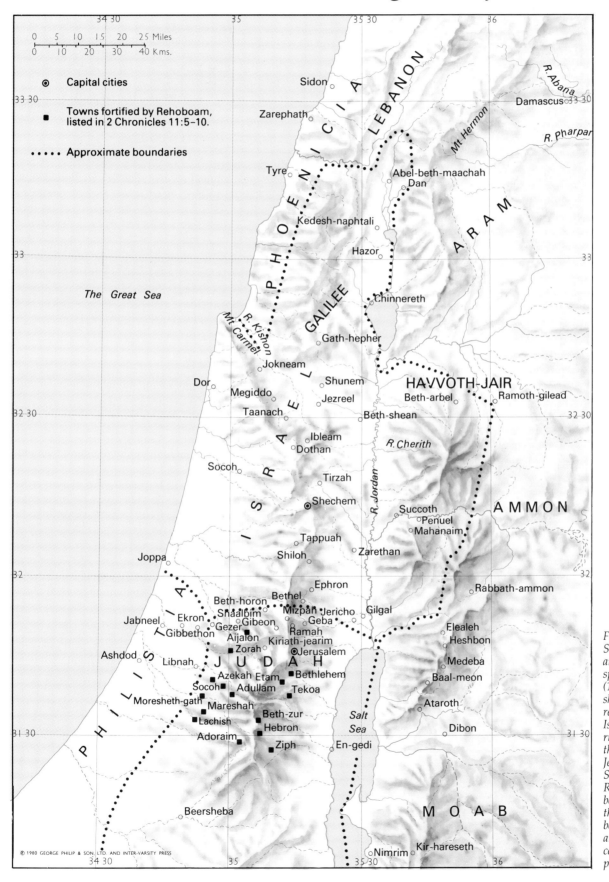

Capital cities

Towns fortified by Rehoboam, listed in 2 Chronicles 11:5–10.

Approximate boundaries

0 5 10 15 20 25 Miles
0 10 20 30 40 Kms.

Sidon

Zarephath

Tyre

PHOENICIA

LEBANON

Abel-beth-maachah
Dan

Kedesh-naphtali

ARAM

Damascus

Mt Hermon

R. Abana

R. Pharpar

Hazor

The Great Sea

GALILEE

Chinnereth

Gath-hepher

Mt Carmel

R. Kishon

Jokneam

Shunem

HAVVOTH-JAIR

Beth-arbel

Ramoth-gilead

Dor

Megiddo

Jezreel

Taanach

Beth-shean

Ibleam

R. Cherith

Dothan

I S R A E L

Socoh

Tirzah

R. Jordan

Shechem

Succoth

AMMON

Penuel
Mahanaim

Tappuah

Shiloh

Zarethan

Joppa

Ephron

Rabbath-ammon

Bethel

Beth-horon

Mizpah

Jericho

Gilgal

Shaalbim

Geba

Jabneel

Ekron

Gibeon

Ramah

Elealeh
Heshbon

Gezer

Gibbethon

Aijalon

Kiriath-jearim

Jerusalem

Zorah

Ashdod

Libnah

JUDAH

Medeba

Bethlehem

Baal-meon

Azekah Etam

Socoh

Adullam

Tekoa

Moresheth-gath

Mareshah

Ataroth

Lachish

Beth-zur

Salt
Sea

Dibon

Adoraim

Hebron

Ziph

En-gedi

PHILISTIA

Beersheba

MOAB

Nimrim

Kir-hareseth

33 30

33

32 30

32

31 30

34 30   35   35 30   36

© 1980 GEORGE PHILIP & SON, LTD AND INTER-VARSITY PRESS

Following the death of Solomon, economic and social tensions split the kingdom (1 Ki. 12). The map shows the two resulting kingdoms of Israel and Judah, ruled respectively by the returned exile Jeroboam and Solomon's son Rehoboam. The N boundary of Israel and the E boundaries of both Israel and Judah are not known with certainty at this period.

Shishak's Palestinian campaign

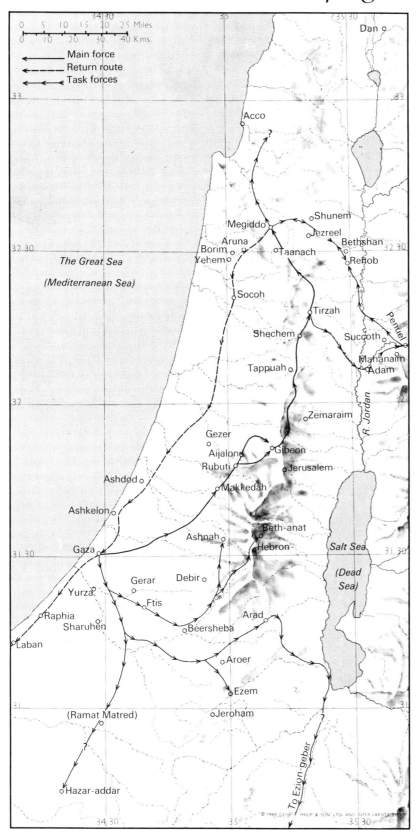

Probable scope and course of the campaign of the Egyptian king Shishak (Sheshonq/Shoshenq I) in Palestine, c.925 BC, reconstructed from his relief-scene.

In the fifth year of Rehoboam's reign (*c.* 926 BC) his kingdom, already weakened by the secession of Israel and war with Jeroboam (*cf.* 1 Ki.14:30), suffered a severe blow. 'Shishak king of Egypt' invaded Judah, capturing its fortified cities and forcing the submission of Jerusalem. The treasures of Solomon's Temple and the royal palace were carried away as tribute as recorded in 1 Ki.14:25-26 and 2 Ch.12:1-9.

Reconstruction from reliefs
The brief biblical accounts of this event can be supplemented by the pharaoh's own reliefs commemorating his achievement. Shoshenq I (*c.*945-924 BC), the founder of Egypt's Libyan 22nd Dynasty, left a relief-scene at the temple of Amun in Thebes, in which are listed the many towns which he captured in Palestine. Because the reliefs are damaged the list cannot be read in its entirety; nevertheless it provides sufficient information for the scope and course of the campaign to be reconstructed in some detail.

Assault on Judah
From Gaza Shoshenq sent a task-force into the Negeb and S Judah while the main army continued NE to the Shephelah, beginning its assault on Judah's fortified towns. The account in 2 Chronicles tells us that Rehoboam and the 'princes of Judah', who were assembled in Jerusalem because of the crisis, were urged by the prophet Shemaiah to submit. Thus when the pharaoh came to Jerusalem it was not to besiege it but merely to take away its treasures as booty (2 Ch.12:5-9). Surprisingly enough, Jerusalem does not feature in Shoshenq's list.

Attack on Israel
Although the biblical accounts refer only to an invasion of Judah, it is evident from Shoshenq's list, and from a fragment of an inscription found at Megiddo, that the Egyptian army next swept through Israel as well. This points to a change in the previously friendly relations between Shoshenq and Jeroboam, who had found asylum at the pharaoh's court when fleeing from Solomon (1 Ki.11:40).

While pressing N to Megiddo with the main army Shoshenq dispatched a task-force into Transjordan, perhaps because Jeroboam had fled there to Penuel (*cf.* 1 Ki.12:25). After further operations from Megiddo, where a commemorative inscription was set up, the army returned to Egypt by way of the coast road.

Shoshenq's purpose had been limited and definite: to gain political and commercial security by subduing his immediate neighbour.

The Moabite Stone

The Moabite Stone (or Mesha Stela) was found at Dhiban (biblical Dibon) in 1868, when the Revd F. Klein, a German missionary, was shown the stone by an Arab sheikh. It was about 3½ ft (c.1.1m) high, 2 ft (c.0.6m) broad and 2 ft (c.0.6m) thick, with a rounded top, and contained thirty-four lines of writing. Klein copied a few words of the inscription and showed them to the German consul, who negotiated to obtain the stone for the Berlin Museum. At the same time, C. S. Clermont-Ganneau tried to obtain it for the Louvre. Sensing its value, the local Arabs broke the stone into several pieces, hoping to make more profit from the fragments. Clermont-Ganneau eventually traced twenty of the fragments and reconstructed the stone in the Louvre. Only about two-thirds of the inscription was recovered, but fortunately Clermont-Ganneau had had a 'squeeze' made of the whole before it was broken. Although imperfect, this made it possible to reconstruct the bulk of the text. The British Museum has a copy of the restored stone.

The first seven lines read:

I (am) Mesha, son of Chemosh-[…], king of Moab, the Dibonite—my father (had) reigned over Moab thirty years, and I reigned after my father,—(who) made this high place for Chemosh in Qarhoh […] because he saved me from all the kings and caused me to triumph over all my adversaries. As for Omri, (5) king of Israel, he humbled Moab many years (lit., days), for Chemosh was angry at his land. And his son followed him and he also said, 'I will humble Moab.' In my time he spoke (thus), but I have triumphed over him and over his house, while Israel hath perished for ever!

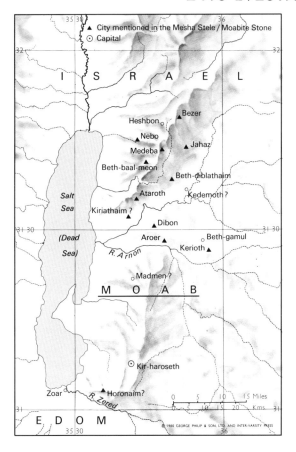

Places in Moab named on the Moabite Stone (Mesha inscription).

The inscription is a valuable complement to the biblical information on the reigns of Omri and Ahab. In language closely akin to Hebrew, it commemorates the successful revolt of Mesha, king of Moab, against Israel. The revolt is recorded in the OT (2 Ki.1:1; 3:4-27), but the stone provides a great deal of additional information.

The first eight lines of the Moabite Stone inscription. The word 'Israel' has been highlighted.

The Moabite Stone

The inscription appears to clash with the biblical account in claiming that Mesha broke free from Israel during Ahab's reign, not after his death as in 2 Kings 1:1. It may be that Ahab lost effective control of Moab while preoccupied with fighting the Aramaeans, and that Mesha reckoned Moab's independence from then; the biblical writer, however, does not regard Moab as free until after the attempt by Ahab's son Joram to regain control had failed.

The Moabite version is valuable in revealing (among other things) that Omri subdued Moab. David had done so earlier (2 Sa.8:2) but control was lost when the kingdom divided.

The stone goes on to record how Ataroth, Jahaz and Nebo were captured, their Israelite inhabitants being devoted to the deity Ashtar-Chemosh (*i.e.* destroyed, *cf.* the Hebrew practice of *ḥērem*, devoting people and things to God by destruction, *e.g.* Jos.6:17). Mesha then relates how he (re)built the towns of Baal-meon, Kiriathaim, Aroer, Beth-bamoth, Bezer, Medeba, Beth-diblathaim and Beth-baal-meon. He also built Qarḥoh, apparently a name for the royal citadel of Dibon. Here he built a high place to his god Chemosh in gratitude for his victory, and equipped the town with reservoirs and a water-channel cut by Israelite slave-labour.

The events recorded on the stone must have occurred between 860 and 840 BC, and the stone was probably set up in Dibon soon after.

The Moabite Stone reconstructed.

Elijah and Elisha

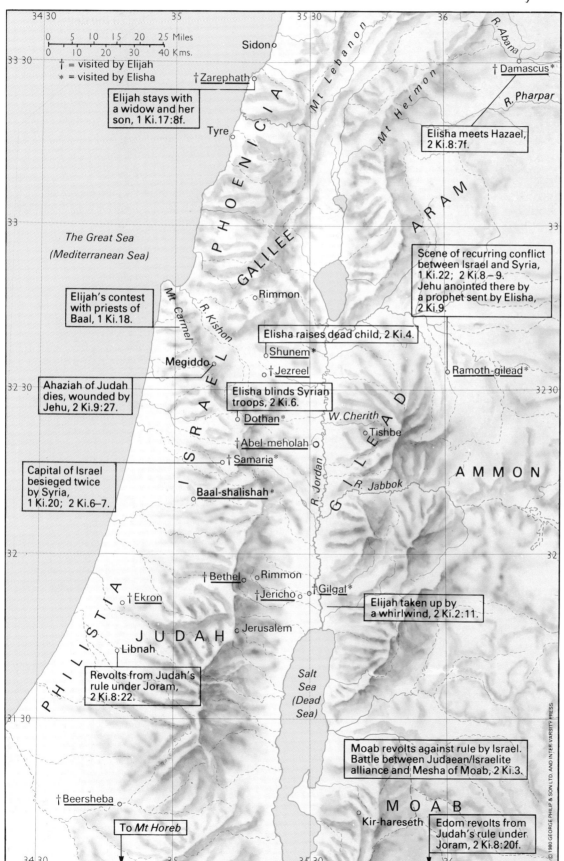

† = visited by Elijah
* = visited by Elisha

†Zarephath

Elijah stays with
a widow and her
son, 1 Ki.17:8f.

Sidon

Mt Lebanon

Mt Hermon

R. Abana

†Damascus *

R. Pharpar

ARAM

Tyre

Elisha meets Hazael,
2 Ki.8:7f.

PHOENICIA

GALILEE

The Great Sea
(Mediterranean Sea)

Scene of recurring conflict
between Israel and Syria,
1 Ki.22; 2 Ki.8–9.
Jehu anointed there by
a prophet sent by Elisha,
2 Ki.9.

Rimmon

Mt Carmel

R. Kishon

Elijah's contest
with priests of
Baal, 1 Ki.18.

Elisha raises dead child, 2 Ki.4.

Shunem *

Megiddo

†Jezreel

Ramoth-gilead *

Ahaziah of Judah
dies, wounded by
Jehu, 2 Ki.9:27.

ISRAEL

JEZREEL

Elisha blinds Syrian
troops, 2 Ki.6.

Dothan *

W. Cherith

Tishbe

GILEAD

†Abel-meholah

R. Jordan

AMMON

†Samaria *

Capital of Israel
besieged twice
by Syria,
1 Ki.20; 2 Ki.6–7.

Baal-shalishah *

R. Jabbok

†Bethel

Rimmon

†Gilgal *

†Jericho

Elijah taken up by
a whirlwind, 2 Ki.2:11.

PHILISTIA

†Ekron

Jerusalem

JUDAH

Libnah

Salt
Sea
(Dead
Sea)

Revolts from Judah's
rule under Joram,
2 Ki.8:22.

†Beersheba

To *Mt Horeb*

Moab revolts against rule by Israel.
Battle between Judaean/Israelite
alliance and Mesha of Moab, 2 Ki.3.

MOAB

Kir-hareseth

Edom revolts from
Judah's rule under
Joram, 2 Ki.8:20f.

0   5   10 15 20 25 Miles
0   10   20   30   40 Kms.

*Main events in the time
of the prophets Elijah
and Elisha, i.e. the
period c. 870-790 BC (the
reigns of Ahab, Ahaziah,
Joram, Jehu, Jehoahaz
and Joash in Israel, and
of Jehoshaphat, Joram,
Ahaziah, Athaliah,
Joash and Amaziah in
Judah). During this
period both Israel and
Judah clashed repeatedly
with the Syrians
(Aramaeans) of
Damascus (on this see
further p. 89). Also
Israel lost control of
Moab, while Judah lost
Edom and the town of
Libnah on the border
with Philistia.*

49

Jeroboam II and Uzziah

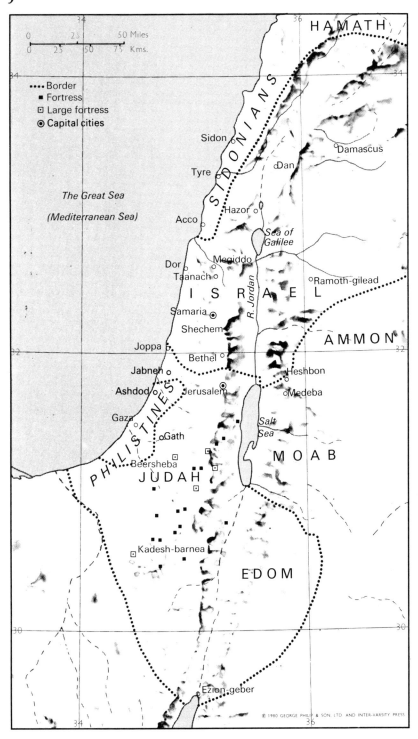

Israel and Judah in the reigns of Jeroboam II and Uzziah.

Jeroboam

By the late ninth century BC, Israel's fortunes were low. The loss of Moab *c.* 850 BC was followed by the loss of Israel's remaining Transjordan territories; Gilead and Bashan were taken from Jehu (*c.* 824-815 BC) by Hazael, king of Damascus (2 Ki.10:32-33). Subsequent campaigns by Hazael and his son Ben-Hadad (II or III) threatened Israel's very existence as an independent state (2 Ki.13:1-7). A change in Israel's fortunes came with J(eh)oash (*c.* 801-786 BC) and his son and co-regent Jeroboam II (*c.* 793-753 BC).

Following up his father's victories over Ben-Hadad (2 Ki.13:25), Jeroboam brought the Aramaean kingdom of Damascus under Israel's dominion (14:28) and restored to Israel its lost Transjordan territories as far S as the Dead Sea (14:25).

Uzziah

Largely contemporary with Jeroboam II, an equally illustrious king reigned in Judah, Uzziah (or Azariah). His fifty-two-year reign (*c.* 791/90-740/39 BC) began and ended with a co-regency (*c.* 791/90-767 BC with his father Amaziah; *c.* 750-740/39 BC with his son Jotham).

In the middle of the previous century, Edom and Libnah had both successfully revolted from Judah's rule (2 Ki.8:20-22). Amaziah reconquered Edom (2 Ch.25:11,14), thus restoring to Judah the port of Elath, which Uzziah rebuilt after becoming sole ruler (2 Ki.14:22). Uzziah also campaigned against the Philistines, conquering Gath, Jabneh and Ashdod and establishing garrison-towns in Philistine territory (2 Ch.26:6). His aim was probably to gain access to the coast directly W of Jerusalem. Libnah, which lay in the Shephelah near the Philistine border (exact location uncertain), was probably regained at this time.

The extent of their power

Arabs living in the S of Judah and the Meunites (probably an Edomite tribe) were also subdued and Ammon was forced to pay tribute (2 Ch.26:7-8). Uzziah maintained a large and well-equipped standing army (2 Ch.26:11-15) and refortified Jerusalem (v.9). He also established forts in the Negeb, where he fostered agriculture on a new scale (2 Ch.26:10).

The stability and prosperity created by Jeroboam II and Uzziah were short-lived, however. Judah became a vassal of Assyria in 733 BC, and in 722 Assyrian armies destroyed Samaria in fulfilment of the warnings given by Amos and Hosea (Ho.13:15-16; Am.6:4-7, 13-14).

Sennacherib's campaign

Hezekiah

Hezekiah (729-687 BC, co-regent with Ahaz 729-716/15 BC) inherited from Ahaz a kingdom submissive to Assyria. Seeking an opportunity to throw off the Assyrian yoke, he strengthened Jerusalem's fortifications and dug the Siloam tunnel to safeguard the water-supply in a time of siege (2 Ki.20:20; 2 Ch. 32:1-8; Is.22:9-11). Support was sought from Egypt (2 Ki.18:21; *cf.* Is.30), and Hezekiah also entertained envoys from a fellow-rebel against Assyria, Merodach-baladan, king of Babylon (2 Ki.20:12-19).

Assyria's king Sennacherib (705-681 BC) moved against his rebellious vassal in 701 BC, the fourteenth year of Hezekiah's sole rule (2 Ki.18:13). The Assyrian account records how he moved S through Phoenicia, receiving the submission of various cities. Further S, Sennacherib took Joppa, Asor, Bene-berak and Beth-dagon, towns which had allied themselves with the rebellious king of Ashkelon, who was sent into exile.

Sennacherib then fought with combined Egyptian and Ethiopian forces at Eltekeh and defeated them. Ekron, whose citizens had called for the Egyptians and Ethiopians to help them, was then captured and the rebels executed. Timnah was also conquered. Thus Sennacherib arrived at the W border of Judah.

Isaiah's version

Isaiah 10:28-32 depicts a different line of advance, bringing the Assyrians to Jerusalem from the N. Either this relates to a task-force which took a different route from the main army, or it is not a factual description at all, but merely an imaginative evocation, uttered before the actual advance, of the mounting panic the attack would bring.

Sennacherib's claims

Sennacherib records that in his invasion of Judah he took forty-six walled towns with their villages (*cf.* 2 Ki.18:13). The conquest of Lachish (2 Ch.32:9) was depicted in a series of reliefs in Sennacherib's SW palace at Nineveh. It was while this siege was in progress that Hezekiah capitulated and offered tribute (2 Ki.18:14-16).

While some scholars refer the remainder of the biblical account, which relates the besieging of Jerusalem and the city's miraculous deliverance (2 Ki.19:35-36), to a hypothetical second campaign by Sennacherib, the evidence does not justify this view. The catastrophic outcome of Sennacherib's campaign was naturally suppressed in the Assyrian account, which ends instead on a victorious note, listing the tribute received in Nineveh.

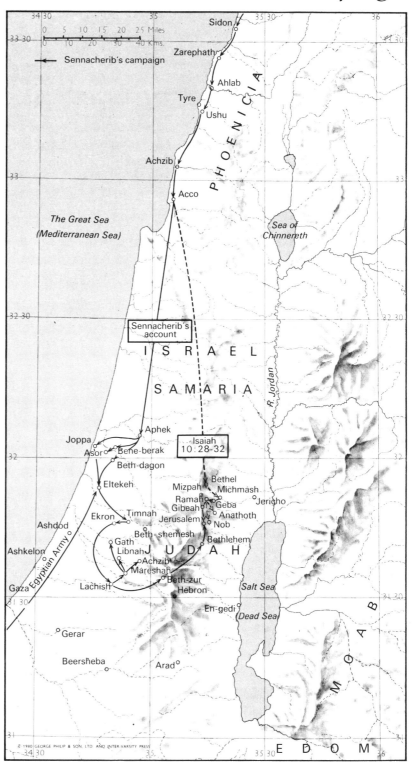

The campaign of Sennacherib against Judah in 701 BC.

Josiah

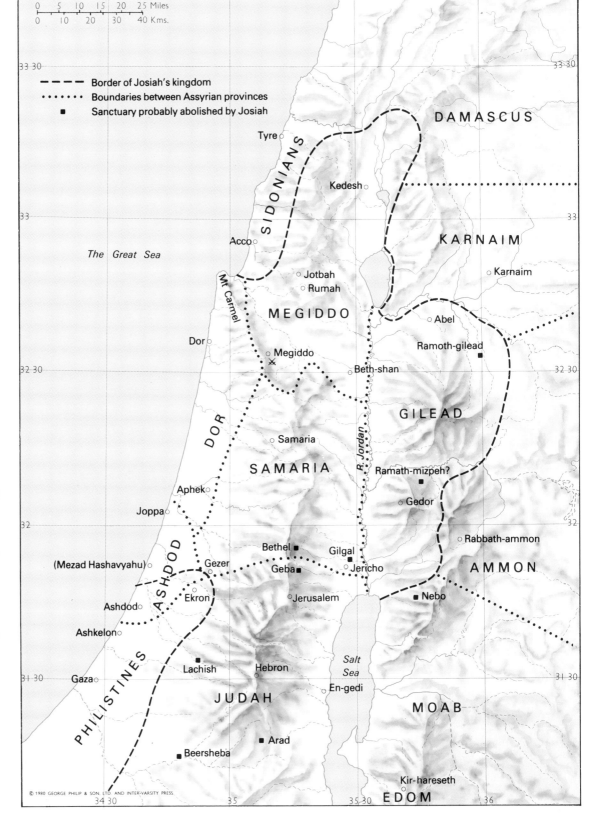

Border of Josiah's kingdom
Boundaries between Assyrian provinces
■ Sanctuary probably abolished by Josiah

0   5   10   15   20   25 Miles
0   10   20   30   40 Kms.

DAMASCUS

Tyre

Kedesh

SIDONIANS

KARNAIM

Acco

The Great Sea

Karnaim

Jotbah
Rumah

MEGIDDO

Abel

Dor

Megiddo
✕

Ramoth-gilead

Beth-shan

GILEAD

Samaria

DOR

R. Jordan

Ramath-mizpeh?

Aphek

Gedor

Joppa

Rabbath-ammon

Bethel
Gilgal
(Mezad Hashavyahu)
Gezer
Geba
Jericho
AMMON

ASHDOD

Ekron

Jerusalem

Nebo

Ashdod

Ashkelon

PHILISTINES

Salt
Sea

Lachish
Hebron
En-gedi

MOAB

Gaza

JUDAH

Arad

Beersheba

Kir-hareseth

EDOM

© 1980 GEORGE PHILIP & SON. LTD. AND INTER-VARSITY PRESS.

The kingdom of Josiah (c. 640-609 BC). From c. 630 BC, as Assyria's power waned, Josiah was able to free Judah from Assyrian control. The fact that he extended his radical religious reforms to the former territory of Israel (2 Ch. 34:6-7) points to the incorporation of the Assyrian provinces of Samaria, Megiddo and Gilead into his kingdom. When Necho II of Egypt set out to aid Assyria against the Babylonians at Harran, Josiah opposed him but was killed in battle at Megiddo (2 Ki. 23:29-30). The enlarged kingdom of Judah temporarily became an Egyptian vassal-state before coming under the control of Babylon in 605 BC (see p. 91f.).

Archaeological sites: Iron Age

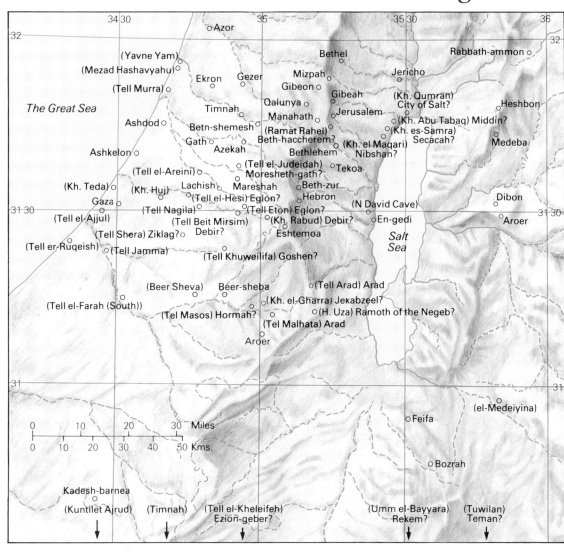

The Great Sea

34 30

Azor

(Yavne Yam)
(Mezad Hashavyahu)
Ekron   Gezer
(Tell Murra)
Timnah
Ashdod
Beth-shemesh
Gath   (Ramat Rahel)
Azekah
Ashkelon
Beth-haccherem?
(Tell el-Areini)   (Tell el-Judeidah)   Tekoa
Moresheth-gath?
(Kh. Teda)   Lachish   Mareshah   Beth-zur
(Kh. Huj)   (Tell el-Hesi) Eglon?   Hebron
Gaza   (Tell Nagila)   (Tell Eton) Eglon?
(Tell el-Ajjul)   (Tell Beit Mirsim)   (Kh. Rabud) Debir?
(Tell Shera) Ziklag?   Debir?   Eshtemoa
(Tell er-Ruqeish)   (Tell Jamma)
(Tell Khuweilifa) Goshen?

Bethel
Mizpah   Jericho
Gibeon
Gibeah   (Kh. Qumran)
Qalunya   City of Salt?   Heshbon
Manahath   Jerusalem
(Kh. Abu Tabaq) Middin?
(Kh. es-Samra)
(Kh. el Maqari)   Secacah?   Medeba
Bethlehem   Nibshan?

(N David Cave)   Dibon
En-gedi   Aroer

Salt
Sea

(Beer Sheva)   Beer-sheba   (Tell Arad) Arad
(Tell el-Farah (South))   (Kh. el-Gharra) Jekabzeel?
(Tel Masos) Hormah?   (H. Uza) Ramoth of the Negeb?
(Tel Malhata) Arad
Aroer

(el-Medeiyina)
Feifa

0   10   20   30   Miles
0   10   20   30   40   50   Kms.

Bozrah

Kadesh-barnea
(Kuntilet Ajrud)   (Timnah)   (Tell el-Kheleifeh)   (Umm el-Bayyara)   (Tuwilan)
Ezion-geber?   Rekem?   Teman?

*S Palestine: some
important Iron Age
excavated sites
(c. 1200– c. 720 BC).*

Whatever the cause of the destructions which marked the Late Bronze (LB) – Iron Age (IA) transition (see pp.38-9), it is evident that the decades around 1200 BC were a time of change in Palestine. There was a marked decline in material culture. Although many archaeologists have labelled the culture of Iron I as 'Israelite', it is worth remembering that this attribution stems purely from the assumption that the Hebrew tribes were entering the land at this period. In fact the culture of Iron I, although relatively impoverished, shows continuity with that of LB in many respects and does not generally point to the arrival of newcomers in Palestine. (An exception is the Philistine pottery which appears on the coastal plain at this time, reflecting the influence of Aegean and Cypriote styles. On the Philistines see p.88.) Even the 'collared rim' jars which W. F. Albright believed to be characteristic of the Israelites can no longer be linked with them in any restricted fashion, since examples have

been found in pre-Israelite Megiddo and at Sahab, in the territory of the Ammonites.

Decline in material culture, however, was not the only change to characterize the beginning of the IA. Although iron had been in use to a limited degree during the Bronze Age (BA), it now began to replace bronze in the manufacture of tools and weapons. Also, plastered (and therefore non-porous) cisterns came into use, making water-storage more viable. These two developments together made possible the growth of settlements in new areas, since forests in the hill-country could be cleared with the new tools, and cisterns made settlements feasible away from permanent water-supplies such as springs. This probably explains the development of numerous villages in areas which had been occupied sparsely or not at all during LB, *e.g.* in the central hill-country, lower Galilee and the Negeb. These settlements include important OT towns such as Ramah, Shiloh,

Archaeological sites: Iron Age

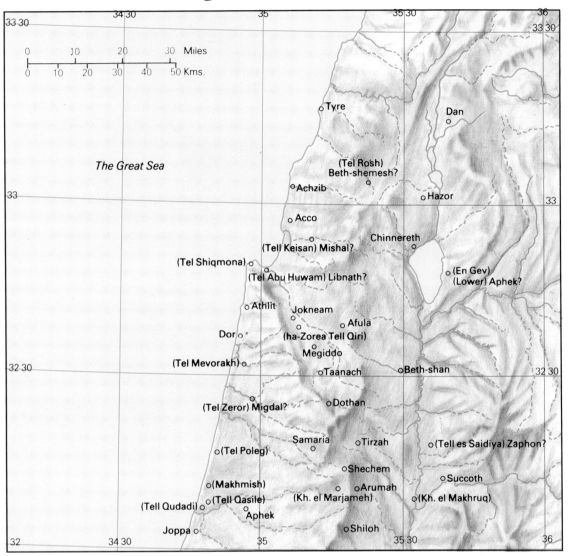

*N Palestine: some
important Iron Age
excavated sites
(c. 1200– c. 720 BC).*

Geba and Mizpah (Tell en-Nasbeh).

The Iron I villages were mostly small and unwalled, but in Iron II (*c.* 1000-800 BC) well-planned fortified towns appeared. While no remains can yet be positively identified as Davidic, strata at Megiddo, Hazor and Gezer have been attributed to Solomon with a fair degree of confidence since 1 Kings 9:15 speaks of Solomon's rebuilding these three towns. Two Solomonic palaces at Megiddo are the earliest examples of a 'royal' style of Israelite architecture which continued throughout the monarchy: monumental buildings of fine ashlar masonry, adorned with Proto-Aeolic stone capitals. Solomon may also have been responsible for a network of small forts in the Negeb between Arad and Kadesh-barnea (both of which were sites of much larger IA fortresses).

Settlements in the IA became relatively dense, especially in Judah during Iron III (*c.* 800-587 BC). Sites are then both more numerous and more crowded. There was

sophisticated urban planning to maximize the use of space (see the plan of Beersheba on p.26). The two major preoccupations of the age were agriculture and defence. Irrigation projects brought cultivation to the Negeb, and royal granaries have been discovered at Beersheba, Lachish, Hazor and Megiddo. Hazor, Gibeon and Jerusalem possessed impressive water-supply systems. Forts were built at many locations in the Judaean wilderness (*cf.* 2 Ch.26:10; 27:4).

The end of the period is marked by destruction at most Judaean sites, resulting from the Babylonian invasions of 597 and 589-87 BC. A few sites were resettled after a short break following these catastrophes, but most were not reoccupied until the return from exile, and some were abandoned permanently. Archaeology thus confirms the impression given by the OT (*cf.* 2 Ki. 25:12; Je. 39-40) that occupation in Judah was relatively sparse during the exile.

Nehemiah

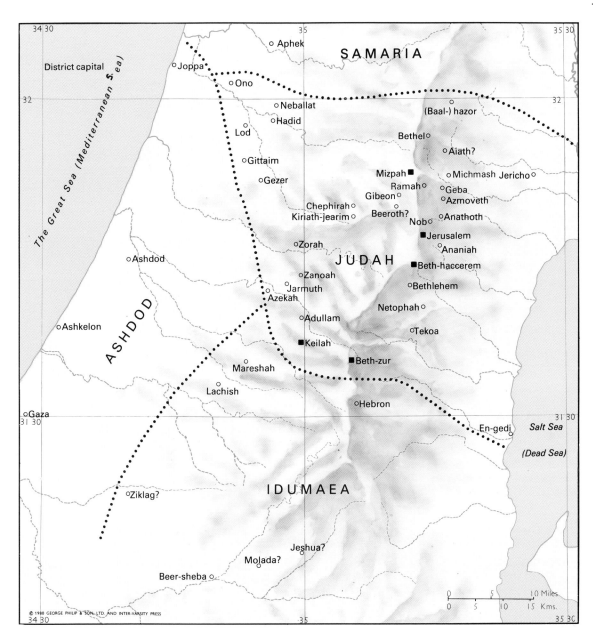

Judah in the time of Nehemiah.

The major settlements of Judah after the return from Exile are named in Ezra 2:1-35 and Nehemiah 7:6-38, while the district governors are referred to in Nehemiah 3. Archaeology has uncovered storage-jar seal-impressions bearing the name 'Yehud' (Judah), and their distribution gives some indication of the extent of Judah in this period. They occur from Mizpah in the N to En-gedi in the S, and from Jericho in the E to Gezer in the W. Compared with its pre-exilic extent, Judah was greatly diminished, the S hill-country being now Idumaea.

Information concerning Judah's neighbours at this time is supplied by the references to those who opposed the rebuilding of Jerusalem's walls. Nehemiah 2:19; 4:1–8; 6:1f. speak of opposition from Sanballat the Horonite, Tobiah the Ammonite, the Ashdodites and Geshem the Arab. That Sanballat was governor of Samaria in 407 BC is attested in papyri from the Jewish colony at Elephantine in Egypt, and he may already have held that office in the time of Nehemiah (*cf.* Ne. 4:2, where he is accompanied by 'the army of Samaria'). Tobiah was the governor of the province of Ammon-with-Gilead, Judah's neighbour to the E. He had influential family ties with Jerusalem (Ne. 6:18). Ashdod shared a border with Judah on the W. The name of Geshem the Arab occurs on a bowl from Egypt's E Delta, where he is referred to as king of Kedar in Arabia. His territory probably included Edom and Idumaea.

Nehemiah

Babylon fell to Cyrus, king of Persia, in 539 BC and in the following year he granted the Jews in exile permission to return home, commissioning them to rebuild the Temple in Jerusalem (Ezr.1:1-4). He restored to them the vessels from the first Temple which Nebuchadrezzar had taken to Babylon and placed in the shrine of his own gods (Ezr.1:7-11; 6:5; *cf.* 2 Ki.25:13ff.).

According to Ezra 2:64 (*cf.* Ne.7:66; 1 Esdras 5:41) a total of 42,360 Jews made the return journey in response to the decree of Cyrus. This figure may refer to the whole period 538-522 BC, but there is no reason to doubt that there was an immediate and enthusiastic return by a great many. On the other hand there were also Jews who had settled comfortably in Babylonia and had no wish to return. Thus the region retained a strong Jewish population and was an important centre of *diaspora* Judaism until the Middle Ages.

Return from exile

The Persian Empire was divided into satrapies, each administered by a Persian commissioner (satrap). Palestine belonged to the satrapy 'Beyond the River' (*cf.* Ezr.4:11, *etc.*), *i.e.* W of the Euphrates. The satrapies were subdivided into provinces, each supervised by a governor. At the time of the return from exile, responsibility for the work of rebuilding the Temple was given to one Sheshbazzar, whom Cyrus had appointed *pēhâ* (Ezr.1:8; 5:14-16). Translating this title as 'governor', some take it to indicate that Judah was granted the status of a province at the time of the return.

Others feel that 'governor' is too specific a translation of *pēhâ*; and that Judah was not detached politically from Samaria until the time of Nehemiah. Whatever the precise administrative arrangements under Cyrus, his decrees (Ezr.1:2-4; 6:3-5) certainly granted Judah religious autonomy in keeping with his general policy.

Temple completed

In spite of initial enthusiasm (Ezr.3:10-13), the work of rebuilding the Temple soon lapsed. There was opposition to the project from other inhabitants of the land. These were not Jews (although they perhaps considered themselves as such, *cf.* Ezr.4:2) but peoples settled in Samaria by the kings of Assyria in the eighth and seventh cents. BC (2 Ki.17:24; Ezr.4:2,10; 'Osnappar' in the latter verse = Ashurbanipal). Their opposition soon halted the work completely (Ezr.4:4,24). The discouraged returnees devoted their energies instead to securing their own comforts, and for this they were rebuked by the prophets Haggai and Zechariah (*e.g.* Hg.1:4), who both began

prophesying in 520 BC. With their encouragement, work on the Temple was resumed after years of neglect (Ezr.4:24-5:2), and was completed in 516 BC (Ezr.6:15).

Opposition did not cease with the successful completion of the Temple. It recurred in the time of Ahasuerus (Ezr.4:6), *i.e.* Xerxes I (486-465 BC), and again under Artaxerxes I (464-423 BC). It is probably in the reign of this latter king (rather than Artaxerxes II, 404-359 BC) that the events of Ezra 7-10, as well as the book of Nehemiah, are to be set (*cf.* also Ezr.4:7-23).

Ezra was sent from Babylonia to Jerusalem by Artaxerxes in 458 BC to enforce observance of the Jewish law. To this end he was given power to make appointments within Judah (Ezr.7:11-26). Another company of exiles returned to Judah with him at this time (Ezr.7:7; 8:1-20), taking a relatively dangerous desert route (perhaps via Tadmor and Damascus) without a military escort (Ezr.8:21-23).

Nehemiah arrived in Jerusalem from Susa in 445 BC, having been appointed governor of Judah (Ne.5:14). In spite of powerful opposition from Sanballat (governor of Samaria) and others, he organized and completed the rebuilding of Jerusalem's walls in 52 days (Ne.4; 6:1-15), encouraging the redevelopment of the underpopulated city (*cf.* Ne.7:4; 11:1-2).

Little is known of events in Judah during the remaining century of Persian rule. In 332 BC Palestine was conquered by Alexander the Great. The division of Alexander's empire among his generals meant that Palestine became a debatable land between Syria and Egypt. In 198 BC it became part of the Syrian Seleucid Empire.

The extravagances of the rich upper classes and the attempts of Antiochus Epiphanes to hellenize his empire (including a demand to worship Greek deities) provoked the Maccabean revolt.

The map on the facing page, with its inset, features S Syria (also known as Coele-Syria) at the time when the Jewish state revolted against the Seleucid Empire from 167 BC. See also Hellenistic Kingdoms (p.98) and Hasmonaean Princes (p.58).

Regional names and boundaries and the major 'Greek' (hellenized) cities are given, as known from various sources. Apart from this the map locates every place mentioned in the first and second books of the Maccabees except Bascama (1 Macc.13:23, site unknown). Judaea has two N boundaries, indicating a growth in territory at this time (1 Macc.11:34,57). The 'land of Tubias' (Pap. Zen.) identifies the 'Jews called Tubiani' of 1 Macc.5:13 (AV) ('our brethren who were in the land of Tob', RSV); the readings 'way of Galilee' and 'ascents of Arbela' are adopted in 1 Macc.9:2.

The Maccabean revolt against the Seleucids

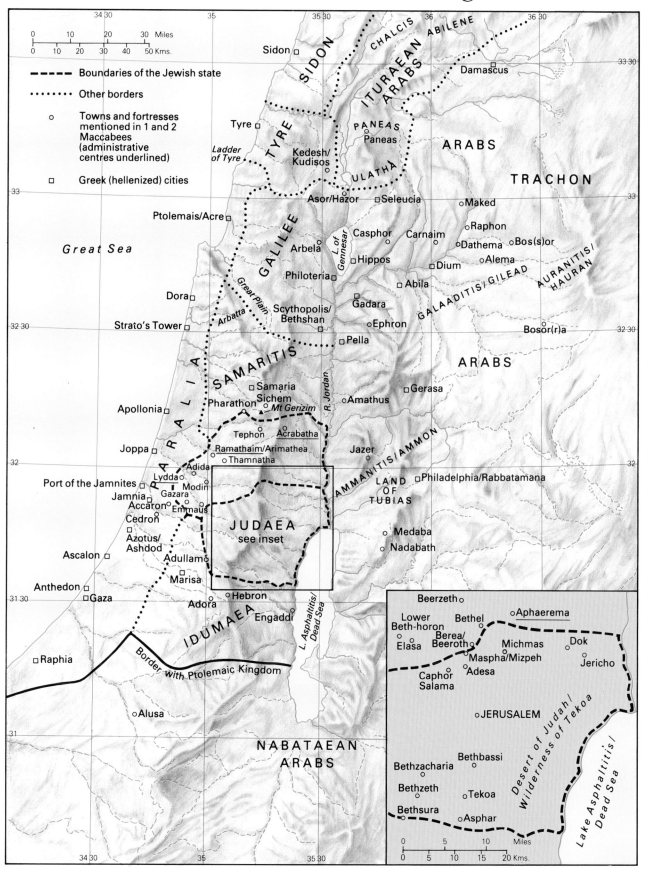

Scale and legend:

0 10 20 30 Miles
0 10 20 30 40 50 Kms.

- - - - Boundaries of the Jewish state

········· Other borders

○ Towns and fortresses mentioned in 1 and 2 Maccabees (administrative centres underlined)

□ Greek (hellenized) cities

Main map labels:

Sidon
CHALCIS
ITURAEAN ARABS
ABILENE
Damascus
PANEAS
Paneas
ARABS
Tyre
Ladder of Tyre
Kedesh/ Kudisos
ULATHA
TRACHON
Asor/Hazor
Seleucia
Maked
Ptolemais/Acre
Casphor
Carnaim
Raphon
Bos(s)or
Great Sea
Arbela
L. of Gennesar
Hippos
Dathema
Alema
AURANITIS/ HAURAN
GALILEE
Philoteria
Dium
Abila
GALAADITIS/ GILEAD
Dora
Gadara
Ephron
Bosor(r)a
Strato's Tower
Scythopolis/ Bethshan
Arbatta
Great Plain
Pella
ARABS
SAMARITIS
Samaria
Gerasa
Apollonia
Pharathon
Sichem
Mt Gerizim
R. Jordan
Amathus
Tephon
Acrabatha
Joppa
Ramathaim/Arimathea
Thamnatha
Jazer
AMMANITIS/AMMON
Adida
Lydda
JUDAEA see inset
LAND OF TUBIAS
Philadelphia/Rabbatamana
Port of the Jamnites
Modin
Gazara
Jamnia
Accaron
Emmaus
Cedron
Medaba
Nadabath
Azotus/ Ashdod
Adullam
Ascalon
Marisa
Anthedon
Gaza
Adora
Hebron
IDUMAEA
Engaddi
L. Asphaltitis/ Dead Sea
Raphia
Border with Ptolemaic Kingdom
Alusa
NABATAEAN ARABS
PARALIA

Inset map (JUDAEA):

Beerzeth
Lower Beth-horon
Bethel
Aphaerema
Elasa
Berea/ Beeroth
Michmas
Dok
Caphor Salama
Maspha/Mizpeh
Adesa
Jericho
JERUSALEM
Desert of Judah/ Wilderness of Tekoa
Bethzacharia
Bethbassi
Lake Asphaltitis/ Dead Sea
Bethzeth
Tekoa
Bethsura
Asphar

0 5 10 Miles
0 5 10 15 20 Kms.

The Hasmonaean princes

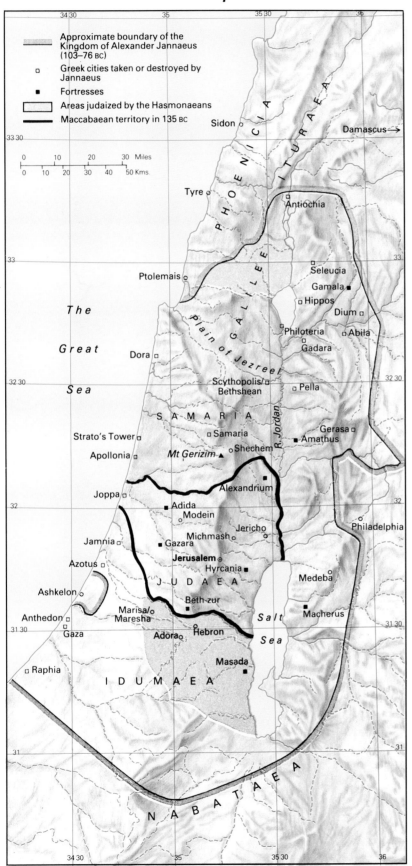

Approximate boundary of the
Kingdom of Alexander Jannaeus
(103–76 BC)

□ Greek cities taken or destroyed by
Jannaeus

■ Fortresses

Areas judaized by the Hasmonaeans

Maccabaean territory in 135 BC

The Seleucid king Antiochus IV Epiphanes
was given advice about Judaea by hellenized
Jews from the high-priestly families of
Jerusalem. In 167 BC royal officials came to
stamp out the traditional Jewish cult. At
Modein pietists refused to comply and the
'Maccabean' revolt broke out, led by Judas the
Maccabee and his brothers. Simon, the last
Maccabee, became head of a free Jewish state
as Seleucid power weakened (see Hellenistic
Kingdoms, p.98) and four generations of his
descendants, the 'Hasmonaeans', men of
high-priestly family descended from
Asamonaeus/Hashmon, ruled the 'community
of the Jews'.

Aristobulus was the first to adopt the title
'king' (104 BC). Simon, Hyrcanus, Aristobulus
and Alexander all expanded Jewish territory
by conquest up to 76 BC. They totally destroyed
some states (cities), including Samaria, Gaza,
Pella and Gadara, and planted Jewish
garrisons or settlers in others (e.g. Joppa,
Gazara: see 1 Macc.14:34). Local populations in
Idumaea and Galilee were forced to adopt
circumcision and Jewish customs (nomoi) if
they wished to stay in their own land (Jos.,
Ant.13.257-8; 13.318).

Under Alexander (103-76 BC) the Jewish state
reached its greatest expansion. But the
freedom created by the weakness of the
Seleucids was to be checked by the growth of
the Roman and Parthian empires (see pp. 99
and 100-101). In 63 BC the Roman general
Pompey made a settlement which reduced
Jewish territory to Judaea (with Idumaea),
Samaria, Galilee and Peraea (an area E of
Jordan settled by Jews). The last Hasmonaeans
fought one another for power until Roman
legions pushed out Parthian invaders and
established an outsider, Herod, as king (37 BC).

Herod had already been declared king of the
Jews by the Roman Senate in 40 BC.

Hasmonaean rulers 142-37 BC

143/2-135/4 Simon the Maccabee
135/4-104 John Hyrcanus I
104-103 Aristobulus I
103-76 Alexander Jannaeus
76-67 Salome Alexandra
67-63 Aristobulus II
(63 Pompey establishes Roman
protectorate)
63-40 Hyrcanus II
40-37 Antigonus
(37- Herod the Great)

*The Holy Land at the time of the Hasmonaean princes,
142-37 BC.*

Qumran

In 1947 and the following years many ancient manuscripts and fragments were discovered in eleven caves in and around the Wadi Qumran, near the NW shore of the Dead Sea. It is to these that the name 'Dead Sea Scrolls' is usually given (though that term is sometimes extended to include other collections from regions W of the Dead Sea, generally of later date). The discovery of these scrolls and the recognition of their antiquity prompted the excavation (1951-55) of the nearby ruins known as Khirbet Qumran. These proved to be the remains of a complex of buildings occupied c. 140 BC–AD 68, with a break between c. 40 and 4 BC. The correspondence between this dating (based chiefly on coins from the ruins) and the likely age of the scrolls, plus the discovery in the ruins of jars like those in which some of the scrolls were found, suggests that the buildings were the headquarters of the community to which the scrolls belonged. A cemetery of over 1,000 burials lying between the ruins and the Dead Sea, investigated as long ago as 1873, is now recognized as the graveyard of the same community.

It is now widely (though not universally) accepted that Khirbet Qumran should be identified with the settlement of Essenes. Pliny the Elder (first century AD) described it in his *Natural History* (5.17) as lying N of En-gedi. Current understanding of the Qumran community is therefore based on evidence from a number of sources: the excavations of Khirbet Qumran (and a subsidiary building 3 km (c. 2 miles) to the S at Ain Feshkha), the contents of the scrolls from the nearby caves, and information on the sect of the Essenes supplied by Pliny, Philo and Josephus.

The Qumran community provided an enigmatic account of its own origins in the scroll now known as the *Damascus Rule*. A possible interpretation is that the community arose among those pious Jews (Ḥasidim) who withstood the hellenization of Judaism under Antiochus Epiphanes (175-164 BC) and endured that monarch's harsh persecutions. Another view sees the community taking shape among those Jews who remained in Babylon after the exile, the group perhaps being inspired to return to Judaea by the victories of Judas Maccabaeus in 164 BC. The *Damascus Rule* implies that for twenty years after 'the age of wrath' (probably the persecutions under Antiochus) the group was without a leader ('like blind men groping for the way'). Then God 'raised for them a Teacher of Righteousness to guide them in the way of His heart'. Reckoning twenty years from Antiochus's persecutions gives a date c. 145 BC, which is compatible with the likely date for the

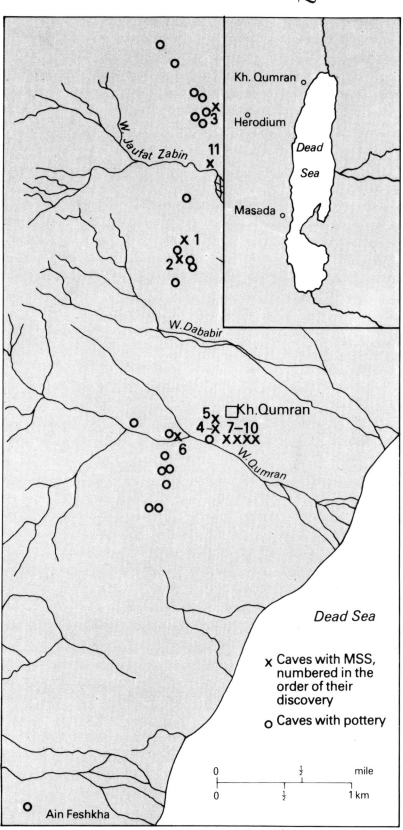

The Qumran area, showing locations of the caves in which pottery and MSS have been found.

Qumran

founding of the settlement at Qumran. It was therefore probably under the leadership of the 'Teacher of Righteousness' that the group left Jerusalem to settle in the wilderness.

The identity of the 'Teacher of Righteousness' is unknown. It is somewhat easier to identify his opponent, a man referred to in the scrolls as 'the Wicked Priest'. From references to this latter character it appears that he held office as High Priest, wielded great political power and died a violent death. These facts point to Jonathan, the

Hasmonaean who succeeded Judas Maccabaeus and who was appointed High Priest in 152 BC. In the view of J. Murphy-O'Connor, the 'Teacher of Righteousness' may have been the legitimate High Priest, deposed to make way for Jonathan's appointment.

Remains of Phase Ia at Qumran (c. 140-110 BC) indicate a very small settlement, but in Phase Ib there was an elaborate reconstruction, pointing to a greatly enlarged community. The site was apparently

Right: aerial view of the Qumran settlement from the N (opposite to the plan on page 62). Compare with the reconstruction on this page, which is viewed from the E.

Artist's reconstruction (based on a model at the Pittsburgh Theological Seminary) of the buildings at Qumran, against a photograph of the surrounding terrain. To the left, at the end of a limestone spur, separated from the buildings by a deep gulley, is Cave 4 (see also the map on page 59). It was here that the majority of the Qumran scrolls were found.

Qumran

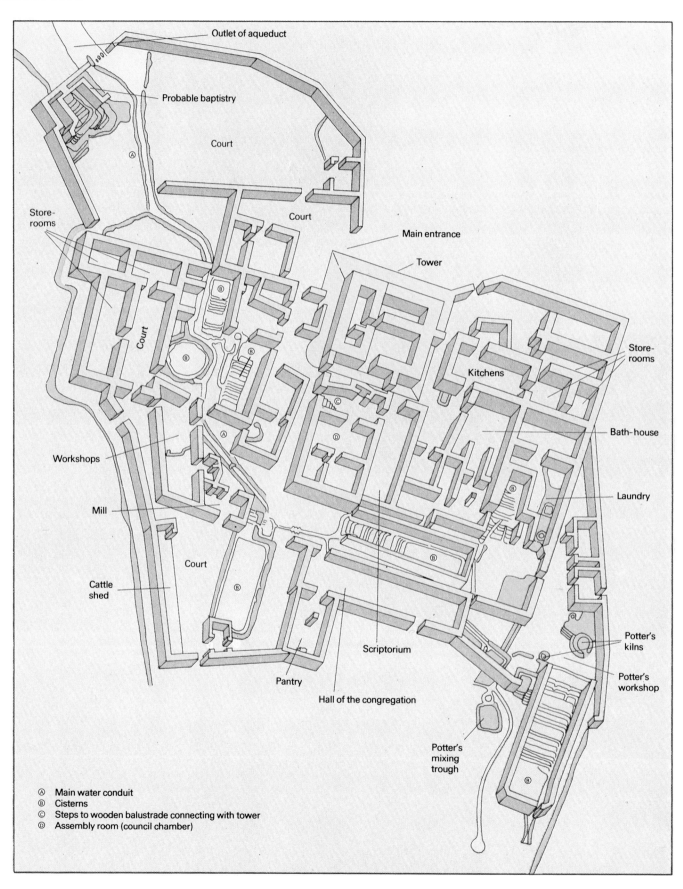

Outlet of aqueduct

Probable baptistry

Court

Court

Store-
rooms

Main entrance

Tower

Court

Store-
rooms

Kitchens

Bath-house

Workshops

Laundry

Mill

Court

Cattle
shed

Potter's
kilns

Scriptorium

Potter's
workshop

Pantry

Hall of the congregation

Potter's
mixing
trough

Ⓐ   Main water conduit
Ⓑ   Cisterns
Ⓒ   Steps to wooden balustrade connecting with tower
Ⓓ   Assembly room (council chamber)

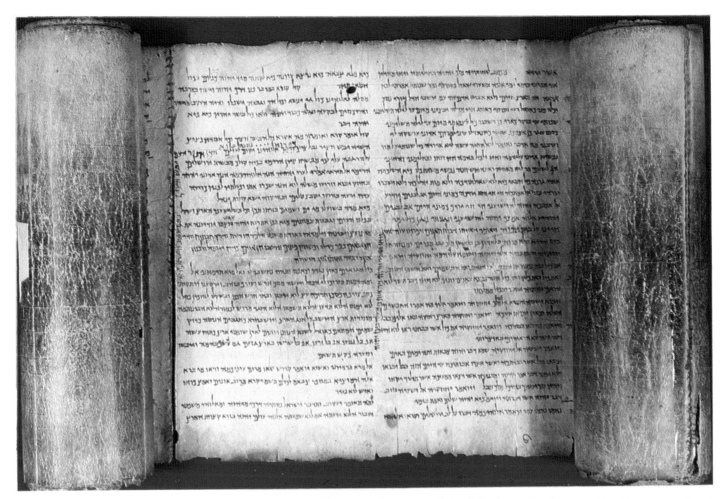

abandoned *c.* 40 BC (perhaps as a consequence of the Parthian invasion) and resettled *c.* 4 BC (beginning of Phase II). In this period essentially the same buildings were in use as in Ib: assembly rooms, scriptorium, kitchen, laundry, pottery and metal workshops, smelting furnaces and flour mills. An aqueduct fed water from cisterns in the hills into an elaborate complex of cisterns within the compound. Phase II came to a violent end in AD 68, *i.e.* during the Jewish war with Rome, the destroyers being in all probability the Roman troops known to have occupied Jericho at that time. The scrolls were presumably hidden in the caves to preserve them when this final disaster threatened.

The scrolls recovered in modern times fall into three categories. About 100 scrolls are books of the OT in Hebrew; all the OT books are represented except Esther. These biblical MSS are 1,000 years older than the oldest copies previously available, and their discovery has greatly increased our knowledge of the textual history of the OT. Secondly there are copies of books of the Apocrypha and Pseudepigrapha, and the third category consists of literature produced by the community itself. Scrolls in this category are of immense importance for understanding the beliefs and practices of the Qumran sectarians.

They reveal a community practising strict self-discipline, interpreting the law even more severely than the most extreme Pharisees. The sect saw itself as the true Israel, with a vital role to play in overthrowing evil at the close of the age, which was held to be imminent. A Davidic messiah was expected, but also a priestly messiah who would have precedence over the former. The OT prophetic writings were interpreted to refer to current and immediately future events, the sect itself figuring largely in their fulfilment.

Events turned out very differently from the way the community expected. It is not known what became of those who escaped the disaster of AD 68; some may have reappraised their beliefs and joined with the early church; some almost certainly made common cause with the Zealots at Masada, where a Qumranian scroll has been found.

Plan of the installations at Qumran in Phases Ib-II, c. 110 BC-AD 68.

The oldest manuscript of a complete book of the Old Testament dates from c. 100 BC and was found at Qumran (Cave 1) in 1947. It is the scroll of Isaiah (IQ Isᵃ) and measures 27 cm × 7.26 m (c. 10½ ins × 23 ft 10 ins). Illustrated is Is. 38:8-40:28.

The Hebrew calendar

The Hebrew calendar showing seasons and festivals with their modern equivalents.

Until *c.*100 BC the Hebrew calendar was based on lunar months which followed the Babylonian practice. The new year began in the spring (March/April) and accommodated the agricultural seasons. To maintain this a second twelfth month (Adar) or sixth month (Elul) was periodically added to control the beginning or 'return of the year' at the time of the spring equinox (1 Ki.20:26). There is no sure evidence that at the time of the final Judaean kingdom there was an administrative new year beginning in autumn (Tishri) at the time of the autumnal equinox ('the going out

of the year', *cf.* Ex. 23:16). Some early names for months are known also from Phoenicia and reflect agricultural and seasonal changes such as Abib, 'ripening of corn' (Ex. 13:4). These names are given in the innermost circle of the chart. Festivals follow both agricultural and historical events (outermost circle). Most local references to the calendar would describe the seasons (see also p.14 Climate; *e.g.* 'seedtime', '(barley)-harvest', 'summer-fruit') but in post-exilic times the Babylonian month names were followed.

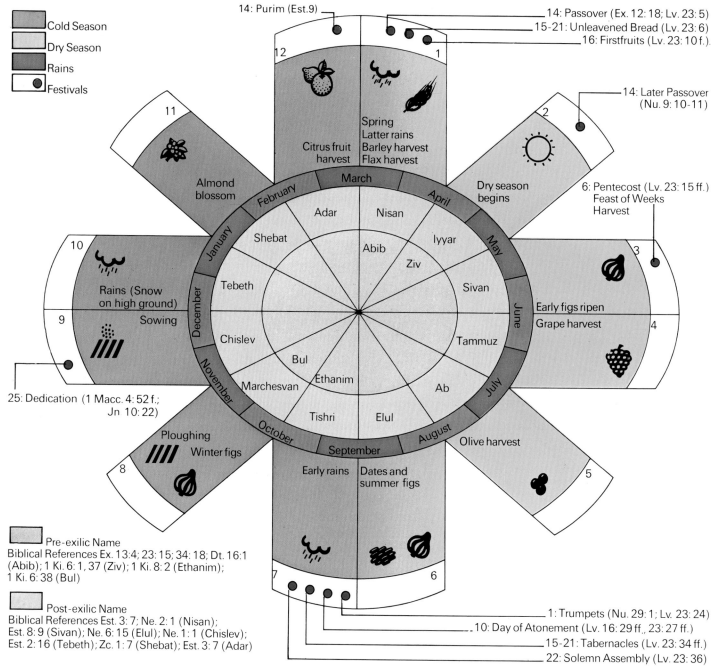

Cold Season
Dry Season
Rains
Festivals

14: Purim (Est.9)

14: Passover (Ex. 12: 18; Lv. 23: 5)
15-21: Unleavened Bread (Lv. 23: 6)
16: Firstfruits (Lv. 23: 10 f.).

14: Later Passover (Nu. 9: 10-11)

6: Pentecost (Lv. 23: 15 ff.) Feast of Weeks Harvest

25: Dedication (1 Macc. 4: 52 f.; Jn 10: 22)

Spring
Latter rains
Barley harvest
Flax harvest

Citrus fruit harvest

Almond blossom

Dry season begins

Early figs ripen
Grape harvest

Rains (Snow on high ground)

Sowing

Ploughing
Winter figs

Olive harvest

Early rains | Dates and summer figs

Adar | Nisan
Shebat | Iyyar
Abib | Ziv
Tebeth | Sivan
Chislev | Tammuz
Bul | Ethanim | Ab
Marchesvan | Elul
Tishri

February | March | April | May | June | July | August | September | October | November | December | January

1: Trumpets (Nu. 29: 1; Lv. 23: 24)
10: Day of Atonement (Lv. 16: 29 ff., 23: 27 ff.)
15-21: Tabernacles (Lv. 23: 34 ff.)
22: Solemn Assembly (Lv. 23: 36)

Pre-exilic Name
Biblical References Ex. 13:4; 23: 15; 34: 18; Dt. 16:1 (Abib); 1 Ki. 6: 1, 37 (Ziv); 1 Ki. 8: 2 (Ethanim); 1 Ki. 6: 38 (Bul)

Post-exilic Name
Biblical References Est. 3: 7; Ne. 2: 1 (Nisan); Est. 8: 9 (Sivan); Ne. 6:15 (Elul); Ne. 1: 1 (Chislev); Est. 2: 16 (Tebeth); Zc. 1: 7 (Shebat); Est. 3: 7 (Adar)

The Holy Land: main routes

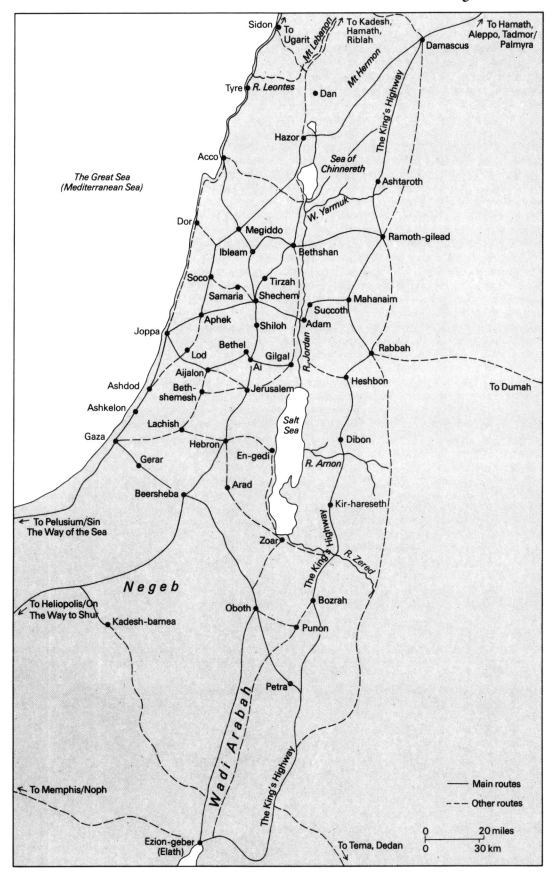

The main routes in the Holy
Land for which there is textual
evidence (solid lines) or which
can be inferred on the basis of
the terrain (dotted lines).

The Holy Land: the economy

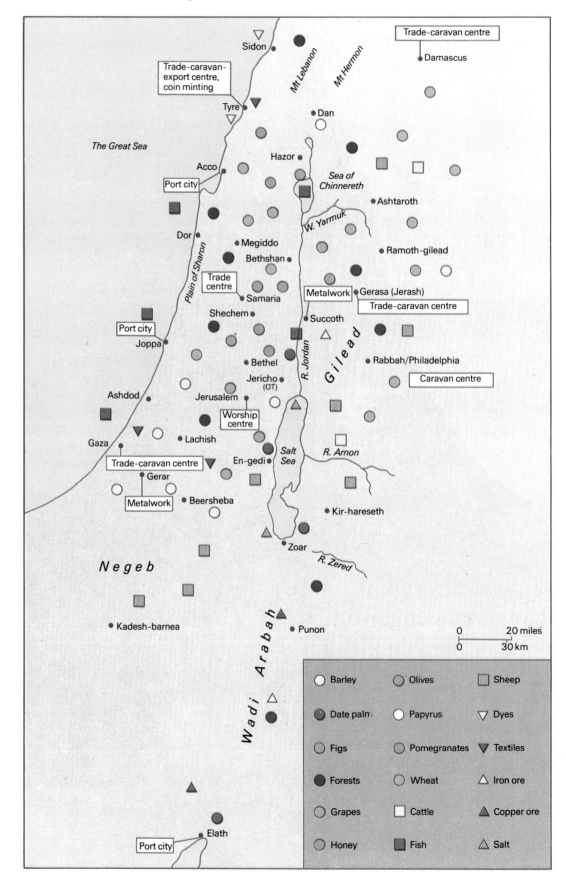

Trade-caravan centre
Damascus

Sidon

Mt Lebanon

Mt Hermon

Trade-caravan-
export centre,
coin minting

Tyre

Dan

The Great Sea

Hazor

Acco

Sea of
Chinnereth

Port city

Ashtaroth

W. Yarmuk

Dor

Megiddo

Ramoth-gilead

Bethshan

Trade
centre

Samaria

Metalwork

Gerasa (Jerash)

Shechem

Succoth

Trade-caravan centre

Joppa

Bethel

Rabbah/Philadelphia

Jericho
(OT)

Caravan centre

Ashdod

Jerusalem

R. Jordan

Gilead

Worship
centre

Gaza

Lachish

Salt
Sea

R. Arnon

Trade-caravan centre

En-gedi

Gerar

Kir-hareseth

Metalwork

Beersheba

Zoar

R. Zered

N e g e b

Kadesh-barnea

Punon

0   20 miles
0   30 km

W a d i   A r a b a h

○ Barley	◐ Olives	▢ Sheep
● Date palm	○ Papyrus	▽ Dyes
○ Figs	◐ Pomegranates	▼ Textiles
● Forests	○ Wheat	△ Iron ore
○ Grapes	□ Cattle	▲ Copper ore
○ Honey	▣ Fish	△ Salt

Port city

Elath

Port city

The economy of the Holy
Land was largely
agricultural. The main
centres for production
and trade in certain
commodities are
indicated here, together
with the regions where
limited mineral
resources were worked
during the biblical
period.

Herod the Great

Herod the Great, king of the Jews, was born c. 73 BC and reigned from 40 to 4 BC. His father, Antipater II, had been appointed procurator of Judaea by Julius Caesar in 47 BC. The son, Herod, was made military prefect of Galilee and then of Coele-Syria (see p.57).

The Parthians (see p.99) invaded Syria and Palestine and set the Hasmonaean Antigonus on the throne of Judaea (40-37 BC). The Roman senate, advised by Antony and Octavian, thereupon gave Herod the title 'King of the Jews'. He fought for three years to make his title effective and then governed Judaea for thirty-three years as a loyal 'friend and ally' of Rome.

He failed, however, to endear himself to his Jewish subjects. He was descended from an Edomite (Idumaean) family, he had wiped out the Hasmonaean rule and had collaborated with his Roman masters. Moreover he erected temples to pagan gods, although his magnificent reconstruction of the Temple at Jerusalem told in his favour.

Herod is remembered for his Temple and for the spectacular fortresses which he built, notably at Masada (see the following pages).

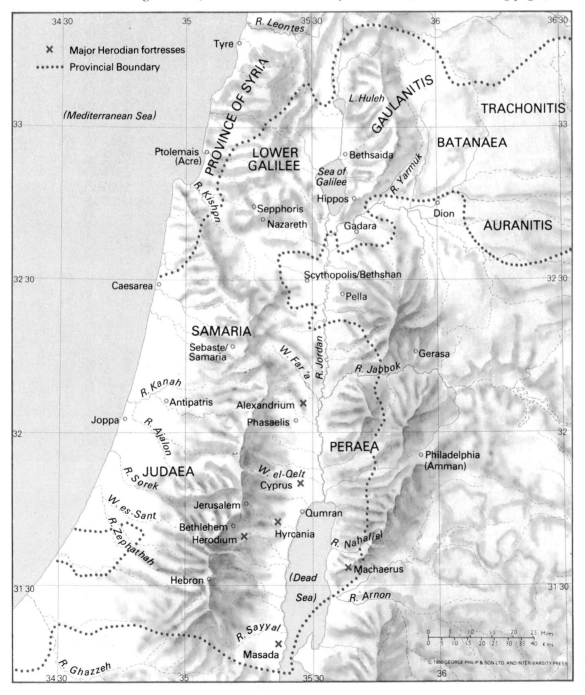

The Kingdom of Herod the Great.

Herod's fortresses

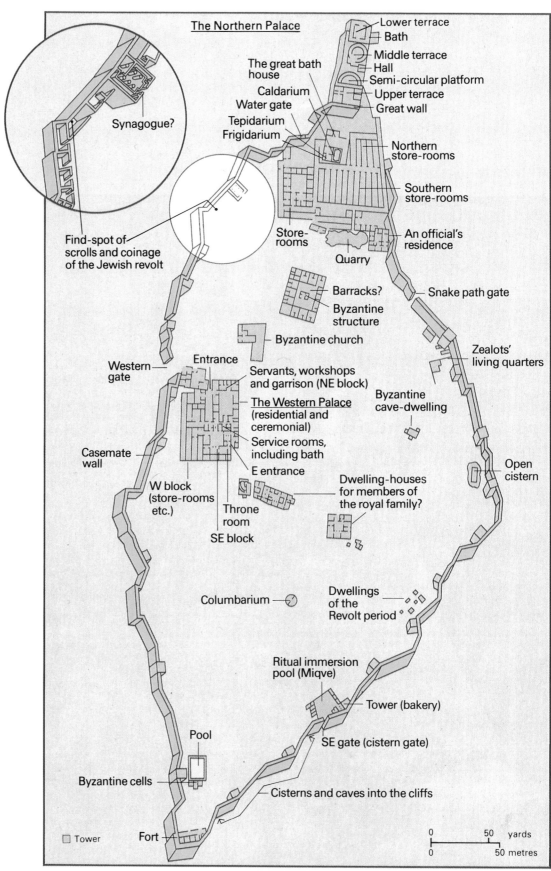

The Northern Palace

Lower terrace
Bath
Middle terrace
Hall
Semi-circular platform
Upper terrace
Great wall

The great bath house
Caldarium
Water gate
Tepidarium
Frigidarium

Northern store-rooms

Southern store-rooms

An official's residence

Synagogue?

Find-spot of scrolls and coinage of the Jewish revolt

Store-rooms

Quarry

Barracks?
Byzantine structure

Byzantine church

Snake path gate

Zealots' living quarters

Western gate

Entrance

Servants, workshops and garrison (NE block)

The Western Palace (residential and ceremonial)

Service rooms, including bath

E entrance

Byzantine cave-dwelling

Casemate wall

W block (store-rooms etc.)

Throne room

SE block

Open cistern

Dwelling-houses for members of the royal family?

Columbarium

Dwellings of the Revolt period

Ritual immersion pool (Miqve)

Tower (bakery)

SE gate (cistern gate)

Pool

Byzantine cells

Cisterns and caves into the cliffs

Tower   Fort

0   50   yards
0   50   metres

Plan of the fortress of Masada.

Masada from the air, viewed from the NW (almost the reverse of the plan opposite). The Roman siege ramp, built in AD 74 when this Jewish outpost fell, can be clearly seen on the right.

Another of Herod's fortresses, Herodium, viewed from the NW.

69

Herod's fortresses

The fortresses of Herod were not merely strong, they were sumptuous and magnificent. The king displayed three of them — Alexandrium, Herodium and Hyrcania — to his Roman friend, M. Agrippa, together with Caesarea and Sebaste (on the sites of Strato's Tower and Samaria), the cities he was proud to have built. The other two, Machaerus and Masada, are on the W and E of the Dead Sea. All except Herodium, which was new, were rebuildings of Hasmonaean fortresses. In Hyrcania, Alexandrium and Machaerus, the Hasmonaean ruler Queen Alexandra had kept her most precious possessions (Jos., *Ant*. 13.417); and these same three fortresses had been surrendered by the Hasmonaean prince Alexander to Gabinius in 57 BC. We do not hear of Masada until Herod takes it from his father's assassins in 42 BC (*Ant*. 14.296; *War* 1.237-238).

Alexandrium was restored in 38 BC by command of Herod during his struggle to realize the pronouncement of the Roman senate making him legally king of Judaea (*Ant*. 14.419). His mother-in-law and wife (the Hasmonaeans Alexandra and Mariamne) were sent there for safety in 30 BC. His two sons by Mariamne, Alexander and Aristobulus, were buried there in 7 BC in the tomb of their ancestors (*Ant*. 15.185 and 16.394). Herod used Hyrcania as a prison (*Ant*. 15.366) after he had repaired it (*War* 1.364). His son by Doris, Antipater, was buried there (*War* 1.664; *Ant*. 17.187). Josephus does not describe either Alexandrium or Hyrcania, and neither has been excavated (the sites are Qarn Sartabeh and Kh. Mird).

Machaerus, restored by Herod between 25 BC and 13 BC, is described by Josephus in some detail (*War* 7.166-189). Here a town was established within a fortified wall protected by towers; from the town an ascent led up to the crest, upon which the citadel was set. Another wall surrounded the crest itself, with high towers at its angles. Inside the citadel Herod built a palace with chambers (halls?) of great size and beauty, and cisterns and an armoury were also provided. The fortress was at the S extremity of Peraea on the borders of the Nabataean kingdom above the baths at Calliroe, which was 20 km (*c*. 13 miles) away by road. It was here that John the Baptist was beheaded at the order of Antipas. The Roman Bassus took it in AD 72. Three seasons of excavations at the site (Qal'at el Mishnaqa, Maqawer) produced only meagre results.

The fortresses illustrated are Herodium and Masada. Herodium was the name of a fortified palace, Herodia of the town at its foot. They mark a point at which a band of Jews was defeated by Herod as he tried to escape the supporters of Antigonus Mattathiah and

Parthian invaders (*Ant*. 14.360). Herod was eventually buried here (*War* 1.673; *Ant*. 17.199). The town became a district administrative capital of Judaea (*War* 3.55). The palace was worthy of a king (*Ant*. 14.360). Some details of the photograph (p. 69) match the description that the hill-crest was 'crowned with a ring of round towers' inside which were 'magnificent' apartments. The crest is in fact a high artificial mound, created by Herod; one sees that he was a man whose imagination was hard to check. And the ring of towers is a ring-wall within which are three half-towers and a round tower. The splendid bath-house is the most impressive feature of the ruins; it contained mosaics and frescoes. Another building is claimed as a very early synagogue.

Masada is also described in detail by Josephus (*War* 7.280-303). It is an isolated natural peak, boat-shaped, and precipitous on all sides; in fact it was so well defended that the Romans who besieged the Zealots there were forced to erect a huge ramp on the W. A wall with thirty-seven high towers in it enclosed the summit; this has been found to be a 'casemate' (a double wall enclosing small chambers). A palace built on the N outside this wall has been found with its baths, mosaics and frescoes. Excavation has also located a large bath-house on the summit, smaller palaces, another large palace, immense cisterns and store-rooms.

Before the recent work of Avigad the sumptuous style and decor of Masada and Herodium were the closest one could come to visualizing the magnificent Hellenistic houses of Jerusalem. (See N. Avigad, *Discovering Jerusalem*, 1984, with its illustrations of mosaics, frescoes and tables *etc*.)

The Tetrarchs

The map on the facing page shows how Herod the Great's kingdom was divided after his death between three of his sons, Archelaus, Antipas and Philip (see page 119 for further details).

The word 'tetrarch' (Gk. *tetra-archēs*, contracted to *tetrarchēs*) was used to denote the ruler of a fourth part of a region. The Romans used it for any ruler of part of a province.

Archelaus took the title 'ethnarch' (Gk. *ethnarchēs*, 'governor') and ruled Judaea, Samaria and Idumaea. The title 'ethnarch' is found in the NT referring to the 'governor' of Damascus (2 Cor. 11:32). Philip was tetrarch of Batanaea, Trachonitis, Ituraea, Gaulanitis and Auranitis, areas NE of the Sea of Galilee.

In the NT the noun 'tetrarch' is used only to refer to Herod Antipas (Mt. 14:1; Lk. 3:19; 9:7; Acts 13:1) but in Luke 3:1 a verb is used to apply to the tetrarchies of Antipas, Philip and Lysanias, tetrarch of Abilene.

The Tetrarchs

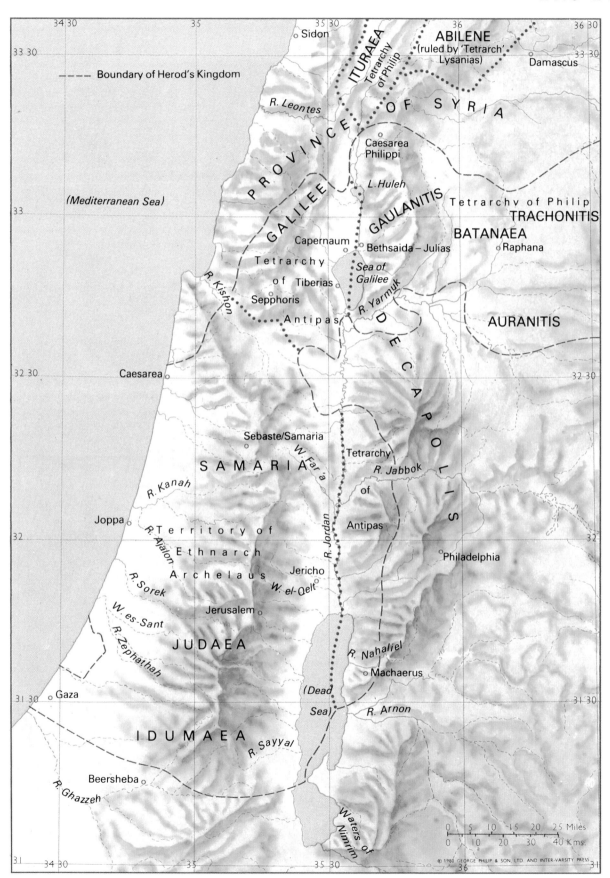

- - - - Boundary of Herod's Kingdom

34.30

33.30

Sidon

ITURAEA

Tetrarchy of Philip

ABILENE
(ruled by 'Tetrarch'
Lysanias)

Damascus

33.30

R. Leontes

PROVINCE OF SYRIA

(Mediterranean Sea)

33

Caesarea
Philippi

L. Huleh

GALILEE

GAULANITIS

Tetrarchy of Philip

TRACHONITIS

BATANAEA

Capernaum

Bethsaida – Julias

Raphana

Tetrarchy

R. Kishon

of   Tiberias

Sea of
Galilee

Sepphoris

R. Yarmuk

D E C A P O L I S

AURANITIS

Antipas

Caesarea

32.30

32.30

Sebaste/Samaria

W. Far'a

Tetrarchy

R. Jabbok

S A M A R I A

of

R. Kanah

Antipas

Joppa

Territory of

R. Ajalon   Ethnarch

Philadelphia

32

R. Sorek   Archelaus

Jericho

R. Jordan

32

W. el-Qelt

W. es-Sant

Jerusalem

R. Zephathah

J U D A E A

R. Nahaliel

Machaerus

31.30

Gaza

(Dead
Sea)

R. Arnon

31.30

I D U M A E A

R. Sayyal

Beersheba

R. Ghazzeh

Waters of Nimrim

0   5   10   15   20   25 Miles

0   10   20   30   40 Kms.

© 1980 GEORGE PHILIP & SON, LTD AND INTER-VARSITY PRESS

34.30   35   35.30   36

31

*The areas
administered
by the tetrarchs in
Palestine.*

71

Galilee

Galilee, taken from the Heb. *gālîl*, 'ring, circle', hence a 'district, region', this is the regional name of part of N Palestine, which was the scene of Christ's boyhood and early ministry. The origin of the name as applied here is uncertain. It occurs occasionally in the OT (*e.g.*Jos. 20:7; 1 Ki. 9:11), and notably in Is. 9:1. The latter reference probably recalls the region's history: it originally formed part of the lands allocated to the twelve tribes, but, owing to the pressure from peoples farther N, its Jewish population found themselves in a kind of N salient, surrounded on three sides by non-Jewish populations — 'the nations'. Under the Maccabees, the Gentile influence upon the Jews became so strong that the latter were actually withdrawn S for half a century. Thus Galilee had to be recolonized, and this fact, together with its diversity of population, contributed to the contempt felt for the Galileans by the S Jews (Jn. 7:52).

Exact demarcation of the Galilee region is difficult, except in terms of the provincial boundaries of the Roman Empire. The name was evidently applied for the N marchlands of Israel, the location of which varied from time to time. In the time of Christ, however, the province of Galilee formed a rectangular territory some 70 km (*c.* 44 miles) from N to S and 40 km (*c.* 25 miles) from E to W, bordered on the E by the Jordan and the Sea of Galilee

and cut off from the Mediterranean by the S extension of Syro-Phoenicia down the coastal plain.

Thus defined, Galilee consists essentially of an upland area, bordered on all sides save the N by plains — the coastlands, the plain of Esdraelon and the Jordan Rift. It is, in fact, the S end of the mountains of Lebanon, and the land surface falls, in two steps, from N to S across the area. The higher 'step' forms Upper Galilee, much of which is at 1,000 m (*c.* 3,283 ft) above sea-level: in NT times it was a forested and thinly inhabited hill country. The lower 'step' forms Lower Galilee, 450-600 m (*c.* 1,478-1,970 ft) above sea level, but falling steeply to more than 180 m (*c.* 591 ft) below sea-level at the Sea of Galilee.

It is to this area of Lower Galilee that most of the Gospel narrative refers. Well watered by streams flowing from the N mountains, and possessing considerable stretches of fertile land in the limestone basins among its hills, it was an area of dense and prosperous settlement. It exported olive oil and cereals, and fish from the lake.

Outside the main stream of Israelite life in OT times, Galilee came into its own in the NT (D. Baly, *The Geography of the Bible*, 1957, p.190). The Roman region was governed successively by Herod the Great (died 4 BC), Herod Antipas and Herod Agrippa.

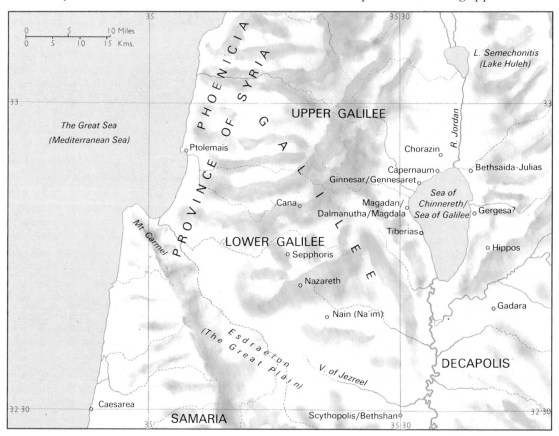

NT Galilee: the scene of Christ's boyhood and early ministry.

The Sea of Galilee

This, then, was the region in which Christ grew up — at Nazareth, in the limestone hills of Lower Galilee. Thanks to its position, it was traversed by several major routeways of the Empire, and was therefore far from being a rural backwater. Its agriculture, fisheries and commerce provided him with his cultural background, and are reflected in his parables and teaching. It provided him with his first disciples and their first mission field.

Today, Galilee and the plain of Esdraelon form the core area of N Israel, but its modern inhabitants have the task of rehabilitating an area which has lost much of the prosperity it enjoyed in NT times. Its forests have been largely replaced by *maquis*, the characteristic scrub of the Mediterranean, and many of its towns and villages, places which Christ knew and visited, have disappeared from the map, leaving hardly a trace behind them.

The Sea of Galilee

The accompanying map shows the NT sites and events associated with the Sea of Galilee. In terms of physical geography the Sea of Galilee is a large fresh-water lake important for its fishing, surrounded by mountains except to the S and the Plain of Gennesaret at its NW. The soil here is fertile, the weather hot:

> The water is sweet to the taste and excellent to drink … and perfectly pure, all the shores of the lake being pebbly or sandy. When drawn it has an agreeable temperature … It becomes as cold as snow after exposure to the air, as is practised on summer nights by the local people.
>
> The lake contains species of fish different in taste and appearance from those found elsewhere (Jos., *War* 1:506-508).

Josephus describes the fertile plain on the N as remarkable in its beauty and properties, growing the walnut, date-palm, fig and olive. It produces grape and fig continuously over ten months of the year. He says it is watered by a most productive spring, called locally 'Kapharnaoum'.

Recent excavation has solved one perennial issue. The site called Tel hum or Talhum is undoubtedly that of NT Capernaum. The claim made by the Franciscan excavators that they have found both the house of Peter (later a place of pilgrimage) and the foundations of the first century synagogue (as well as substantial remains of one from the fourth or fifth) deserves careful consideration.

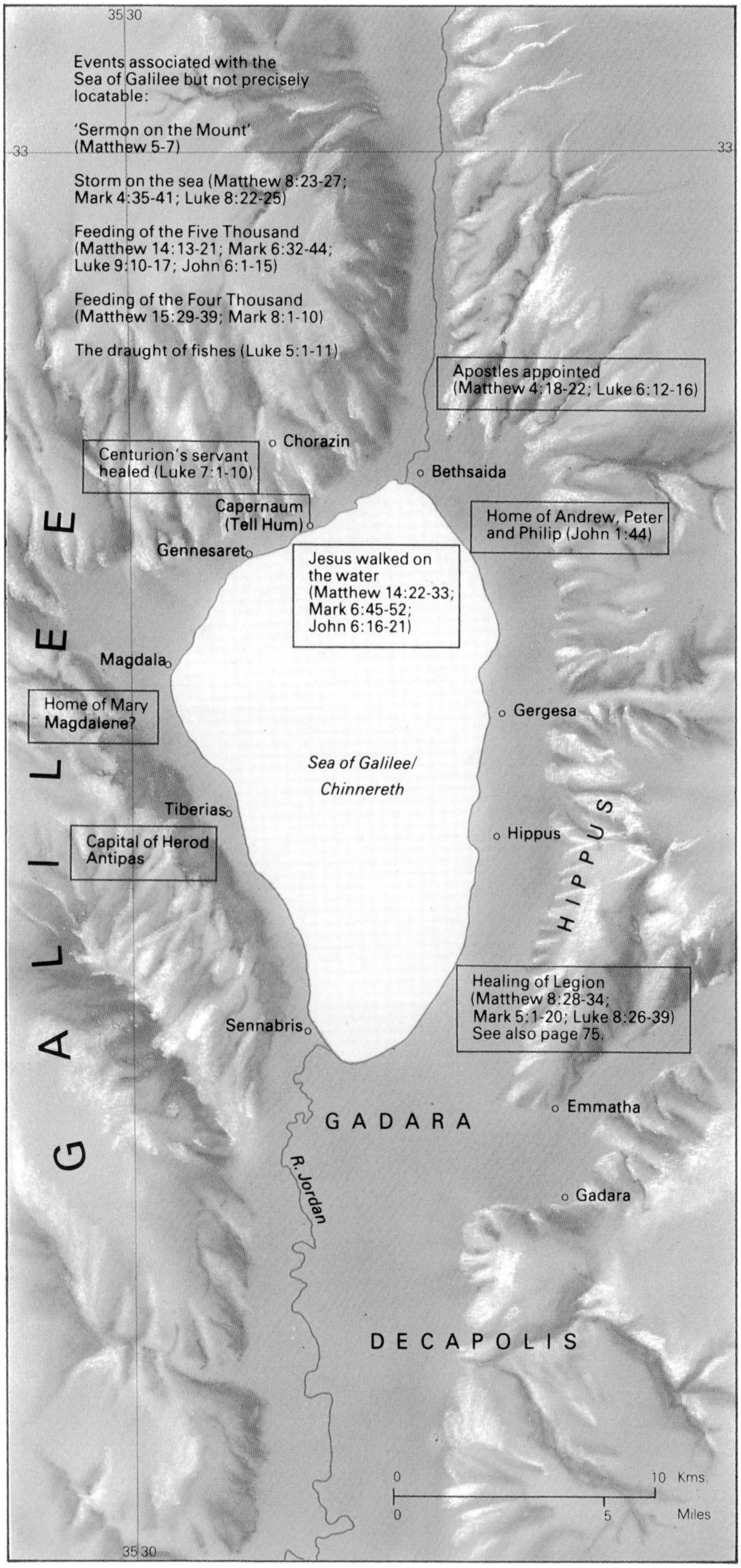

The Sea of Galilee and its associations with the ministry of Jesus.

Events associated with the Sea of Galilee but not precisely locatable:

'Sermon on the Mount' (Matthew 5-7)

Storm on the sea (Matthew 8:23-27; Mark 4:35-41; Luke 8:22-25)

Feeding of the Five Thousand (Matthew 14:13-21; Mark 6:32-44; Luke 9:10-17; John 6:1-15)

Feeding of the Four Thousand (Matthew 15:29-39; Mark 8:1-10)

The draught of fishes (Luke 5:1-11)

Apostles appointed (Matthew 4:18-22; Luke 6:12-16)

Chorazin

Bethsaida

Centurion's servant healed (Luke 7:1-10)

Capernaum (Tell Hum)

Gennesaret

Home of Andrew, Peter and Philip (John 1:44)

Jesus walked on the water (Matthew 14:22-33; Mark 6:45-52; John 6:16-21)

Magdala

Home of Mary Magdalene?

Gergesa

Sea of Galilee/ Chinnereth

Tiberias

Capital of Herod Antipas

Hippus

HIPPUS

Healing of Legion (Matthew 8:28-34; Mark 5:1-20; Luke 8:26-39) See also page 75.

Sennabris

GADARA

Emmatha

R. Jordan

Gadara

DECAPOLIS

GALILEE

0   10 Kms.

0   5   Miles

The Decapolis

The term 'Decapolis' first occurs in Mk.5:20 and 7:31 and Mt.4:25. It refers to a group of hellenized states, free in the Greek sense of having their own citizens and council. The cities in Gilead which belong to the group, and also Scythopolis, are all certainly old hellenistic foundations, which probably implies that they were military colonies in origin, each with its own nucleus of Macedonian (or Greek) veterans. One may suppose that the aristocracies remained Greek, that the cities adhered to the 'gymnasial' style of training and education inveighed against in 2 Macc.4:12, and that their citizens had no friendly feelings towards the Jews. They had been conquered by Alexander Jannaeus (see page 58) and freed by the Roman Pompey. Josephus says (*Ant.* 14.4.4; *War* 1.7.7) that Pompey restored them to the province of Syria. The fact that some of them issued coins with an era beginning in 64/63 BC, when Pompey set them free, shows the importance of this event in their history. They constituted a group of cities well-disposed to each other and with common trading interests, values and institutions. But they cannot have constituted a league in the technical sense, or we would hear of a federal capital, federal assemblies and the like, as we do with Megalopolis at the time of the Arcadian League in the Peloponnese (4th cent. BC).

The territory of a number of them – Hippos, Gadara, Scythopolis and Pella – was adjacent to and touched on the Sea of Galilee or the River Jordan. Abila, Dion, Gerasa and Philadelphia are also in Transjordan. The loose nature of the 'league' is demonstrated by the fact that three different lists appear in the three sources which name them. The earliest (*c.* AD 75) is that of Pliny, who names Scythopolis, Hippos, Gadara, Pella, Philadelphia, Gerasa (Galasa), Dion, Canatha, Damascus and Raphana.

Decapolis, the Greek name for the group of ten hellenized cities and their territories. Cities underlined are the ten named by Pliny.

Ancient Hippos, a city of the Decapolis, was situated at the summit of a flat-topped hill, ascended by a winding path. Its prominent position may have prompted Jesus' reference to a city on a hill which cannot be hidden (Mt.5:14).

The ministry of Jesus

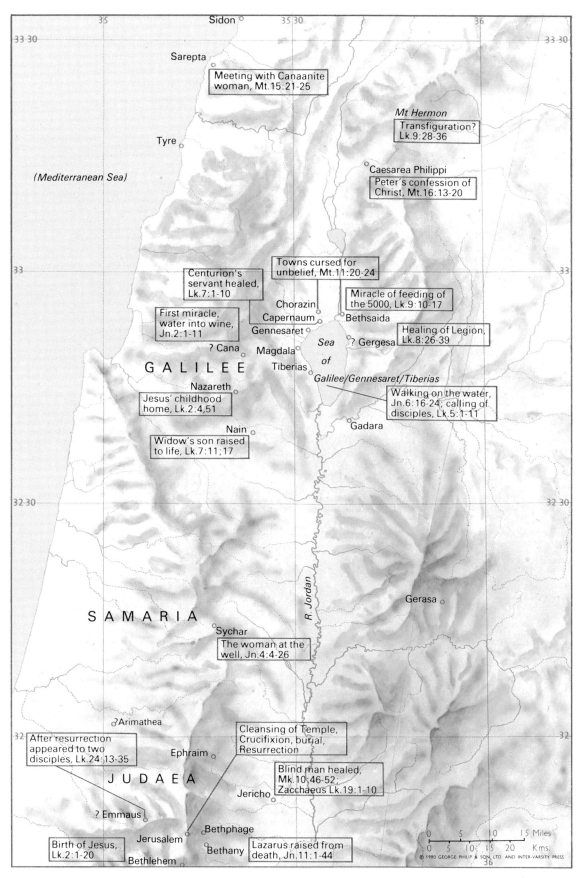

Sidon

33 30

Sarepta

Meeting with Canaanite
woman, Mt.15:21-25

Mt Hermon

Transfiguration?
Lk.9:28-36

Tyre

Caesarea Philippi

(Mediterranean Sea)

Peter's confession of
Christ, Mt.16:13-20

33

Towns cursed for
unbelief, Mt.11:20-24

Centurion's
servant healed,
Lk.7:1-10

Miracle of feeding of
the 5000, Lk.9:10-17

Chorazin

First miracle,
water into wine,
Jn.2:1-11

Capernaum
Gennesaret

Bethsaida

Healing of Legion,
Lk.8:26-39

? Gergesa

*Sea
of*

? Cana

Magdala

Tiberias

G A L I L E E

Galilee/Gennesaret/Tiberias

Nazareth

Walking on the water,
Jn.6:16-24; calling of
disciples, Lk.5:1-11

Jesus' childhood
home, Lk.2:4,51

Gadara

Nain

Widow's son raised
to life, Lk.7:11;17

32 30

R. Jordan

Gerasa

S A M A R I A

Sychar

The woman at the
well, Jn.4:4-26

?Arimathea

Cleansing of Temple,
Crucifixion, burial,
Resurrection

After resurrection
appeared to two
disciples, Lk.24:13-35

Ephraim

32

J U D A E A

Blind man healed,
Mk.10:46-52;
Zacchaeus Lk.19:1-10

Jericho

? Emmaus

Bethphage

Jerusalem

Birth of Jesus,
Lk.2:1-20

Bethany

Lazarus raised from
death, Jn.11:1-44

Bethlehem

0   5   10   15 Miles
0 5 10 15 20 Kms.
© 1980 GEORGE PHILIP & SON, LTD. AND INTER-VARSITY PRESS

*Some significant
locations in the ministry
of Jesus*

Greek New Testament manuscripts

1.

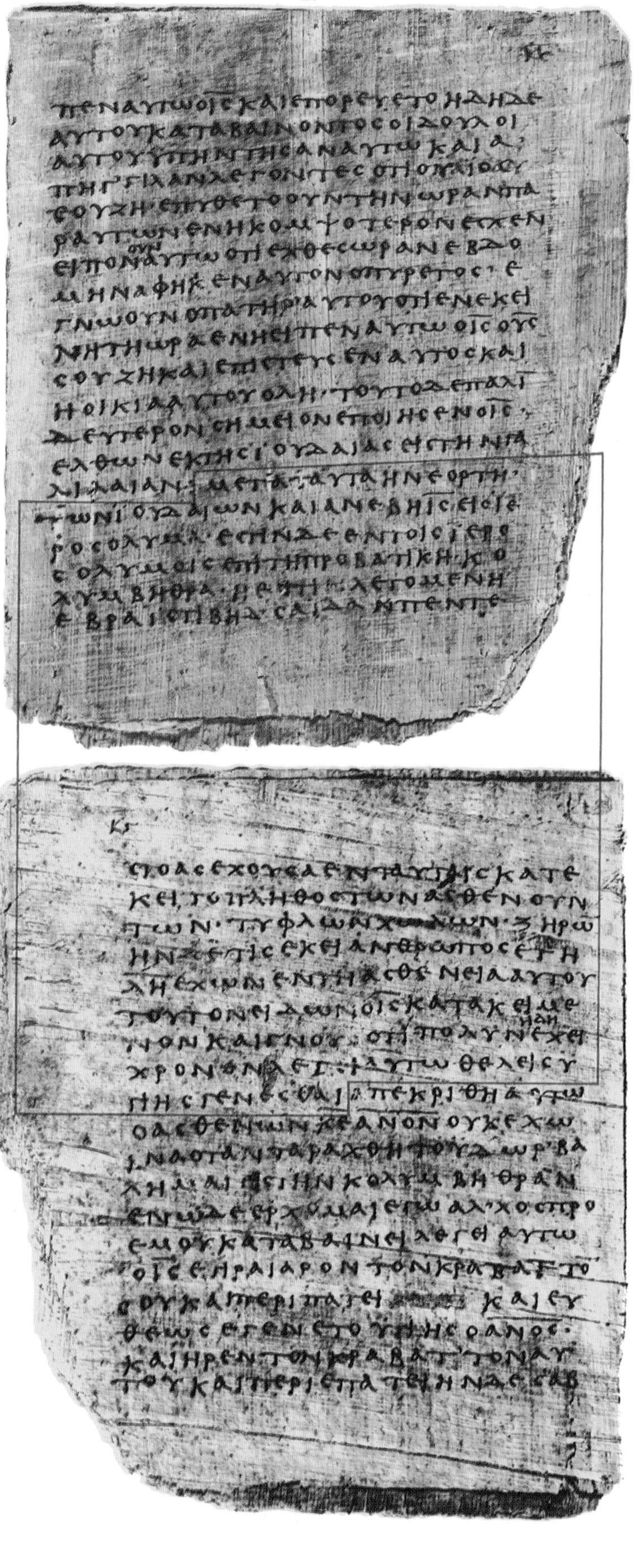

2.

4.51	πεν αυτω ο $\overline{ις}$ και επορευετο ηδη δε
	αυτου καταβαινοντος οι δουλοι
	αυτου ϋπηντησαν αυτω και α ΄
	πηγ΄γιλαν λεγοντες οτι ο ϋιος
52	σου ζη · επυθετο ουν την ωραν πα
	ρ αυτων εν η κομψοτερον εσχεν
	ουν
	ειπον αυτω οτι εχθες ωραν εβδο
53	μην αφηκεν αυτον ο πυρετος ΄ ε
	γνω ουν ο πατηρ΄ αυτου οτι εν εκει
	νη τη ωρα εν η ειπεν αυτω ο $\overline{ις}$ ο $\overline{υς}$
	σου ζη και επιστευσεν αυτος και
54	η οικια αυτου ολη · τουτο δε παλι
	δευτερον σημειον εποιησεν ο $\overline{ις}$ ΄
	ελθων εκ της ϊουδαιας εις την γα
5. 1	λιλαιαν · μετα ταυτα ην εορτη
	των ϊουδαιων και ανεβη $\overline{ις}$ εις ϊε
2	ροσολυμα · εστιν δε εν τοις ϊερο
	σολυμοις επι τη προβατικη · κο
	λυμβηθρα · η επιλεγομενη
	εβραϊστι βηδ΄σαϊδα[[ν]] πεντε
3	στοας εχουσα εν ταυταις κατε
	κειτο πληθος των ασθενουν
	των · τυφλων χωλων · ξηρω
5	ην δε τις εκει ανθρωπος ετη
	$\overline{λη}$ εχων εν τη ασθενεια αυτου
6	τουτον ειδων ο $\overline{ις}$ κατακειμε·
	νον και γνους οτι πολυν εχει ηδη
	χρονον λεγει αυτω θελεις ϋ
7	γιης γενεσθαι απεκριθη αυτω
	ο ασθενων $\overline{κε}$ ανον ουκ εχω
	ϊνα οταν ταραχθη το ϋδωρ΄ βα
	λη μαι εις την κολυμβηθραν
	εν ω δε ερχομαι εγω αλ΄λος προ
8	εμου καταβαινει λεγει αυτω
	ο $\overline{ις}$ εγιραι αρον τον κραβαττο
9	σου και περιπατει και ευ
	θεως εγενετο ϋγιης ο $\overline{ανος}$ ·
	και ηρεν τον κραβατ΄τον αυ
	του και περιεπατει ην δε σαβ

3.

5.1   meta tauta en eorte
ton ioudaion kai anebe is eis ie

2 rosoluma· estin de en tois iero
solumois epi te probatike· ko
lumbethra· e epilegomene
ebraisti bed'saida(n) pente

(start of next page)

3 stoas echousa en tautais kate
keito plethos ton asthenoun
ton· tuflon cholon· xero

5 en de tis ekei anthropos ete
le echon en te astheneia autou

6 touton eidon o is katakeime ede
non kai gnous oti polun echei
chronon legei auto theleis u
gies genesthai

4.

5.1   after this there-was a-festival
of-the Jews and went-up Js into Je/

2 rusalem· There-is and in the Jeru/
salem at the sheep-(gate)· a-res/
ervoir· the -one also-called
in-Hebrew Bed'saida five

(start of next page)

3 porticoes having in these was-ly/
ing a-multitude of-the af/
flicted· of-the-blind of-the-lame· of-the-
paralysed

5 there was and a-certain there man for-
years
thirty-eight keeping in the infirmity of-
him

6 him seeing the Js ly/
ing-down and realising that for-much he-
was-keeping already
time he-says to-him do-you-wish w/
ell to-become

5.

Jn. 5:1–6: After this there was a festival of the Jews, and Jesus went up into Jerusalem. And there is in Jerusalem at the sheep-(gate) a pool, also called Bedsaida, which has five porticoes. In these was lying a multitude of the afflicted, blind, lame. And there was a certain paralysed man there, who had suffered with his infirmity for thirty-eight years. Jesus, seeing him lying down, and realizing that he had suffered a long time, said to him, 'Do you want to become well?'

This double spread will enable the reader to gain some idea of what Greek MSS of the New Testament look like and how a passage of NT Greek differs from a passage of English. In English the word-order is often vital to the sense of a phrase, but in Greek the sense is governed by word endings. Thus the Greek word-order is much freer than its English equivalent.

The MS chosen is one of two papyri of John's Gospel. This is a very early example, dating from the late second century AD and first made known relatively recently.

1. Photographs of the manuscript
The photographs of the MS (far left) and the separate reproduction of its Greek in an edited form are both from *Papyrus Bodmer II, Supplement* (1962) by V. Martin. The text written on these pages covers John 4:50 – 5:9.

On this papyrus all the letters are capitals. This is true of all early Greek MSS. There is no word-division and often no sentence-division. 'Punctuation' is added only at selected points where the scribe feels that the sense might not be established without it.

2. Printed Greek
In column 2 the text has been printed in lower case letters with word-breaks, and placed alongside the original for comparison. The Bible's chapter and verse references have also been added.

3. English transcription
The extract indicated by the red border in columns 1 and 2 appears at 3 as a transcription of the Greek into English letters. This extract is John 5:1–6, and is broken in the original by the end of the page. A comparison between 2 and 3 shows the difference between Greek and English letters.

4. Word-by-word English
The next version is a word-by-word English translation of the extract. This version gives some idea of how the Greek word-order differs from the English.

5. Literal translation
The final version is a literal English translation, switching to normal English word-order. It does not correspond to any published translation of this passage.

This MS, known as P66, is the only early one which makes it clear that the scribe has separated 'pool' from 'sheep' in John 5:2 and so understood the sense as '...at the sheep (gate) a pool...'. The word 'gate' can be supplied with confidence since the sheep-gate is known from Nehemiah chapter 3.

Archaeological sites: Herodian period

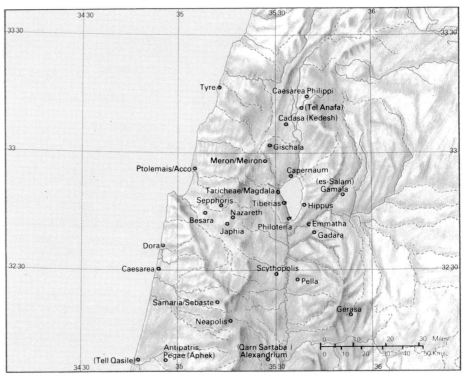

N Palestine: some important Herodian (New Testament) excavated sites.

Remains of the early hellenistic period·in Palestine and Transjordan are rare compared with those of the Maccabean/Hasmonaean period; and remains of the Hasmonaean period (including fortresses at Gezer and Beth-zur, and the N line of forts erected by Alexander Jannaeus (Jos., *War* 7.170) near Tel Aviv-Jaffa) are rare compared with Herodian remains. At Jerusalem Avigad found that for the Herodian period he could reconstruct not merely walls and topography but the daily life of the wealthy Jerusalemites (*Discovering Jerusalem*, p.81). The map indicates remains from the old Greek cities and the new Herodian foundations; from Herod's fortresses (pp. 68-69); from the Nabataeans (including the unusual finds of Glueck at Kh. et-Tannur, as described in *Deities and Dolphins, the Story of the Nabataeans*, 1965); and from the local strongholds of the land.

Inscriptions are notably important among archaeological finds. Several from Jerusalem are of interest. We have two copies of the *stelai* (upright stone slabs or tablets) which forbade Gentiles access to the Inner Temple (first centuries BC/AD):

No non-Jew to proceed beyond the barrier and enclosure which surrounds the sacred place; any man who (does so and) is caught is himself responsible for his death, which is the consequence.

Such *stelai* were set up in Latin and Greek round the Inner Temple. Josephus describes

them with almost the same words as the inscription (*War* 5.194; *Ant.* 15.417). The incidents of Acts 21:26-29 must be connected with the same prohibition: the riot which broke out then was caused by pious Jews who believed that Paul had brought a Greek within the forbidden area.

A Jerusalem ossuary (bone chest) inscription names one of the masons who worked on Herod's Temple (Simon, builder of the Temple); another refers to Nicanor, who provided the most splendid gates for it: 'Bones of the sons of Nicanor, who provided the Gates'. The combination 'Jesus, son of Joseph' occurs on another ossuary (both were common names of the period). The tomb of 'Alexander, son of Simon, of Cyrene' and his sister Sarah from Cyrenaican Ptolemais may plausibly be linked with 'the man called Simon from Cyrene, the father of Alexander and Rufus'.

The ruins of many ancient synagogues are to be found in Palestine. For a long time the earliest were thought to be those at Capernaum, Chorazin and Kefar Biram in Galilee, which were dated late second/early third centuries AD. Now it is claimed that assembly-halls of the first century AD at Masada and Herodium were synagogues. Franciscan excavators argue that the Capernaum synagogue is later than had been thought (late fourth/early fifth centuries AD), but have dated basalt foundations under its hall to an earlier synagogue, possibly of the time of Jesus. Gutman also places the Gamala synagogue early, perhaps earlier than Masada

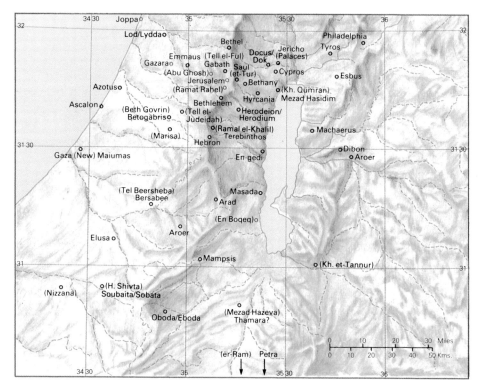

S Palestine: some important Herodian (New Testament) excavated sites.

or Herodium (see *Ancient Synagogues Revealed*, ed. L. I. Levine; *Judaism in Stone*, H. Shanks). But in fact the earliest evidence for a Palestinian synagogue comes from an inscription at Jerusalem, carved in the first century BC/AD by the grandson of a man who had already been 'head of synagogue' (*archisunagogos*): a certain Theodotus who built the place 'for the reading of the Law and study of its precepts', attaching to it a hospice for visitors from abroad, who were provided with their own baths and chambers.

Outside Jerusalem the most notable find in terms of inscriptions is the stone which was re-used in the theatre at Caesarea, but had been set up by Pontius Pilate. He is named 'prefect of Judaea' (at about the time when the title of minor equestrian governors was to change from 'prefect' to 'procurator'); and the wording states that he set up a shrine in honour of Tiberius.

Important Herodian remains outside Jerusalem have come to light in the new city-foundations of Herod the Great (Sebaste, Caesarea), at his winter-palace in Jericho (it snows in Jerusalem in the winter, whereas the climate of Jericho is sub-tropical) and in his fortresses Masada and Herodium. More recently less spectacular finds have come from Antipatris (Aphek). In the Samaritan hills the old city of Samaria was re-founded by Herod as Sebaste to honour Augustus (Lat. *augustus* = Gk. *sebastos*). Ancient Israelite walls were rebuilt and reinforced with round towers; a temple was dedicated to Augustus (the cult of

the emperor was a political phenomenon, a way of acknowledging that the Roman Empire gave peace and prosperity to the provinces); and a sports-stadium was founded. All have been located by excavation. At Caesarea the great Herodian harbour (mole) has been explored by an underwater team; its lines are clearly visible in aerial photographs. Italian excavators have found parts of the city-wall of Strato's Tower (the name of the town before it became Caesarea Maritima), and the Herodian theatre with its seats and stage and most unusual painted plaster floors. The winter-palace at Jericho includes a great *opus sectile* hall, a sunken garden, a pool, Roman-style baths, and the specifically Roman building technique of *opus reticulatum* (a net-like facing of small stones set in the concrete of the walls), also found at Caesarea Philippi.

The Herodian palace-fortresses exhibit the same luxurious style and flamboyant imagination as Herod everywhere displayed. A 'Herodian style' in terms of the ornament used for floor-mosaics and wall- and ceiling-frescoes is found in his fortresses, palaces and cities; it has links with the funerary art of Jerusalem. Moreover the leaping imagination proclaimed by the conception of the Temple Mount (and the precinct at Hebron) is matched by the N palace at Masada, perched on a terrace above a sheer ravine, and by the artificial truncated cone created for a ring-wall of defence at Herodium.

For details and illustrations of these fortresses see pages 68-70.

Paul's 'missionary journeys'

It is customary to depict the apostle Paul's ministry as three 'missionary journeys' and a final journey to Rome. The following headings, however, may provide a better picture.

Mission to Galatia

About AD 46 Paul and Barnabas, commissioned by the church in Antioch, embarked on an evangelistic tour. It took them across the island of Cyprus and through 'S Galatia' (Acts 13-14). Their strategy, which became a pattern for the Pauline missions, was to preach first in the synagogue. Some Jews and Gentile 'Godfearers' accepted the message and became the nucleus for a local assembly. When the mass of Jews rejected the gospel, sometimes with violence, the focus of the preaching shifted to the Gentiles (*cf.* Acts 13:46f.). Despite these perils and the defection at Perga of their helper, John Mark, the mission succeeded in establishing a Christian witness in Pisidian Antioch, Iconium, Lystra, Derbe and possibly Perga.

Mission to Greece

Because of differences with Barnabas (over taking John Mark with them again) Paul took a new companion, Silas, on his second missionary tour (Acts 15:40-18:22). From Antioch they travelled overland to the churches of 'S Galatia' and at Lystra added young Timothy to the party. Forbidden by the Holy Spirit to evangelize W, they journeyed N through 'N Galatia', where some converts may have been made (*cf.* Acts 16:6; 18:23). At Troas Paul in a vision saw a 'man of Macedonia'

beckoning to him. Thus his evangelization of Greece began. In Macedonia missions were established in Philippi, Thessalonica and Beroea; in Achaia, or S Greece, Athens and Corinth were visited. In the latter city Paul remained almost two years founding a Christian fellowship that was to be the source of both joy and trial in the future. The Holy Spirit now moved Paul to turn his eyes once more upon the earlier forbidden province of Asia. Departing from Corinth, he stopped briefly at Ephesus, the commercial metropolis of Asia, and left as an advance party his Corinthian colleagues Priscilla and Aquila. In a quick trip back to Antioch – *via* Jerusalem – Paul completed his 'second missionary journey'.

The Aegean ministry

In many ways the Aegean period (*c.* AD 53-58; Acts 18:23-20:38) was the most important of Paul's life. The province of Asia, so important for the later church, was evangelized; and the Christian outposts in Greece secured. During these years he wrote the Corinthian letters, Romans and perhaps one or more of the Prison Epistles (Ephesians, Philippians, Colossians and Philemon), which in the providence of God were to constitute a holy and authoritative Scripture for all generations. For the apostle this was a time of triumph and defeat, of gospel proclamation and threatening heresies, of joy and frustration, of activity and prison meditation. The risen Christ used all these things to mould Paul into his image and to speak through Paul his word to the church.

From Antioch Paul travelled overland through the familiar Galatian region to Ephesus. There he met certain 'disciples', including Apollos, who had known John the Baptist and, presumably, Jesus (Acts 18:24ff.). Paul doubtless made a number of short trips out from Ephesus, and at length, some three years after his arrival, he made a final visit to the churches in the Aegean area. Through Troas he came to Macedonia, where he wrote 2 Corinthians and, after a time, travelled S to Corinth. There he spent the winter and wrote a letter to the 'Romans' before retracing his steps to Miletus, a port near Ephesus. After a touching farewell Paul, 'bound in the Spirit' and under threatening clouds, sailed towards Jerusalem and almost certain arrest. This did not deter him, for Asia had been conquered and he had visions of Rome.

Ministry in Caesarea and voyage to Rome

Paul disembarked at Caesarea and, with a collection for the poor, arrived at Jerusalem at

Paul's missions to Galatia and to Greece.

Pentecost (Acts 21:23f.; *cf.* Rom. 15:25ff; 1 Cor. 16:3f.; 2 Cor. 9). Although he was careful to observe the Temple rituals, Jewish pilgrims from Ephesus, remembering 'the apostle to the Gentiles', accused him of violating the Temple and inciting the crowds to riot. He was placed under arrest but was permitted to address the crowd and later the Sanhedrin.

To prevent his being lynched, Paul was removed to Caesarea, where Felix, the Roman governor, imprisoned him for two years (*c.* AD 58-60, Acts 23-26). At that time Festus, Felix's successor, indicated that he might give Paul to the Jews for trial. Knowing the outcome of such a 'trial', Paul, as a Roman citizen, appealed to Caesar. After a moving interview before the governor and his guests, King Agrippa and Bernice, he was sent under guard to Rome. Thus, under circumstances hardly anticipated, the risen Christ fulfilled the apostle's dream and his own word to Paul: 'You must bear witness also at Rome' (Acts 23:11). Paul had a stormy sea voyage and, after being wrecked, spent the winter on Malta (*c.* AD 61). He reached Rome in the spring and spent the next two years under house-arrest 'teaching about the Lord Jesus Christ quite openly' (Acts 28:31).

Paul's Aegean ministry.

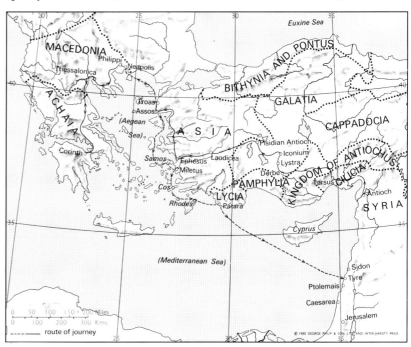

Paul's journey to Rome.

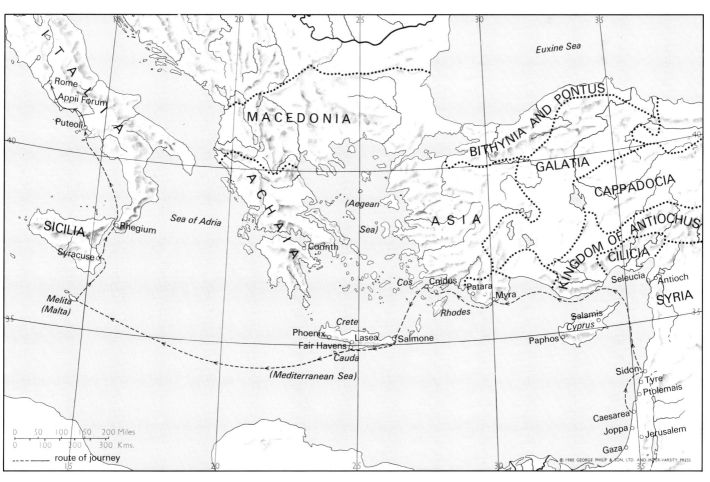

Asia Minor: the 'Seven Churches'

The 'Seven Churches' are those which received messages of encouragement and rebuke from God, through the revelation to John on the island of Patmos (Rev. 1:9 – 3:22). They were all situated in the Roman province of Asia, in the W of what is now Turkey. In order of mention they are:

1. Ephesus

Ephesus was the most important city in the province but is now uninhabited. It was situated at the mouth of the Caÿster River between the mountain range of Coressus and the sea. A magnificent road 11 m (c. 36 ft) wide and lined with columns ran down through the city to the fine harbour, which served both as a great export centre at the end of the Asiatic caravan-route and also as a natural landing-point from Rome. The city has been undergoing excavation for many years and is probably the most extensive and impressive ruined site of Asia Minor. This site was originally sacred to the worship of the Anatolian fertility goddess, later identified with Greek Artemis and Latin Diana.

The church in Ephesus is addressed first of the seven (Rev. 2:1-7), as being the most important church in the *de facto* capital, and as being the landing-place for a messenger from Patmos and standing at the head of a circular road joining the seven cities in order. This church is flourishing, but is troubled by false teachers, and has lost its 'first love'. The false apostles (2:2) are most probably like the Nicolaitans, who seem to have advocated compromise with the power of paganism for the Christian under pressure. The Ephesians were steadfast, but deficient in love.

The 'Seven Churches of Asia' of Rev.1-3 and the island of Patmos where John received the revelation.

2. Smyrna

Smyrna is modern Izmir, the second largest city in Asiatic Turkey.

The gospel probably reached Smyrna at an early date, presumably from Ephesus (Acts 19:10). The 'angel of the church in Smyrna' is the recipient of the second of the letters of the 'seven churches ... in Asia' (Rev. 2:8-11). As in other commercial cities, the church encountered opposition from the Jews (Rev. 2:9; *cf.* 3:9). The description of the Christ as the one who was dead and lived again (v.8) may allude to the resurgence of the city to new prosperity after a long period in obscurity. The 'crown' (v.10) was rich in associations at Smyrna. It may suggest the victor's wreath at the games, or current forms of eulogy which used the image of the beauty and glory of the city and its buildings. *Cf.* also James 1:12. The call to faithfulness (v.10) is a call to the church to fulfil in the deepest way the historic reputation of the city.

3. Pergamum

Pergamum is listed third of the 'seven churches' (Rev. 2:12-17); the order suits its position in geographical sequence. This was the place 'where Satan's throne is' (Rev. 2:13). The phrase has been referred to the complex of pagan cults, of Zeus, Athena, Dionysus and Asclepius, established by the Attalid kings, that of Asclepius Soter (the 'saviour', 'healer') being of special importance. These cults are illustrative of the religious history of Pergamum, but the main allusion is probably to emperor worship. This was where the worship of the divine emperor had been made the touch-stone of civic loyalty under Domitian. It marked a crisis for the church in Asia. Antipas (v.13) is probably cited as a representative (perhaps the first) of those who were brought to judgment and execution here for their faith.

4. Thyatira

The Thyatiran church was the fourth of the 'seven churches' that are in Asia' (Rev.1:11). Some of the symbols in the letter to the church (Rev.2:18-29) seem to allude to the circumstances of the city. The description of the Christ (v.18) is appropriate for a city renowned for its brass-working (*chalkolibanos*, translated 'fine brass', may be a technical term for some local type of brassware). The terms of the promise (vv.26-27) may reflect the long military history of the city. 'Jezebel' (the name is probably symbolic) was evidently a woman who was accepted within the fellowship of the church (v.20). Her teaching is nowhere recorded but probably advocated a measure of compromise with some activity which was implicitly pagan.

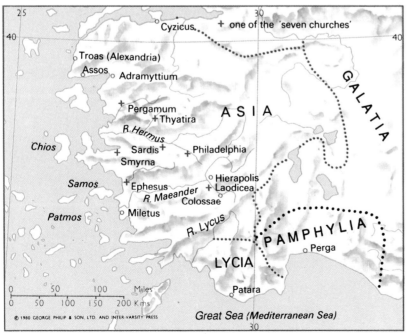

Early church congregations

5. Sardis

Sardis was the capital of the ancient kingdom of Lydia and was renowned for its wealth, especially under Croesus.

The letter to 'the angel of the church in Sardis' (Rev. 3:1-6) suggests that the early Christian community there was imbued with the same spirit as the city, resting on its past reputation and without any present achievement, and failing, as the city had twice failed, to learn from its past and be vigilant. The symbol of 'white garments' (vv.4-5) was rich in meaning in a city noted for its luxury clothing trade; the faithful few who are vigilant shall be arrayed to share in the triumphal coming of their Lord.

6. Philadelphia

The letter to 'the angel of the church in Philadelphia' (Rev. 3:7-13) probably alludes to some of the circumstances of the city. As Philadelphus was renowned for his loyalty to his brother, so the church, the true Philadelphia, inherits and fulfils his character by its steadfast loyalty to Christ (vv.8,10). As the city stands by the 'open door' of a region from which its wealth derives, so the church is given an 'open door' of opportunity to exploit (v.8; *cf.* 2 Cor.2:12). The symbols of the 'crown' and the 'temple' (vv.11-12) point to a contrast between the games and religious festivals of the city. In contrast with the impermanence of life in a city prone to earthquake, those who 'overcome' are promised the ultimate stability of being built into the temple of God.

7. Laodicea

Laodicea was a city of SW Phrygia. It was founded by the Seleucid Antiochus II in the third century BC and called after his wife Laodice. It was a prosperous commercial centre, lying near Hierapolis and Colossae in the valley of the Lycus, a tributary of the Maeander.

The last of the letters to 'the seven churches … in Asia' was addressed to Laodicea (Rev.3:14-22). Its imagery owes relatively little to the OT, but contains pointed allusions to the character and circumstances of the city. For all its wealth, it could produce neither the healing power of hot water, like its neighbour Hierapolis, nor the refreshing power of cold water to be found at Colossae, but merely lukewarm water, useful only as an emetic. The church was charged with a similar uselessness: it was self-sufficient rather than half-hearted. Like the city, it thought it had 'need of nothing'. In fact it was spiritually poor, naked and blind, and needed 'gold', 'white garments' and 'eyesalve' more effective than its bankers, clothiers and doctors could supply (v.18). Like citizens inhospitable to a traveller who offers them priceless goods, the Laodiceans had closed their doors and left their real Provider outside. Christ turns in loving appeal to the individual (v.20).

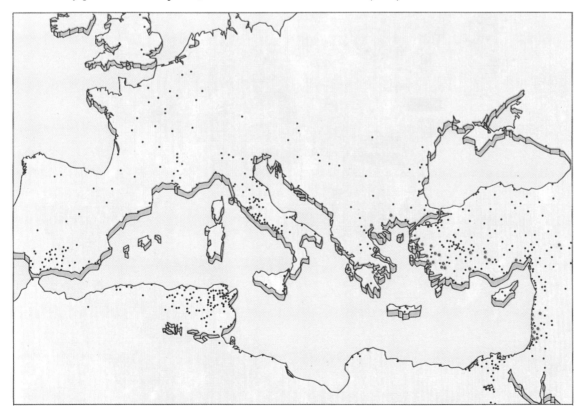

Early church congregations of the first century AD (shown in red) and churches founded before Diocletian's persecution of AD 304 (black).

The 'Table of the Nations'

The Table of Nations, according to Gn. 10, showing the descendants of Noah's sons, Shem, Ham and Japheth.

Genesis 10 provides a list of 'the families of the sons (or descendants) of Noah, according to their genealogies (or generations), in their nations' (v.32). The thinking represented by the list is complex, however, and in some cases it clearly depicts something other than the straightforward descent of racial groups from individuals. For example, the presence of Sheba (= Saba in SW Arabia) among the descendants of both Shem and Ham (vv.7,28) probably reflects both the Semitic origin of the Sabaeans and the historical fact that Sabaeans migrated across the Red Sea and settled among Hamitic groups (*i.e.* Egyptians and Ethiopians) with whom they became racially and culturally mingled.

Many of the names in the Table have been identified with those of racial, geographical and political entities known from outside the Bible. On the basis of these identifications we can say that the names in the first section (Japheth, vv.2-5) represent peoples of the N and NW of the Ancient Near East, those in the second (Ham, vv.6-20) represent generally the peoples of the S, and those in the third (Shem, vv.21-31) the peoples who settled from Syria in the N, through Mesopotamia as far as Arabia in the S.

Japheth	Ham	Shem
Gomer	Cush	Elam
Ashkenaz	Seba	Asshur
Riphath	Havilah	Arpachshad
Togarmah	Sabtah	Shelah
Magog	Raamah	Eber
Madai	Sheba	Peleg
Javan	Deban	Joktan
Elishah	Sabteca	Almodad
Tarshish	Nimrod	Sheleph
Kittim	Mizraim	Hazarmaveth
Dodanim	Ludim	Jerah
Tubal	Anamin	Hadoram
Meshech	Lehabim	Uzal
Tiras	Naphtuhim	Diklah
	Pathrusim	Obal
	Casluhim	Abimael
	Philistines	Sheba
	Caphtorim	Ophir
	Put (Phut)	Havilah
	Canaan	Jobab
	Zidon	Lud
	Heth	Aram
	Jebusite	Uz
	Amorite	Hul
	Girgashite	Gether
	Hivite	Mash
	Archite	
	Sinite	
	Arvadite	
	Zemorite	
	Hamathite	

Descendants of an individual are placed below and to the right of the ancestor's name

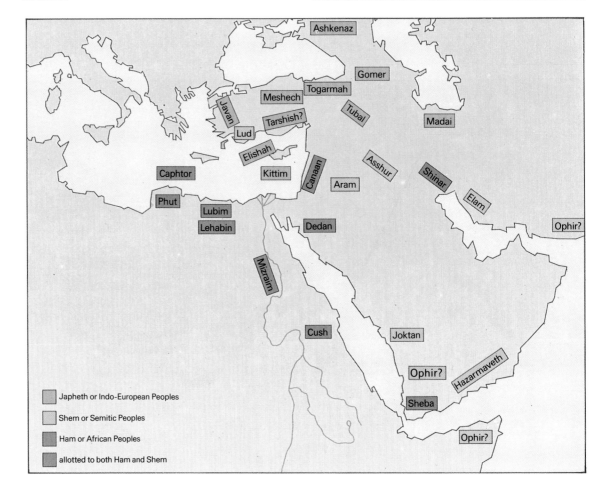

Map based on the 'Table of Nations' in Gn.10, showing possible connections between the names in the Table and the names of peoples or regions known from extra-biblical inscriptions.

Japheth or Indo-European Peoples

Shem or Semitic Peoples

Ham or African Peoples

allotted to both Ham and Shem

Sumer and Akkad

In early antiquity Babylonia (modern S Iraq) was known as Akkad (the N part of the region) and Sumer (the S, bordering the Persian Gulf).

Sumer

In the fourth millennium BC the Sumerians were responsible for many of the hallmarks of later civilization, including fine art and architecture, and pictographic writing (*c.* 3100 BC), ancestor of the later cuneiform script. The period *c.* 3000-2500 BC in Sumer saw the advent of kingship and the growth of city-states centred at Uruk (OT Erech, Gn.10:10), Kish, Ur, Lagash, Umma, Abu Salabikh and Shuruppak (whose governor Ziusuddu is the hero of the Sumerian flood story). There were frequent clashes between cities as their rulers sought dominion over their neighbours. A new unity came to the region in 2371 BC when the Semitic ruler Sargon of Akkad brought the whole of Sumer under his control.

Akkad

In the OT Akkad (or Accad) is mentioned as one of the cities founded by Nimrod (Gn.10:10). The precise location of this city, known as Agade in Sumerian, is unknown. Inscriptions show, however, that the powerful dynasty founded by Sargon flourished there until *c.* 2230 BC. The reigns of Sargon and his successor Naram-Sin were looked back on as a golden age of political strength and commercial prosperity. Their armies reached as far as Syria, Elam and S Anatolia.

Later, when Babylon became the capital of the region, the term 'Akkad' continued to be employed to describe the whole of N Babylonia until the late Persian period. It is used in this way in the records of the kings of Assyria and Babylonia.

Around 2230 BC Akkad was overrun by the Gutians from the E hills. However, the invaders never succeeded in imposing their rule on the whole of Babylonia, and Lagash, under its ruler Gudea (*c.* 2150 BC), remained independent and dominated Ur and the S cities. Eventually, under Ur-Nammu (2113-2096 BC), Ur became the centre of a Neo-Sumerian dynasty (Third Dynasty of Ur, 2113-2006? BC).

The new dynasty was prosperous, and Ur's influence reached as far as Assur and Byblos. Eventually, however, severe famines, invaders from Elam and Semitic semi-nomads from the W, deserts brought the epoch to an end. (For the later history of Babylonia see pages 91-93.)

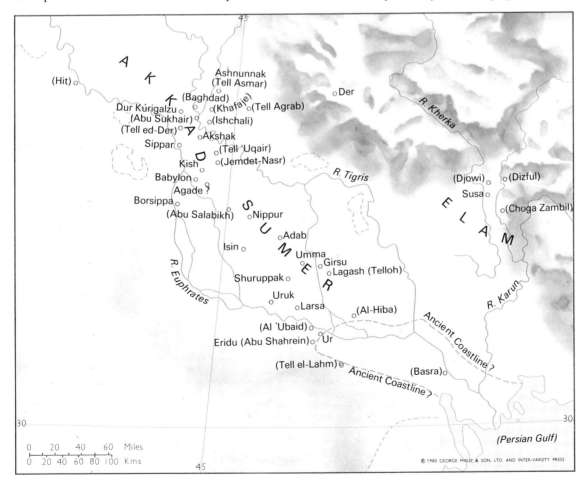

Sumer and Akkad, the S and N regions respectively of ancient Babylonia.

Egypt

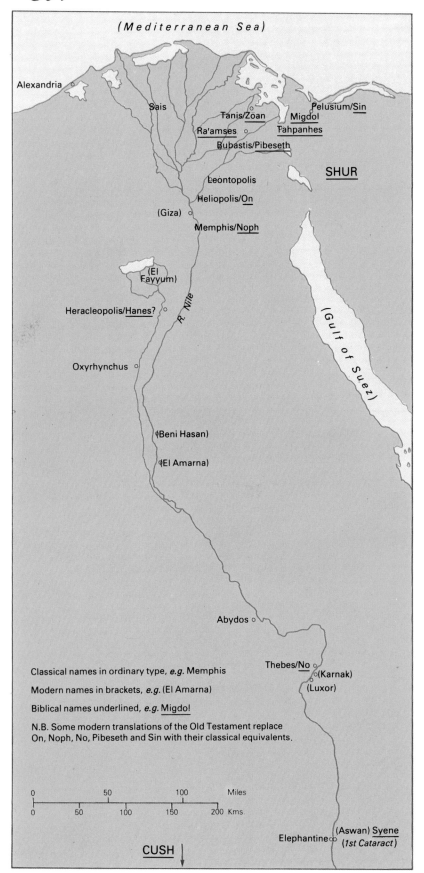

(Mediterranean Sea)

Alexandria

Sais

Tanis/Zoan

Pelusium/Sin

Migdol

Ra'amses

Tahpanhes

Bubastis/Pibeseth

SHUR

Leontopolis

Heliopolis/On

(Giza)

Memphis/Noph

(El Fayyum)

Heracleopolis/Hanes?

R. Nile

Oxyrhynchus

(Gulf of Suez)

(Beni Hasan)

(El Amarna)

Abydos

Thebes/No

(Karnak)

(Luxor)

Classical names in ordinary type, *e.g.* Memphis

Modern names in brackets, *e.g.* (El Amarna)

Biblical names underlined, *e.g.* Migdol

N.B. Some modern translations of the Old Testament replace On, Noph, No, Pibeseth and Sin with their classical equivalents.

| 0 | 50 | 100 | Miles |
| 0 | 50 100 | 150 | 200 Kms. |

Elephantine

(Aswan) Syene

(1st Cataract)

CUSH

In the Nile Valley, as in Mesopotamia, civilization developed *c.* 3000 BC. When Abraham visited Egypt (Gn. 12:10–20), perhaps *c.* 2000 BC, its civilization was therefore already 1,000 years old, and the Great Pyramid of Cheops at Giza had stood for six centuries.

By Abraham's time (the beginning of the Middle Kingdom) Egypt was entering its second period of greatness (see chart on p.116 for periods of Egyptian history with dates). It was probably in the late Middle Kingdom or the Second Intermediate Period that Jacob's family settled in the E Delta. On the date of the Exodus see pp. 38-9.

Egypt's third period of greatness, the New Kingdom (*c.* 1550–1070 BC), saw the creation of an empire, chiefly through the campaigns of Tuthmosis III (*c.* 1490–1436 BC). Egypt became the paramount power of the Near East, with the princes of Syria-Palestine her tribute-paying vassals. Under the religious reformer Akhenaten (*c.* 1367-1350 BC) Egypt's hold on the region weakened. Akhenaten moved the capital from Thebes to Akhet-Aten (El Amarna), where the famous Amarna letters (correspondence from the Canaanite city-states) were found. During the 19th Dynasty (*c.* 1300–1200 BC) Egypt's dominance in Syria-Palestine was reasserted by Seti I and Ramesses II, but after the reign of the last great warrior-pharaoh Ramesses III (*c.* 1190–1160 BC) control was finally lost, allowing the rise of an independent Hebrew kingdom.

Solomon had close commercial and diplomatic ties with Egypt (1 Ki. 7:8; 9:16; 10:28–29). After Solomon's death Shishak campaigned in Palestine (see p. 46), but made no attempt to recover the former empire. Assyria conquered Egypt in 671 BC. The prophet Nahum (3:8–10) refers to Ashurbanipal's sack of Thebes (No-Amon) in 663 BC.

The prophets frequently refer to the declining power of Egypt in the Late Period, often naming major cities such as Zoan (Tanis, the effective capital *c.* 1100–660 BC), Memphis, Thebes, Heliopolis, Bubastis, Pelusium and Tahpanhes (Is. 19:11–13; 30:1–5; Je. 46; Ezk. 30–32).

After the fall of Jerusalem in 587 BC, Jews settled in the Delta and 'the land of Pathros', *i.e.* Upper Egypt between Memphis and Aswan (Je. 44:1). In the fifth century BC a Jewish community flourished on the island of Elephantine near Aswan.

Egypt 'from Migdol to Syene' (Ezk. 29:10), i.e. from the N Delta to the border with Cush, showing locations mentioned in the OT with a selection of other sites. For more detail of the E Delta in connection with the Exodus route, see page 31.

The Kingdoms of Transjordan

The inhabitants of Transjordan impinged significantly on Israel's history, usually in the role of enemies.

Israel first clashed with the peoples of Transjordan in the time of Moses. The king of Edom, whose territory reached Kadesh in the W and included the King's Highway in the E (Nu. 20:16–17), and probably stretched from the Wadi Zered in the N to the Gulf of Aqabah in the S, refused Israel permission to traverse his kingdom on their way to Canaan (Nu. 20:18–21). Balak the king of Moab, whose S boundary was the Wadi Zered, was even more hostile, hiring the prophet Balaam to curse the new nation (Nu. 22–24). He was joined in this opposition by the chiefs of the Midianites, who seem at this time to have shared territory with Moab (Nu. 22:4ff.; 25:1–18; 31:1–12), though later their home lay S of Edom. Balak's predecessor had lost the territory N of the river Arnon (Nu. 21:26) to Sihon, king of the Amorites, who ruled from Heshbon (Nu. 21:13, 27–30). Sihon also opposed Israel's passage but was defeated in battle (Nu. 21:23–25); thus Israel occupied the territory between the Arnon and the Jabbok, as far E as the boundary with the Ammonites. Og the king of Bashan also opposed Israel, but was likewise defeated (Nu. 21:33–35).

The Moabites, Midianites and Ammonites all feature as oppressors of Israel in the Judges period (Jdg. 3:12–20; 6 – 8; 11:4–33). At the beginning of Saul's reign Nahash the king of Ammon besieged Jabesh-gilead but was defeated by Saul (1 Sa. 11:1–11), who also campaigned successfully against Edom and Moab (1 Sa. 14:47). Later, Moab, Ammon and Edom were totally subjugated by David (2 Sa. 8:2, 12, 14; 12:26–31).

Edom was always an opponent of Judah and earned the condemnation of the prophets (e.g. Je. 49:7–22; Ob. 1–14; cf. Ps. 137:7). After the fall of Jerusalem in 587 BC, Edomites settled in Judah S of Hebron, and the area became known as Idumaea.

For Israel's relations with Moab during the later monarchy, see pp. 47–48.

The Ammonites raided Judah along with Moabites and Edomites in the time of Jehoshaphat, perhaps c. 850 BC, but Judah was saved when her enemies began fighting among themselves (2 Ch. 20:1–30). In the following century Uzziah and Jotham both received tribute from the Ammonites (2 Ch. 26:8; 27:5). They remained inveterate enemies of Judah, however (cf. 2 Ki. 24:2; Je. 40:11–14), and were fiercely denounced by the prophets (e.g. Je. 49:1–6; Zp. 2:8–11).

For description of the land, see page 23.

The Kingdoms and peoples of Transjordan in the OT period.

The Philistines and Phoenicians

Philistia and Phoenicia. There is still uncertainty concerning the identification of the sites of some of the cities of the Philistine pentapolis (five towns). Philistine pottery occurs characteristically at coastal sites from Joppa southwards and inland to border sites such as Gezer and Debir, but has also been found as far N as Megiddo and as far E as Tell Deir 'Alla.

Map labels:
Karatepe, Zinjirli, Ugarit (Ras Shamra), Kition, Arvad, Simyra, The Great Sea (Mediterranean Sea), R. Orontes, Byblos, Berytus, Sidon, Zarepta, Tyre, Damascus, Achzib, Hazor, Acco, Lebanon Mts, Dor, Megiddo, Beth-shan, (Tell el-Qasileh), (Tell Deir 'Alla), Joppa, Jordan, Ekron, Jerusalem, Ashdod, Beth-shemesh, Ashkelon, Lachish, Gaza, Gath?, Debir, (Tell el-'Ajjul), Gerar, (Tell en-Nagila), Beersheba, (Tell el Farah (south))

■ Town of the Philistine 'pentapolis' (Jos. 13:3; Isa. 6:17)
✕ Major Phoenician city
● Towns under Phoenician influence

0   25   50 Miles
0   25 50 75 100 Kms.

© 1980 GEORGE PHILIP & SON LTD. AND INTERVARSITY PRESS.

Philistines

According to Amos 9:7 the Philistines came from Caphtor (Crete or Cyprus). An attempted invasion of Egypt by the 'Sea Peoples', including Philistines (*prst*), was repulsed by Ramesses III in 1185 BC, after which the Philistines fell back on S Canaan, where distinctive pottery attests their arrival. Subsequently they occupied much of the coastal plain S of Carmel.

Although the OT attests the presence of (proto-) Philistines in S Canaan from an early date (Gn. 26), it was after their major influx in the twelfth century BC that they became a persistent thorn in Israel's side (Jdg. 13 – 16; 1 Sa. 4ff.). David subdued them (2 Sa. 5:17–25), but during the divided monarchy there was frequent fighting along the border with Judah (1 Ki. 15:27; 2 Ch. 21:16–17; 26:6).

A serious invasion occurred in the reign of Ahaz (*c.* 732–716 BC), when the Philistines captured several towns in the Shephelah and resettled them (2 Ch. 28:18; *cf.* Is. 9:11–12). The last reference to Philistines in the Bible comes from the post-exilic period when Zechariah prophesied against them (Zc. 9:5–7).

The culture of the Philistines was largely that of Canaan, in spite of their foreign origins. The three gods of the Philistines mentioned in the Bible, Ashtaroth (1 Sa. 31:10), 'Baal-zebub, the god of Ekron' (2 Ki. 1:1–6), and Dagon (Jdg. 16:23; 1 Sa. 5:1–5), were worshipped widely in the ancient Near East.

The term 'Palestine' derives from the name of the Philistines and their territory. It was first used in a broader sense, to designate S Syria generally, by Herodotus (*c.* 450 BC).

Phoenicians

By the twelfth century BC, Israelite and Philistine settlement in the S, and Aramaean pressure inland, had restricted the Canaanites to the coastal strip N of Carmel, where they emerged as the sea-faring Phoenicians of the first millennium BC.

By the ninth century BC, as a result of their initiative in maritime ventures, the Phoenicians had colonies in Sardinia, Cyprus (Kition) and Karatepe (N Taurus). By the eighth century BC the important colony of Carthage in N Africa had also been founded, and there were other settlements in Tunisia and Sicily.

David and Solomon had commercial treaties with Hiram of Tyre, the chief Phoenician port of their day (2 Sa. 5:11; 1 Ki. 5:1–12; 9:27; 10:22). Ahab's wife, Jezebel, was the daughter of Hiram's successor Ethbaal. The marriage unfortunately brought Phoenician religion into Israel on a large scale (1 Ki. 16:32; 18:19). The major cities of Tyre and Sidon are frequently mentioned by the OT prophets (*e.g.* Is. 23; Je. 47:4; Ezk. 27 – 28; Joel 3:4; Zc. 9:2–4).

The Aramaeans

Around 1100 BC a number of Aramaean states came into existence to the N and NE of Palestine. Saul (*c.* 1050–1010 BC) and David (*c.* 1010–970 BC) both fought against Zobah, David defeating its king Hadadezer on two occasions (1 Sa. 14:47; 2 Sa. 8:3; 10:6–19). Hadadezer was a powerful ruler, able to command the support of other Aramaean states, including Bit-Idini (Beth-Eden) beyond the Euphrates (*cf.* 2 Sa. 10:6, 8, 16, 19). David also defeated the Aramaeans of Damascus who came to Hadadezer's aid, subsequently annexing 'Aram of Damascus' (2 Sa. 8:5–6). The king of Hamath (Toi or Tou), an erstwhile enemy of Hadadezer, became David's ally (vassal?) (2 Sa. 8:9–10).

Solomon is reported to have taken 'Hamath-Zobah' (2 Ch. 8:3–4), which probably means that he put down a revolt in the region where Zobah adjoined Hamath. He had no success, however, in dealing with a later rebellion. Rezon, a former servant of Hadadezer of Zobah, became the leader of a band of marauders operating from Damascus. Eventually, he became king in Damascus and opposed Solomon for the rest of the latter's reign (1 Ki. 11:23–25). Under Rezon's

successors in Damascus (Hezion, Tabrimmon and Ben-hadad I, listed in 1 Ki. 15:18), whose reigns probably spanned the period *c.* 925–850 BC, Damascus became a powerful Aramaean state which posed a grave threat to Israel.

It is uncertain whether the Ben-hadad who fought against Ahab (1 Ki. 20:1–34; 2 Ki. 6:24 – 7:20) and was assassinated in the latter's reign (2 Ki. 8:7–15) was Ben-hadad I with a long reign (*c.* 900–843 BC?) or a second king of the same name (*c.* 860–843 BC). His murderer Hazael, who seized the throne, was even more vigorous in his attacks on Israel, taking Tranjordan from Jehu (2 Ki. 10:32–33) and reducing the kingdom to desperate straits under Jehoahaz (2 Ki. 13:1–7). However, under Jehoash lost territory was regained and Damascus itself was subjugated by Jeroboam II (2 Ki. 13:25; 14:25, 28).

Damascus next appears as Israel's ally. In 734 BC Rezin of Damascus and Pekah of Israel threatened Judah, but Ahaz appealed for Assyrian aid and Tiglath-pileser III destroyed Damascus in 732 BC (2 Ki. 16:5–9). More N Aramaean states also fell before the armies of Assyria (*cf.* 2 Ki. 18:34; 19:12–13).

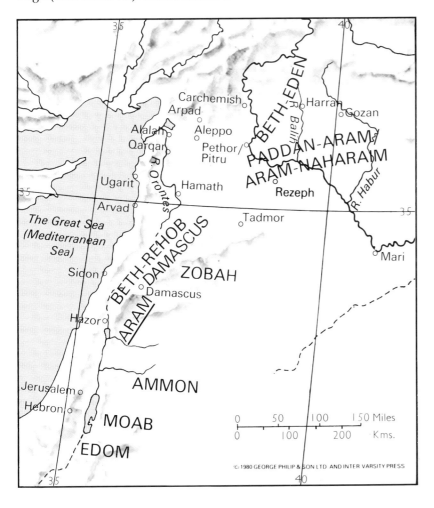

Aramaean states of the period of the Israelite monarchies.

89

The Assyrian Empire

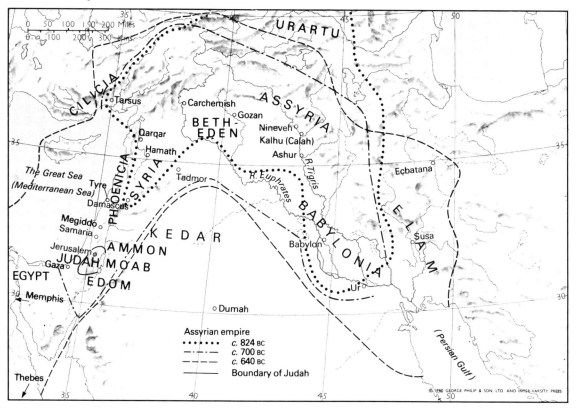

The Assyrian Empire at three stages during its period of expansion, c.880-640 BC.

Although Assyria had made considerable conquests during the period c.1300–1100 BC, between c.1100 and 900 BC its power was contained by the activities of Aramaean tribes in the W. Under Tukulti-Ninurta II (890–884 BC) and his son Ashurbanipal II (883–859 BC) Assyria embarked once more on vigorous military action. Ashurbanipal subdued the Middle Euphrates region and the tribes of the E hills, and in the W reached Lebanon and Philistia. This was the beginning of a period of sustained Assyrian pressure against the W.

Ashurbanipal's son Shalmaneser III (858–824 BC) further extended Assyria's domains. In response to his capture of Carchemish in 857 BC, ten W kings opposed him at Qarqar in 853. Shalmaneser records that the forces opposing him included 2,000 chariots and 10,000 men supplied by 'Ahab the Israelite'. The battle seems to have been indecisive, but by 841 BC the W coalition had broken up. In that year Shalmaneser received tribute from the kings of Tyre and Sidon, and from Jehu of Israel. However, the latter years of Shalmaneser's reign saw his empire weakened by rebellion, and by his death in 824 BC all the conquered W territories were lost.

Assyria's imperialism revived under Tiglath-pileser III (745–727 BC). He consolidated Assyrian control in Babylon and then subdued the regions to the N and W. In 734 BC he marched down the coast of Phoenicia and Philistia as far as Gaza, partly in response to

Ahaz's request for aid against Israel and Damascus (2 Ki. 16:5–7). He destroyed Damascus in 732 BC, and took from Israel her N territories (2 Ki. 15:29) from which he created an Assyrian province; the land remaining to Samaria became a subject-state. Judah actually fared little better, since Ahaz accepted vassaldom himself in return for Assyrian aid (2 Ki. 16:7–18). Notwithstanding Hezekiah's attempted rebellion, and the miraculous discomfiture of the army which Sennacherib sent against him (see p.51), Judah remained a vassal state until the final years of the empire's existence.

When Israel's king Hoshea withheld tribute and made overtures to Egypt, Tiglath-pileser's son Shalmaneser V (726–722 BC) besieged Samaria (2 Ki. 17:1–5). The city fell after three years (in 722 BC) and Israel became a province of the empire (2 Ki. 17:6, 24).

Lower Egypt was brought under Assyria's rule by Esarhaddon in 672 BC, and though it rebelled in 669 BC it was reconquered by Ashurbanipal (668 – c. 627 BC) under whom the empire reached its greatest extent. However, it then began to disintegrate rapidly. Under attack from Babylonia and the Medes, Assyria lost its grip on the W states. In Judah, this freedom was manifested by Josiah's reforms. After the fall of Nineveh (foretold by Nahum and Zephaniah) in 612 BC, Ashur-uballit attempted to rule from Harran but was defeated in 609 BC by the Babylonians.

The Babylonian Empire

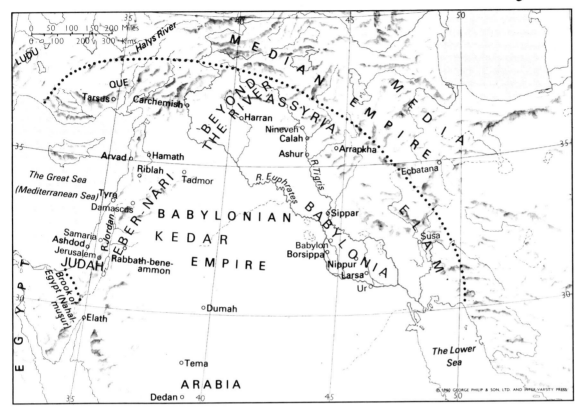

The extent of the short-lived Babylonian Empire.

Early history

For the early history of Babylonia, down to *c.* 2000 BC, see p. 85 (Sumer and Akkad).

From the power struggles which followed the collapse of the Third Dynasty of Ur (*c.* 2006 BC), Babylon eventually emerged as the seat of an Amorite dynasty (First Dynasty of Babylon, 1894-1595 BC). The sixth king of this line, Hammurapi (1792-1750 BC) is well-known for his collection of 282 laws.

The collapse of this dynasty under Hittite attack in 1595 BC was followed by a period of rule by the Kassites from the E hills (1595–1174 BC). During the following centuries, Babylonia remained weak, though independent except for brief periods of Assyrian control. In 745 BC Tiglath-pileser III of Assyria consolidated this control, proclaiming himself 'King of Sumer and Akkad' and claiming the throne of Babylon. Assyria ruled Babylon thereafter until 626 BC, apart from brief periods when Babylon was in the hands of rebel kings such as Marduk-apla-iddina, the biblical Merodach-baladan (2 Ki. 20:12–19).

Following the death of the Assyrian king Ashurbanipal (669–627 BC), the local Babylonian tribes supported the Chaldean Nabopolassar against the Assyrian Sin-shar-ishkun, and Nabopolassar became king of Babylon in 626 BC, beginning the Neo-Babylonian or Chaldean Dynasty (626–539 BC). Chaldea was the later name for Sumer, and in periods when Chaldean kings ruled Babylon,

especially during the Neo-Babylonian dynasty, 'Chaldean' was used as a synonym for 'Babylonian' (*e.g.* Is. 13:19; 47:1, 5; 48:14, 20; Ezk. 23:23).

With the fall of Nineveh to the Babylonians and Medes in 612 BC, the Assyrian empire was effectively finished. In 605 BC Nabopolassar's crown-prince, Nebuchadrezzar, defeated the Egyptians at Carchemish, thus taking the whole of Syria-Palestine under Babylon's control (2 Ki. 24:7; Je. 46:2) and bringing a new Babylonian empire into existence. Jerusalem's king Jehoiakim, a vassal of the Egyptian pharaoh Neco II, submitted to Nebuchadrezzar (2 Ki. 24:1). Daniel and other hostages were taken from Jerusalem to Babylon at this time (Dn. 1:1–7).

While in Palestine in 605 BC, Nebuchad-rezzar received news that Nabopolassar had died. He rode back to Babylon where he claimed the throne on 6 September. (This information is supplied by the Babylonian Chronicle, an important and reliable source for the period.) In 604 BC Nebuchadrezzar received tribute from all the kings of Syria-Palestine.

In 601 BC Babylon clashed again with Egypt and sustained heavy losses. This may have been the event which inspired Jehoiakim to rebel (2 Ki. 24:1). In response the re-equipped Babylonian army marched into Palestine again in December 598 BC. The Babylonian Chronicle records how Nebuchadrezzar 'besieged the

The Babylonian Empire

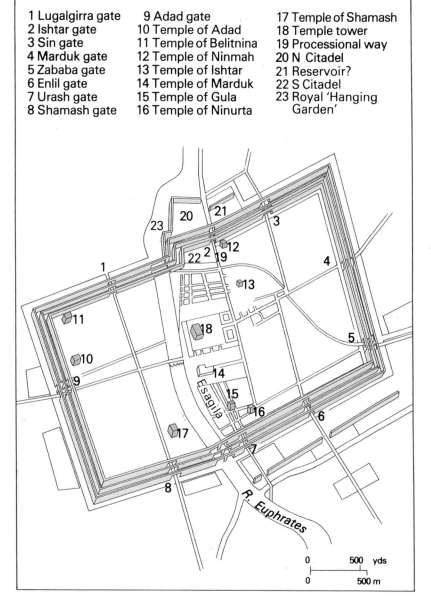

1 Lugalgirra gate
2 Ishtar gate
3 Sin gate
4 Marduk gate
5 Zababa gate
6 Enlil gate
7 Urash gate
8 Shamash gate
9 Adad gate
10 Temple of Adad
11 Temple of Belitnina
12 Temple of Ninmah
13 Temple of Ishtar
14 Temple of Marduk
15 Temple of Gula
16 Temple of Ninurta
17 Temple of Shamash
18 Temple tower
19 Processional way
20 N Citadel
21 Reservoir?
22 S Citadel
23 Royal 'Hanging Garden'

Babylon at the time of Nebuchadrezzar, 605-562 BC.

city of Judah, capturing it on the second day of Adar (= 16 March 597 BC). He captured its king, appointed a ruler of his own choice and, having taken much spoil from the city, sent it back to Babylon. The OT tells how Jehoiakim's young successor Jehoiachin was taken into exile after a reign of only three months, along with other members of the royal court and the administration, warriors and artisans (2 Ki. 24:8–16). The new vassal-king appointed by Nebuchadrezzar was Jehoiachin's uncle, Mattaniah, who acquired the name Zedekiah on ascending the throne (2 Ki. 24:17).

Nine years later, in spite of the advice of Jeremiah (*cf.* Je. 27:1–15), Zedekiah also rebelled. The ensuing two-year siege of Jerusalem by the Babylonian army, interrupted

briefly by an Egyptian intervention (Je. 37:5–10), ended with the capture of the city in 587 BC. Zedekiah was taken to Nebuchadrezzar in Riblah, where he was blinded and sent into exile in Babylon. Jerusalem was then totally destroyed and more of the people deported. Judah was left a dependent province under Gedaliah (2 Ki. 25:1–22; Je. 52:29). In 582/81 BC, a further deportation to Babylon took place (Je. 52:30).

Nebuchadrezzar
Probably many of the craftsmen taken from Judah to Babylon by Nebuchadrezzar were put to work in his project for refurbishing the city. This work of restoration was begun by Nabopolassar and was continued by Nebuchadrezzar and his wife Amytis. Modern excavations, combined with the evidence of thousands of inscribed tablets, have made possible a fairly detailed reconstruction of the city as rebuilt by Nebuchadrezzar. He rebuilt the temples of Marduk and Nabû (Nebo), and equipped the city with a system of multiple defence walls, the outer one large enough for chariots to be driven along the top. There were eight gates, the famous Ishtar gate on the N side marking a great processional way through the city. This was some 920 m (*c.* 3,020 ft) long, its walls decorated with scenes composed of enamelled bricks. It led to the temple of Marduk, Esagila and the ziggurat (temple tower). From it another road led W to cross the Euphrates, linking the ancient capital with the city on the W bank. Nebuchadrezzar also provided the city with new canals. His great works of restoration are the subject of his boasting in Daniel 4:30.

Of the last thirty years of Nebuchadrezzar's reign little is known. Hence there is no corroboration of the madness which afflicted him for seven months (or 'times') according to Daniel 4:23–33. He was succeeded by his son Amēl-Marduk (562–560 BC), the Evil-merodach of 2 Kings 25:27–30, which mentions him for his favourable treatment of the exiled Jehoiachin.

Amēl-Marduk was assassinated in a plot led by Nebuchadrezzar's son-in-law Neriglissar, who then took the throne (560–556 BC). He was succeeded by his son Labaši-Marduk, who reigned only nine months before Nabonidus seized power. Nabonidus appears to have been an eccentric individualist and was for ten years exiled from Babylon, staying in Tema (N Arabia) where he seems to have exercised local influence. He returned just before Babylon fell to the Persian king Cyrus in 539 BC (in fulfilment of Is. 44:24–28; 45:13; *etc.*). His son Belshazzar, who had acted as co-regent during his exile, was killed (Dn. 5:30) and Nabonidus was exiled to Carmenia.

*The Ishtar Gate, Babylon.
7th-6th century BC.*

*The ruins of Babylon:
the S Citadel.*

93

The Persian Empire

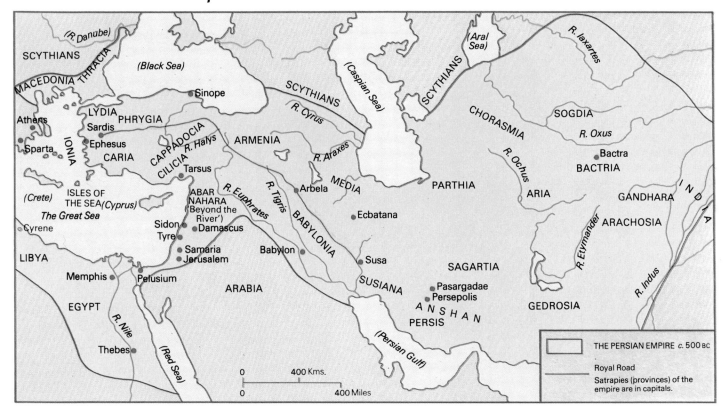

The Persian Empire in the fifth century BC, *extending 'from India to Ethiopia' (Est. 1:1).*

Cyrus II (the Great) of Persia came to the throne in 559 BC. He effectively founded the Persian (Achaemenid) Empire in 550 BC when he conquered his erstwhile overlord Astyages of Media. In 547 BC he marched through Assyria (then part of the Babylonian Empire) and defeated Croesus of Lydia (Lud), taking his capital at Sardis. By 540 BC he was threatening Babylonia itself, and in 539 he entered Babylon without a fight, 'in peace, joy and jubilation' (inscription on the Clay Cylinder of Cyrus), welcomed by its people as the restorer of the worship of Marduk.

There is no evidence of battles being fought in Palestine by Cyrus; it is likely that Syria and Palestine fell to him automatically with the conquest of Babylon. His empire thus stretched from the Iranian highlands in the E to the border of Egypt in the W. It was divided into districts (satrapies) and Palestine belonged to the fifth of these, Abar Nahara, *i.e.* 'Beyond the River (Euphrates)'.

In his first year Cyrus issued a decree by which he 'gathered together all the inhabitants (who were exiles) and returned them to their homes', at the same time restoring deities of peoples conquered by Nebuchadrezzar to their own renovated temples (Clay Cylinder inscription). The release of the Jews and the rebuilding of the Jerusalem Temple (Ezr. 1:1–4) occurred in this context.

Two edicts of Cyrus concerning the Jews are recorded in the OT. The one quoted in Ezra

6:3–5 is in Aramaic, the administrative language used throughout much of the Persian Empire. It reveals that Cyrus was prepared to meet the cost of rebuilding the Temple from the royal treasury. He was not giving the Jews a blank cheque, however; the edict specifies the dimensions and the materials to be used. The edict in Ezra 1:2–4 is in Hebrew, probably a translation or paraphrase of an Aramaic original. Cyrus' apparent acknowledgement of Yahweh in v. 2 has led some to doubt the authenticity of this edict, but it is entirely in keeping with his practice; *e.g.* in Babylonia Cyrus honoured Marduk not his own gods.

Cyrus' son and successor, Cambyses (530–522 BC), conquered Egypt in 525 BC (though it subsequently rebelled and had to be reconquered a number of times), and his successor, Darius I (522–486 BC), reached India. Thus in the Book of Esther, the events of which are set in the reign of Xerxes I (Ahasuerus, 486–465 BC), we read of 'the satraps and the governors and the princes of the provinces from India to Ethiopia, a hundred and twenty-seven provinces' (Est. 8:9).

The disastrous outcome of Xerxes' invasion of Greece in 481–479 BC foreshadowed the eventual demise of the Persian Empire some 150 years later. In 334 BC, Alexander of Macedon (the Great) invaded the empire, following Xerxes' route in the reverse direction and by 331 BC conquered all the major cities.

The cultural heritage of Greece

In their small, independent cities (*poleis*) – self-governing states – the Greeks developed a culture with sophisticated forms, theories and practices in the fields of poetry, literature (history, rhetoric, drama, *etc.*), thought (philosophy, myth-allegory, science) and art. Greek culture continued to develop in all these fields after Alexander's conquests, but in political and cultural terms it became also a prestigious export, the province often of a cultured minority like the poets, scientists and scholars whom Ptolemy Philadelphus gathered around him at Alexandria, where they had the largest library in the Greek world (20,000 volumes catalogued in the first twenty years).

It is worth noting that in Egypt the schoolmaster and the man who directed the gymnastic-training of boys had special tax immunities, like the victors in the Games at Alexandria. The Greek tradition of competitive culture, both intellectual and physical, as a school of training for the leisured class (who effectively governed), took root as the hallmark of the claim to be *Greek* (it was not essentially a racial matter).

The Greeks continued to prize learning. The great centres of culture included Cyrene, Tarsus (whence we have the names of many scholars and philosophers from the second century BC on, but their works are lost), Rhodes (300–50 BC), the islands Cos and Samos (third century BC) and Syracuse (on Sicily), where the mathematical theorist and ingenious inventor (*eureka*!) Archimedes lived. Athens remained the major university-town of the Greek world with new forms of drama and new schools of philosophy. The Academy, the Lyceum, the Stoa, the Garden (schools of Plato, Aristotle, Zeno and Epicurus) flourished.

The highest centre of scholarship and poetry was Alexandria, developed as a cultural centre by Ptolemy II Philadelphus (285–246 BC). Here scholars and poets whose leisure was bought by royal patronage argued as to whether one could continue to imitate the lengthy epics of Homer (how to imitate perfection!), or whether the shorter form of a few hundred lines, displaying craftsmanship and cleverness, should not be one's delight.

The pastoral poems and mimes of Theocritus are impressive products, but so is the long 'Voyage of the Argo' (a new epic) by Apollonius of Rhodes. The scholars were trying to 'establish' the text of Homer, the tragedians, *etc.*; they began to use accents, punctuation and quantity-marks as tools of precision. They were immensely industrious: Aristarchus of Samothrace (217–145 BC) wrote commentaries on more than 800 works of Greek literature. In science Euclid, Aristarchos of Samos and Eratosthenes of Cyrene (as well

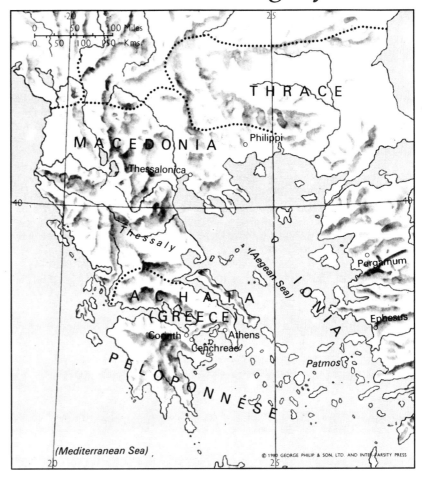

as Archimedes) were great names. New medical theories of the body's 'humours' and new techniques of surgery, were developed by the Alexandrian schools.

This tradition then passed to Rome, which became the new centre of Greek culture, formulating a new Roman literature and philosophy in reaction to its Greek models. It began with translations of Greek works by captured slaves, followed by visits of Greek philosophers and teachers of rhetoric. The ideas and forms of the Alexandrian poets and their classical predecessors penetrated to Catullus and Horace and Vergil. Menander's Greek 'Comedy of Manners' was taken up by Terence and Plautus in Latin. The Roman Empire provided a secure political frame for such leisured activity. In the E half of the Roman Empire Greek remained also the language of business, law and administration (Latin in the W). Educated Romans were expected to read and understand Greek as well as Latin.

That hellenism penetrated the Jewish 'Diaspora' (those dispersed from the Holy Land) is also clear from the works of Philo of Alexandria, and the need for the *Septuagint* (a Greek translation of Hebrew scriptures).

Greece (ancient Achaia) and the adjoining provinces of Macedonia and Thrace.

95

The cultural heritage of Greece

Athens: the Acropolis, showing the dominant position of the Parthenon, built between 447 and 438 BC.

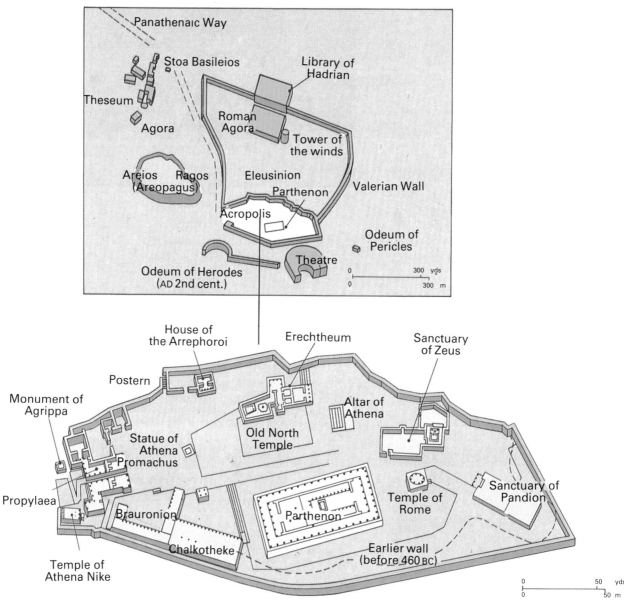

Panathenaic Way

Stoa Basileios

Library of Hadrian

Theseum

Roman Agora

Agora

Tower of the winds

Areios Ragos (Areopagus)

Eleusinion

Parthenon

Valerian Wall

Acropolis

Odeum of Pericles

Theatre

Odeum of Herodes (AD 2nd cent.)

0 300 yds
0 300 m

House of the Arrephoroi

Erechtheum

Sanctuary of Zeus

Postern

Monument of Agrippa

Altar of Athena

Statue of Athena Promachus

Old North Temple

Propylaea

Sanctuary of Pandion

Brauronion

Parthenon

Temple of Rome

Temple of Athena Nike

Chalkotheke

Earlier wall (before 460 BC)

0 50 yds
0 50 m

Ruins of Corinth. The Acropolis ('Acrocorinth') dominates the city in the plain below. View along Lechaeum road towards the city centre.

Plan of the centre of Corinth, refounded as a Roman colony in 44 BC, incorporating the remains of the Greek city dating from c.540 BC.

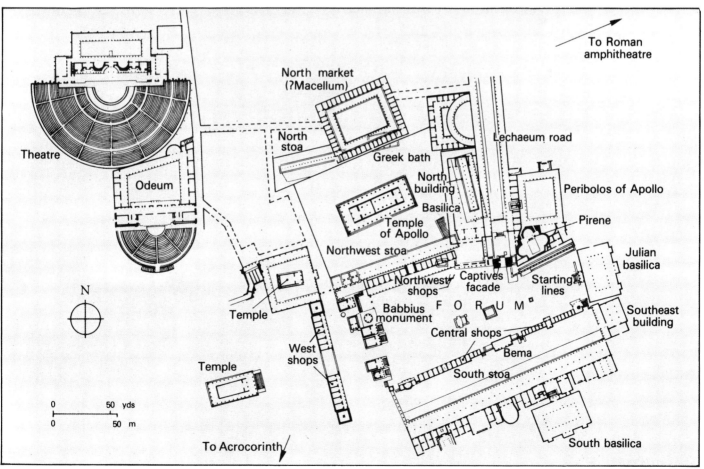

The Hellenistic Kingdoms

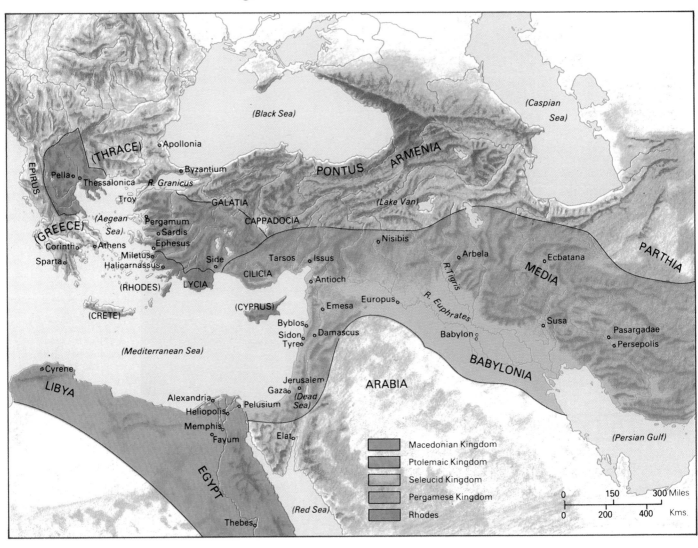

*The Hellenistic
Kingdoms during
Maccabean times (after
188 BC).*

Alexander (who died in 323 BC) conquered the Persian empire; his generals split it between them. They and their successors also planted colonies of Greek veterans at strategic military points and on important trade-routes, mainly in the old towns and cities, where the native urban aristocracies became 'hellenized'. Ptolemy Lagi secured Egypt (323 BC), Seleucus secured Babylon (312 BC) and the Antigonids Macedonia. In 301 BC Seleucus occupied N Syria, where he founded Antioch, his capital; Ptolemy occupied S Syria, perhaps as far N as Damascus. The Ptolemaic province is called 'Syria and Phoenicia' in the Zeno papyri (259–258 BC). But the map illustrates a later time (the Maccabaean revolt began in 167 BC), after 188 BC, when the Seleucid Antiochus III (223–187 BC) had taken S Syria from the Ptolemies or Lagids.

The Seleucid realm looks enormous, but in fact it was already facing checks both to the W and to the E; the Ptolemaic realm, though smaller, was more secure, more stable and more prosperous. Though Antiochus IV (175–164 BC) still possessed nearer Iran (Media and Persis), the Parthians were about to overrun it and advance to the Euphrates. In the W the Roman senate had forced Antiochus III out of Asia Minor after the battle of Magnesia (Treaty of Apamea, 188 BC), giving the lost Seleucid territory to Rome's allies, the smaller Greek states of Pergamum and Rhodes. From this time on Roman political pressure dogged and weakened the Seleucid house.

In 64 BC Syria became a Roman province, the Seleucid house extinguished; in 30 BC Egypt was annexed, the Ptolemaic house gone.

Comparison with map 99 (the Parthian Empire in 51 BC) will show the ancient trade-routes on which many of the Seleucid cities were located.

For lists of the Seleucid rulers of Syria and the Ptolemaic rulers of Egypt see pages 116 and 117.

The Parthian Empire

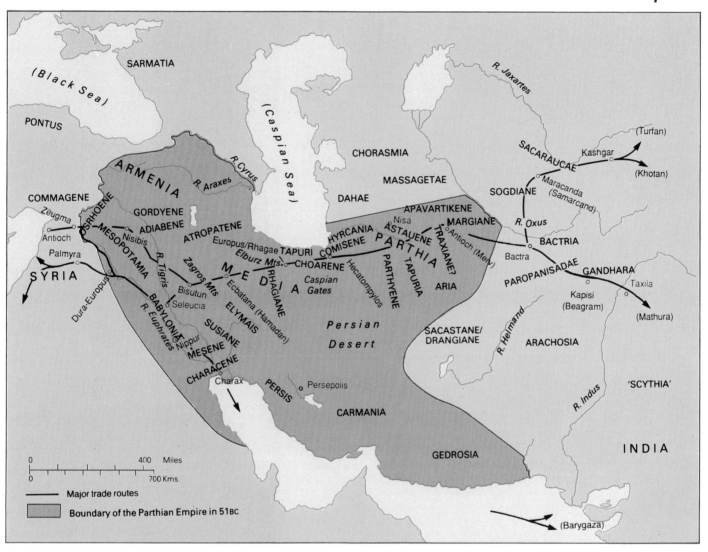

The Parthian Empire.

The Parthians, first heard of in the late third century BC as the Aparni or Parni, were then powerful enough to overcome the Seleucid governor (see map 57) of a province which the Persians had called *Parthava*. From this province they henceforth took their name, when they later erupted W against first the Seleucids and then the Romans.

Around 150–140 BC Mithradates founded their empire at Seleucid expense. Mithradates I (171–137 BC) took both nearer Iran (Media and Persis) and the river lowlands (Babylonia and Elam in the S, Mesopotamia in the N) from the Seleucid kingdom, leaving little more than Syria itself in the hands of Tryphon (142-138 BC).

Mithradates II (123–87 BC) came even further W, entering Dura-Europus in 113 BC. He claimed that the Parthians were descended from Artaxerxes Mnemon the Achaemenid, and used the old Persian title 'King of Kings' on his coins. Around 94 BC he pushed the NW

boundaries of the Parthian empire through the small N Mesopotamian princedoms of Adiabene, Gordyene and Osrhoene. But Parthian attempts on Armenia were checked by Pompey.

In 54 BC the Roman Crassus attacked the Parthians in the desert of N Mesopotamia. At Harran (Carrhae) the Roman eagles were lost in a humiliating disaster. In 51 BC the Parthians invaded the Roman province of Syria and reached Antioch, but were driven back by Cassius Longinus. In 41 or 40 BC the Parthian prince Pacorus, son of Orodes II (57–37 BC), aided by a Roman renegade Labienus, conquered Syria, Phoenicia (except Tyre) and Palestine, but was defeated and killed by Ventidius in 38 BC. Pacorus had supported the last Hasmonaean prince, Antigonus Mattathiah, against Herod (who fled to Masada). But the Roman legions secured the throne for Herod, and proved too powerful for the Parthians.

The Roman Empire

Pompey's 'Eastern Settlement' (64–63 BC), in the latter days of the Roman Republic, was followed by such carnage in the power-struggles in Italy that when Octavian (Augustus) at last founded a stable administration he was seen as the saviour of Roman civilization; 'Men could hope for nothing more from the gods... than Augustus bestowed on the Republic...' (Velleius Paterculus).

In NT times the Roman Empire provided stability, order and the rule of law for those countries it conquered. Augustus established the fact that the emperor (not the senate) controlled the frontier-armies in Asia Minor, Syria and Egypt, and in Europe on the Rhine and the Danube. He created a standing army of twenty-eight legions, some 6,000 heavy infantry in each, supplemented by cavalry and light-armed auxiliaries. It was normal for up to thirteen legions to defend the Rhine-Danube border, and four legions were placed in Syria against the Parthians (see map 99).

In the E problems of administration, pacification, civilization and defence were partly solved by the 'buffer-states', client-dependencies ruled on behalf of Rome by kings, ethnarchs and tetrarchs (in descending rank). Some of the princes were total aliens to the peoples they ruled; others were native (as at Commagene, in Nabataean Arabia, at Emesa).

Herod of Judaea was between these two: not Jewish, not of a high priestly line, but local, half Idumaean, half Arab (son of Antipater and Kypros), from the area forcibly judaized by John Hyrcanus (135–104 BC) (see pp. 58 and 67). For Rome the Jews were *the* classic instance of a people difficult to govern because of their acute religious sensitivities. Herod dealt firmly with his people, and maintained law in his land, a prerequisite of prosperity. Other territories were therefore added to him by Augustus. Apparently the Ituraean rulers of Chalcis and Abilene proved less able: Batanaea, Auranitis, Trachonitis, Paneas, Ulatha and Gaulanitis all became Herodian territories (see Lk. 3:1).

Augustus also established a principle of succession in his own family which gave further stability to the Empire. Few changes were made by these 'Julio-Claudians' (Tiberius, Caligula, Claudius and Nero) during the years AD 14 to 68. Cappadocia, Lycia and Mauretania became provinces; parts of Britain were conquered. The Jews of Judaea, Idumaea and Samaritis asked for direct Roman rule instead of Herod Archelaus. A succession of obscure 'prefects', experienced administrators of middle (equestrian) rank rather than the aristocrats who governed the large provinces, came and went until AD 41: Coponius, Ambivius, Rufus, Gratus, Pontius Pilate, Marcellus and Marullus. These men governed

for the emperor direct, whereas in some other provinces the governors were responsible to the senate.

Agrippa, who came to rule all of Herod's former kingdom (Judaea, AD 41–44 only) and was the personal friend of Caligula (Gaius) and of Claudius, was a popular ruler, mourned by his people and praised for his piety. Jewish Palestine reverted to direct Roman rule after he died, but this no longer satisfied the people. The procurators from AD 44 to 66 were increasingly heavy-handed and unpopular (Felix, Albinus and Florus are singled out as blameworthy by Josephus), and the rule of law gave way to corruption and brigandage. Jewish aristocrats who showed pro-Roman sympathies were assassinated by extreme Zealots, called Knifemen (Sicarii). Nero was 'vicious and vain, cruel and lustful' (Scullard); he won the hatred of senate, people, armies, Jews and Christians, and he died heirless in AD 68.

In AD 66 the Judaean nationalists revolted,

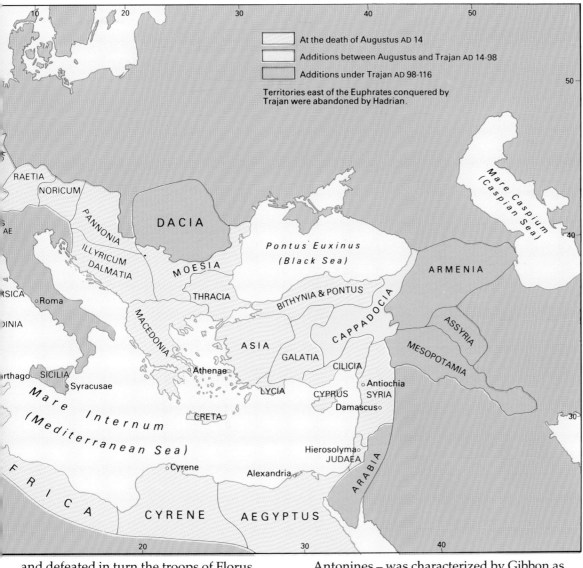

The Roman Empire.

Legend on map:

At the death of Augustus AD 14

Additions between Augustus and Trajan AD 14-98

Additions under Trajan AD 98-116

Territories east of the Euphrates conquered by
Trajan were abandoned by Hadrian.

and defeated in turn the troops of Florus, Agrippa II and the Syrian legate (governor). It took the resources of the experienced general Vespasian and his son Titus (with three legions, auxiliaries and allied forces) to secure the country in AD 67–70, and overcome Zealot resistance in the fortresses of Herodium, Machaerus and Masada from AD 71 to 74. Halfway through the struggle Vespasian hurried back to Rome. After three rivals — Galba, Otho and Vitellius — had failed (the year is called 'Year of the Four Emperors') he established himself as emperor in AD 69. His short-lived dynasty (only his sons Titus and Domitian followed him, and the line ended in AD 96) ruled at a time when Judaea received a senatorial (aristocratic) governor who commanded a permanent legion (Legio X Fretensis).

The period of Nerva, Trajan, Hadrian, Antoninus Pius and Marcus Aurelius (AD 96–180) – by a convenient fiction known as the Antonines – was characterized by Gibbon as the most prosperous period of the Roman Empire. A civic-minded upper class of provincials served on their city councils, and became citizens and senators (even emperors: Trajan was a Spanish senator). Client-kingdoms, their task of pacification complete, were swallowed up in provinces. When Agrippa II died in AD 93 (?), Ituraea reverted to the province of Syria, as did Chalcis and Emesa at about that time. Trajan's military successes against the Parthians were regarded as an 'adventure' by Hadrian, who reverted to the Flavian frontiers again. In Judaea Hadrian himself precipitated a second revolt in AD 135 (known, from the name of its leader, as the Bar-Kokhba revolt) by his plan to re-found Jerusalem as Aelia Capitolina, dedicated to the Capitoline Jupiter. The revolt was overcome by the legions, and the province reconstituted as Syria Palaestina under a governor of consular rank with two legions.

The growth of Jerusalem

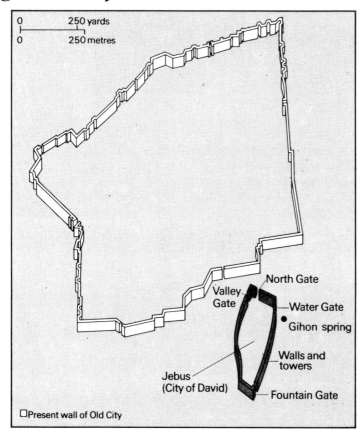

0 — 250 yards
0 — 250 metres

North Gate
Valley Gate
Water Gate
Gihon spring
Walls and towers
Jebus (City of David)
Fountain Gate

☐ Present wall of Old City

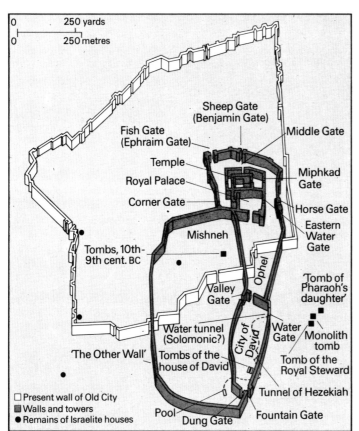

0 — 250 yards
0 — 250 metres

Sheep Gate (Benjamin Gate)
Fish Gate (Ephraim Gate)
Middle Gate
Temple
Royal Palace
Miphkad Gate
Corner Gate
Horse Gate
Mishneh
Eastern Water Gate
Tombs, 10th–9th cent. BC
Ophel
Tomb of Pharaoh's daughter
Valley Gate
Water tunnel (Solomonic?)
City of David
Water Gate
Monolith tomb
'The Other Wall'
Tombs of the house of David
Tomb of the Royal Steward
Tunnel of Hezekiah
Pool
Dung Gate
Fountain Gate

☐ Present wall of Old City
◼ Walls and towers
● Remains of Israelite houses

There is some archaeological evidence for a settlement at Jerusalem before 2000 BC, but it is in the following millennium that the city begins to emerge into history. It is referred to in the Egyptian Execration Texts of the eighteenth century BC, and a section of wall of this date was excavated on the E slope of the SE hill by Kathleen Kenyon. If the *Salem* of Gn. 14:18 is Jerusalem (*cf.* Ps. 76:2), its existence at the time of Abraham has biblical warrant. Elsewhere, the mountain on which Isaac was offered is identified with the Temple Mount of later Jerusalem (*cf.* Gn. 22:2; 2 Ch. 3:1). Jerusalem is named again in the Amarna letters of the fourteenth century BC, where its king is one Abdi-Khiba.

When the Israelites entered Canaan they attacked Jerusalem but were only partially successful in conquering it (Jdg. 1:8, 21), and it remained a stronghold of the Jebusites until David's time. The Jebusite city was confined to the SE ridge, being dependent on the Gihon spring for its water-supply.

David conquered the city (2 Sa. 5:6–10), making it his new capital. By creating a capital on the border between Judah and Benjamin, he probably hoped to end inter-tribal rivalry. David had royal quarters built there (2 Sa. 5:11), and installed the ark within the city (2 Sa. 6:12–19), but the work of building a Temple to house it fell to Solomon (1 Ki. 6:1ff.). Solomon also created a new and impressive palace-complex (1 Ki. 7:1–8; 9:24). This building activity took place to the N of the old Jebusite city, and a new wall was built to enclose the enlarged area (1 Ki. 3:1; 9:15).

It is not clear how the city spread to include the W ridge. Archaeological evidence places this extension in the eighth century BC, when Jerusalem and Judah reached a new peak of strength under Azariah/Uzziah (*cf.* 2 Ch. 26:9), but there is disagreement over whether the S part of this was occupied or only the N. It is possible that the extension remained unwalled until the reign of Hezekiah, and that the 'other wall' which he built outside the existing one (2 Ch. 32:5) was the first attempt to enclose and fortify this area. The W extension may well be the section of the city later referred to as the Second Quarter or Mishneh (2 Ki. 22:14).

Jerusalem was destroyed by Nebuchadrezzar in 587 BC, and although resettled later that century, it was not rebuilt as a walled city until the time of Nehemiah (mid-fifth century BC) on a smaller scale than the pre-exilic city.

Above: Jebus, the site of the City of David, Jerusalem, on the SE hill, Mt Zion.

Below: Jerusalem from Solomon to Hezekiah, showing extensions to the N and W, including the Temple area.

Hellenistic Jerusalem

Antiochus Epiphanes plundered the Temple. In 168 BC he built the Akra (Citadel) at Jerusalem, and established in it a Syrian garrison which dominated the city until 141 BC. The location of this garrison is disputed but, since excavation has found no traces of settlement on the W hill in the Persian, Ptolemaic and Seleucid periods, it was probably S of the Temple Mount. The history of the Akra can be followed in 1 Macc. It is unlikely that its remains will ever be found: when Simon the Maccabee at last rid the city of its garrison, he razed the Akra to the ground, and levelled the hill on which it had stood:

> He summoned an Assembly, and persuaded the people …and they all devoted their energies to levelling the hill. After unceasing toil day and night for three full years they reduced it to ground-level, and made it flat and smooth. And when the Citadel and the hill on which it had stood were gone the Temple stood out above all else (Jos. *Ant.* 13.216–7).

Under the last Maccabees or the Hasmonaean princes Jerusalem expanded onto the W hill (later second century BC). Excavation by Johns, Amiran/Eitan and Broshi has identified the 'First Wall' of Josephus as Hasmonaean in the W line (the Citadel of today and the Turkish Wall going S from it), while Bliss and Dickie have uncovered the S line (also Hasmonaean). Most recently the assumed N line, based on Josephus, has been confirmed by excavation. Possibly too the Gate Gennath has been found by Avigad (*Discovering Jerusalem*, pp. 50, 69).

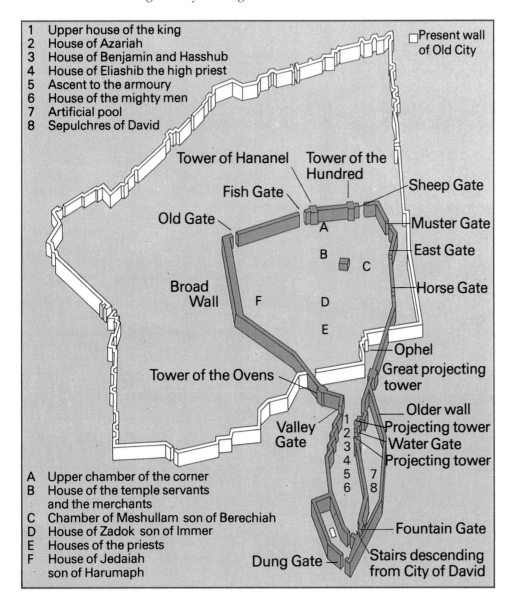

1. Upper house of the king
2. House of Azariah
3. House of Benjamin and Hasshub
4. House of Eliashib the high priest
5. Ascent to the armoury
6. House of the mighty men
7. Artificial pool
8. Sepulchres of David

☐ Present wall of Old City

Tower of Hananel
Tower of the Hundred
Fish Gate
Old Gate
Sheep Gate
Muster Gate
East Gate
Horse Gate
Broad Wall
Tower of the Ovens
Ophel
Great projecting tower
Older wall
Projecting tower
Water Gate
Projecting tower
Valley Gate
Fountain Gate
Stairs descending from City of David
Dung Gate

A Upper chamber of the corner
B House of the temple servants and the merchants
C Chamber of Meshullam son of Berechiah
D House of Zadok son of Immer
E Houses of the priests
F House of Jedaiah son of Harumaph

Probable reconstruction of Jerusalem as rebuilt by Nehemiah in the fifth century BC.

Jerusalem in New Testament times

Herodian Jerusalem

Roman generals forced their way into the city in 63 and 54 BC, a Parthian army plundered it in 40, and three years later Herod the Great took it by conquest. Perhaps before his advent the 'Second North Wall' described by Josephus was built by one of the last Hasmonaean rulers, enclosing an area N of the First Wall. Herod enjoyed the goodwill of the emperor Augustus; territories which Pompey had detached from the Hasmonaean state returned to the Herodian one. He built walls and towers in Jerusalem, cities and fortresses beyond it. The city-plan on this page shows some of his notable projects: the Temple Mount, the Antonia fortress and the Upper Palace (the royal palace in the Upper City) with its three great towers.

It was the palace in the Upper City which served as the residence of the Roman governors after Herod (AD 6–41, 44–66). This was the *praetorium* where Jesus was brought to trial before the prefect Pontius Pilate. Only substructures have survived for the excavators to find. The cloisters of Bethesda near the Sheep Gate (Jn. 5:2) may have been part of the same building project as the Temple and the Antonia. The Upper City, where the Royal Palace was located, was the quarter of the wealthy aristocrats. Excavations have now uncovered this magnificence (Avigad, *Discovering Jerusalem*, ch. 3).

A 'Third North Wall' was begun by Agrippa (AD 41–44), but he was warned to desist by the Romans. It remained unfinished when the great war with Rome (Jewish War) broke out, the Zealot revolt of AD 66–70 (74).

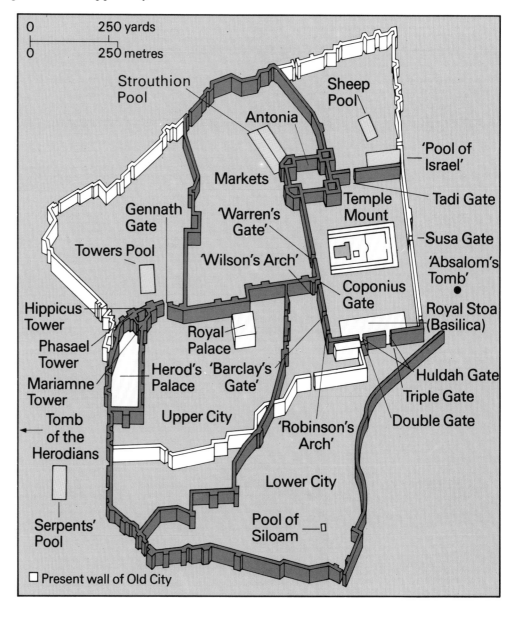

Jerusalem at the time of Herod the Great.

Archaeological opinion is divided over the location of the second and third N walls, but whichever view one adopts, the traditional tomb of Jesus now in the Church of the Holy Sepulchre remains firmly outside the city-wall. In AD 70 Titus systematically destroyed the fortifications and walls of Jerusalem. He left three towers standing at the NW of the Upper Palace; one still remains (incorporated into the modern 'Citadel' inside the Jaffa Gate). The streets and houses burnt down by the troops of Titus are currently being located and recognized by archaeologists Avigad and Mazar.

After AD 70
Further disaster lay ahead. The Bar-Kokhba Revolt in AD 132 led to the expulsion of all Jews from Jerusalem, and its re-foundation as Aelia Capitolina (dedicated to Jupiter Capitolinus). Not until the fourth century AD could Jews return to 'the holy city'.

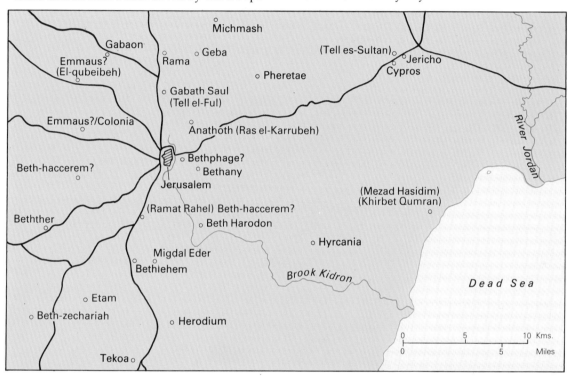

The area surrounding Jerusalem in New Testament times, showing two possible sites for Emmaus. This map does not indicate elevation but Jerusalem is c. 3,800ft (c. 1,170m) above the level of the Dead Sea.

Part of a map made as a mosaic on the floor of St George's church at Medeba, Jordan. This section shows Jerusalem with its streets, gates and churches, sixth century AD.

105

The city from the air

A recent aerial photograph of Jerusalem from the W.

The photograph reproduced above, with its accompanying key on the facing page, complement the description of the historical growth of Jerusalem (pages 102-104) and the location of the city (page 105). The distant view of the Dead Sea sets the photograph in the context of that map.

Imagination is needed to picture the city as it would have appeared in ancient times. Although much of archaeological value is preserved, many predominant buildings are post-biblical in origin, such as the Dome of the Rock and, of course, the churches. The present-day walled area (the 'Old city') was not given its definitive shape until the sixteenth century when Suleiman the Magnificent built the walls.

The line of walls now visible should be compared with the plans on pages 102-104 (which mark Suleiman's walls clearly), with the drawing on page 109 and the photographs on pages 110-111.

Excavations have shown conclusively that the earliest city was on the SE hill, an area now wholly outside the city walls (the S wall was retracted N in the second century AD). It must be clearly borne in mind that the original Zion lay on the E ridge; by the time of Josephus the name was already erroneously attached to the SW hill.

Few traces remain from the pre-Jebusite period, but it may be inferred that a small town grew on the SE ridge, within easy reach of the spring Gihon in the valley to the E. The Jebusites enlarged the city to a limited extent, most notably by the construction of terraces E, so that their E wall lay well down the slope towards the spring. This terracing and E wall seem to have needed frequent maintenance and repair till their final destruction by the Babylonians in the early sixth century BC, after which the E wall was again retracted to the ridge. Present opinion is inclined to consider the word 'Millo' (*e.g.* 2 Sa. 5:9; 1 Ki. 9:15), which derives from a Heb. root meaning 'fill', to refer to this terracing.

In times of peace it was common practice for houses to be built outside the walls, which from time to time necessitated new walls and fortifications. David's and Solomon's city extended N, in particular, the Temple being built on the NE hill; the royal palace was probably situated in the area between the older city and the Temple area.

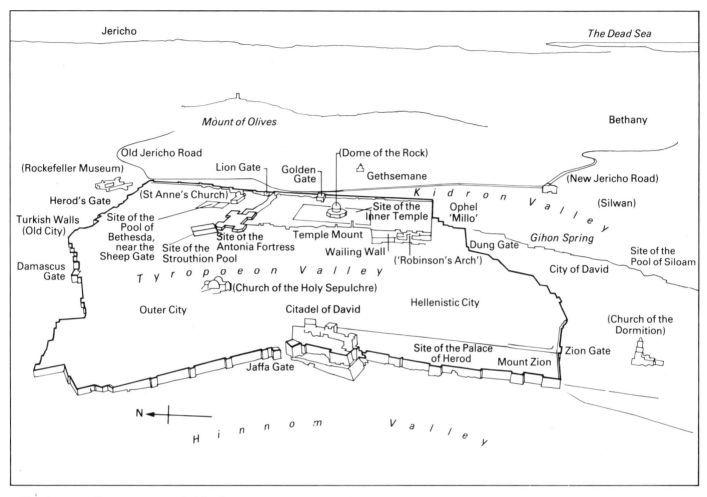

Key to the map:

Jericho

The Dead Sea

Mount of Olives

Bethany

Old Jericho Road

(Rockefeller Museum)

Lion Gate

Golden Gate

(Dome of the Rock)

Gethsemane

(New Jericho Road)

Herod's Gate

(St Anne's Church)

K i d r o n   V a l l e y

(Silwan)

Turkish Walls (Old City)

Site of the Pool of Bethesda, near the Sheep Gate

Site of the Antonia Fortress

Site of the Strouthion Pool

Site of the Inner Temple

Temple Mount

Wailing Wall

('Robinson's Arch')

Ophel 'Millo'

Dung Gate

Gihon Spring

City of David

Site of the Pool of Siloam

Damascus Gate

T y r o p o e o n   V a l l e y

(Church of the Holy Sepulchre)

Hellenistic City

(Church of the Dormition)

Outer City

Citadel of David

Site of the Palace of Herod

Mount Zion

Zion Gate

Jaffa Gate

N

H i n n o m   V a l l e y

Key to the photograph opposite, showing both ancient and modern sites and their relationship.

This intermediate area is probably the 'Ophel' of such passages as 2 Ch. 27:3 (the name means 'swelling', and was used of the citadel of other cities too, *e.g.* Samaria, *cf.* 2 Ki. 5:24, NEB); but some scholars apply the term to the whole E ridge S of the Temple. The Jebusite city, or perhaps more strictly the central fortress of it, already bore the name 'Zion' (the meaning of which is uncertain, perhaps 'dry area' or 'eminence') at the time of David's capture, after which it was also called 'the city of David' (*cf.* 2 Sa. 5:6–10; 1 Ki. 8:1). The name 'Zion' became, or remained, synonymous with Jerusalem as a whole.

It was in the prosperous days of the eighth century BC that the city first spread to the W ridge; this new suburb seems to have been called the Second Quarter or Mishneh (2 Ki. 22:14). A wall later enclosed it, built either in Hezekiah's reign (*cf.* 2 Ch. 32:5) or somewhat later. It is certain that this extension included the NW hill, but whether the SW hill was now occupied is as yet unresolved. Israeli archaeologists conclude that it was, and that the Pool of Siloam was inside the city walls in Hezekiah's reign; but K. M. Kenyon maintained otherwise.

Jerusalem was sacked by Nebuchadrezzar's troops in 587 BC; most of the buildings were destroyed, and the city walls were demolished. The Temple was rebuilt at the end of the century, and Jerusalem had a small population once again; but it was not until the mid-fifth century that the Persian authorities permitted the rebuilding of the city walls, by Nehemiah.

No doubt Nehemiah rebuilt earlier walls so far as was practicable, but it is clear from excavations that the W ridge was abandoned, and also the E slopes of the SE hill. The Jebusite terracing had been too thoroughly demolished for repair, and Nehemiah therefore retracted the E wall to the ridge itself.

The development of the city in the inter-testamental period and the three walls of Josephus are discussed on pages 104-105.

The city lay in ruins between AD 70 and the Bar-Kokhba revolt sixty years later. The emperor Hadrian then rebuilt the city, naming it Aelia Capitolina; his city was much smaller than its predecessor, with the permanent retraction of the S wall. During the Christian era, the size of Jerusalem has been by no means constant.

The Temples of Solomon and Herod

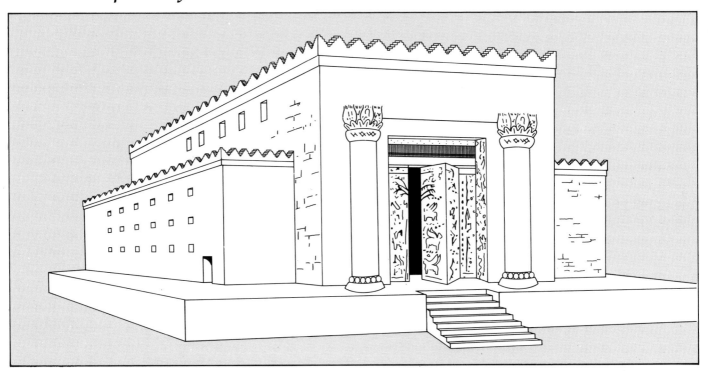

Steven's reconstruction of Solomon's Temple, showing the twin free-standing pillars (Jachin and Boaz), the vestibule porch and side storage chambers.

Solomon's Temple

That it stood within the area now called 'Haram esh-Sherif' at the E side of the 'Old City' of Jerusalem is undisputed. The precise location within the vast enclosure is less certain. The highest part of the rock (now covered by the building known as 'The Dome of the Rock') may have been the site of the innermost sanctuary or of the altar of burnt-offering outside (2 Ch. 3:1; *cf.* 2 Sa. 24:25). This rock was presumably part of the threshing-floor of Araunah (Ornan), bought by David for a sum given as 50 silver shekels (2 Sa. 24:24) or 600 gold shekels (1 Ch. 21:25).

Nothing of Solomon's structure remains above ground, nor were any definite traces found in the diggings sponsored by the Palestine Exploration Fund. Indeed, it is likely that the work of levelling the rock and building up the great retaining walls for the courtyard of Herod's Temple obliterated earlier constructions.

The passages 1 Ki. 6–7 and 2 Ch. 3–4 must be the bases of any reconstruction of Solomon's Temple. The Temple proper was an oblong, orientated E and W. It is reasonable to assume that, like Ezekiel's Temple, it stood on a platform (*cf.* Ezk. 41:8). No dimensions are given for the surrounding area. Again following Ezekiel's plan, it seems that there were two courtyards, inner and outer; a suggestion supported by 1 Ki. 6:36; 7:12; 2 Ki. 23:12; 2 Ch. 4:9.

The bronze altar for burnt offerings stood in the inner court (1 Ki. 8:22, 64; 9:25). It was 20 cubits* square and 10 cubits high (2 Ch. 4:1). Between this and the porch was the bronze laver holding water for ritual washings (AV 'molten' or 'brazen sea', 1 Ki. 7:23–26). This great basin, 10 cubits in diameter, rested upon four groups of four bronze oxen orientated to the four compass-points. These were removed by Ahaz (2 Ki. 16:17).

A flight of steps would have led up from the inner court to the porch (Heb. *'ûlām*). The entrance was flanked by two pillars, Jachin and Boaz, with elaborately ornamented capitals. Their purpose remains indeterminate; they were not part of the structure. Gates probably closed the passage (*cf.* Ezk. 40:48).

The porch was 10 cubits long and 20 cubits wide.

W of the porch was the large chamber in which the ordinary rituals were performed. This 'holy place' (AV 'temple'; Heb. *hêkāl*, a word derived through Canaanite from Sumerian *é·gal*, 'great house') was 40 cubits long, 20 in breadth, and 30 high. It was shut off from the porch by double doors of cypress wood, each composed of two leaves.

Latticed windows near the ceiling lighted the holy place (1 Ki. 6:4). Here stood the golden incense-altar, the table for showbread, and five pairs of lampstands, together with the instruments of sacrifice. The double doors of cypress leading to the inner sanctuary were rarely opened, probably only for the high priest at the atonement ceremony.

* The 'cubit' varies, but is usually the distance from elbow to finger-tip, about 15-17 ins (38-43 cm).

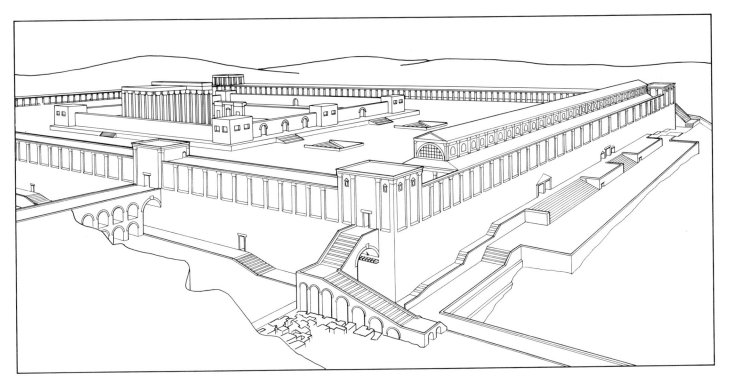

The inner sanctuary was a perfect cube of 20 cubits. Although it might be expected that the floor was raised above the *hêkāl*, there is no hint of this. Within stood two wooden figures side by side, 10 cubits high. Two of their wings met in the centre above the ark of the covenant, and the other wing of each touched the N and S walls respectively (1 Ki. 6:23–28). In this most holy place the presence of God was shown by a cloud (1 Ki. 8:10f.).

Each room was panelled with cedar wood and the floor planked with cypress (or pine, Heb. *bᵉrôš*). The walls and doors were carved with flowers, palm trees and cherubim, and overlaid with gold in the way approved for ancient temples, as inscriptions testify. No stonework was visible.

The outer walls of the inner sanctuary and the holy place were built with two offsets of one cubit to support the joists of three storeys of small chambers all around. Thus the ground-floor chambers were five cubits wide, those above six, and the uppermost seven. A door in the S side gave access to a spiral staircase serving the upper floors. These rooms doubtless housed various stores and vestments, provided accommodation, maybe, for the priests in course, and sheltered the offerings of money and goods made by the worshippers.

Much has been made of the proximity of the royal palace to the Temple and the inference drawn that it was the 'Chapel Royal'. While admitting such a relationship (emphasized by the passage connecting the two buildings –

2 Ki. 16:18 refers to it as 'the covered way for the sabbath'), it should be remembered that it was appropriate for the viceroy of Yahweh to reside near to the house of God; entry was not restricted to the king.

Later history

Ancient temples generally served as state treasuries, emptied to pay tribute or filled and decorated with booty according to the power of the land. If, for some reason, a ruler paid little attention to the temple it would lose its revenue and rapidly fall into disrepair (*cf.* 2 Ki. 12:4-15). Solomon's Temple was no exception. The treasures which he had gathered in the Temple were raided in the reign of his son, Rehoboam, by Shishak of Egypt (1 Ki. 14:26). Later kings, including even Hezekiah, who had adorned the Temple (2 Ki. 18:15f.), used the treasure to purchase allies (Asa, 1 Ki. 15:18) or to pay tribute and buy off an invader (Ahaz, 2 Ki. 16:8). The idolatrous kings added the appurtenances of a Canaanite shrine, including the symbols of pagan deities (2 Ki. 21:4; 23:1-12), while Ahaz introduced an altar of foreign type, displacing the laver, at the time of his submission to Tiglath-pileser III (2 Ki. 16:10-17). By the time of Josiah (*c.* 640 BC), three centuries after its construction, the Temple was in need of considerable repair, which had to be financed by the contributions of the worshippers (2 Ki. 22:4). In 587 BC it was looted by Nebuchadrezzar and sacked (2 Ki. 25:9, 13-17). Even after the destruction men came to sacrifice there (Je. 41:5).

Herod's Temple. This drawing shows the S approaches to the Temple Mount from the SW, where terraced steps descend from the W entry to the Royal Stoa (foreground). It should be related to the plan on p.104 and the views on pp.106–107 and 110-111. Within this vast and magnificent enclosure, open to Gentiles, was the Inner Temple, reserved for Israel .

Herod's Temple

Herod's Temple

The building of Herod's Temple, commenced early in 19 BC, was an attempt to reconcile the Jews to their Idumaean king rather than to glorify God. Great care was taken to respect the sacred area during the work, even to the training of 1,000 priests as masons to build the shrine. Although the main structure was finished within ten years (c. 9 BC), work continued until AD 64.

As a basis for the Temple buildings and to provide a gathering-place, an area about 450 m (c. 1,478 ft) from N to S and about 300 m (c. 985 ft) from E to W was made level. In places the rock surface was cut away, but a large part was built up with rubble and the whole enclosed by a wall of massive stone blocks (normally about 1m (c. 3 ft) high and up to 5 m (c. 16 ft) long cf. Mk. 13:1). At the SE corner, overlooking the Kidron ravine, the inner courtyard was about 45 m (c. 148 ft) above the rock. Perhaps the parapet above this corner was the pinnacle of the Temple (Mt. 4:5). Stretches of this wall still stand. One gateway pierced the N wall (Tadi Gate), but was apparently never used, and one led through the wall on the E (under the present Golden Gate). Traces of the two Herodian gates on the S side are still visible beneath the Mosque of el-Aqsa. Ramps led upwards from these to the level of the court. Four gates faced the city on the W. One at least was approached by viaducts across the Tyropoeon valley.

At the NW corner the fortress of Antonia dominated the enclosure, its garrison always at hand to subdue any unrest in the Temple (cf. Lk. 13:1; Acts 21:31–35). The high priest's robes were stored therein as a token of subjection.

Top left: the SE corner of Herod's Temple from the Mt of Olives. In this early morning view the S wall is in shadow on the right of the picture (the wall projecting from its centre is later work and should be ignored). The steps leading up to the S wall correspond to the nearer flight, below the small double gate on the S wall, in the drawing on the previous page.

Middle left: the Great Join, at the S end of the E wall of the Temple Mount (looking S). The further masonry is a section of wall added to an older one by Herod. Note the difference between the smoothly finished Herodian stones and the rougher bosses of the older ones. There is an arch (formerly a vault supporting steps leading up to an entry) in the Herodian walling. The older masonry is compared by Kenyon with the Persian architecture in Phoenicia (at Eshmun near Sidon, and at Byblos), and assigned to Zerubbabel (c. 516 BC).

Bottom left: Herodian masonry of Temple Mount, detail. These stones are laid as ashlars (square-cut stones) in regular horizontal rows (averaging 3-4ft, c. 0.9-1.3m, in height) without mortar and with precise joints. The 'peg' used for winching has been left on the stone.

The outer court of the Temple was surrounded by a portico, inside the walls. As described by Josephus (*Ant.* 15. 410–416), the S porch had four rows of columns and was called the Royal Porch. The porticoes of the other sides each had two rows. Solomon's Porch stretched along the E side (Jn. 10:23; Acts 3:11; 5:12). In these colonnades the scribes held their schools and debates (*cf.* Mk. 11:27; Lk. 2:46; 19:47) and the merchants and money-changers had their stalls (Lk. 19:45–46; Jn. 2:14–16). The inner area was raised slightly above the Court of the Gentiles and surrounded by a balustrade. Notices in Gk. and Lat. warned that no responsibility could be taken for the probable death of any Gentile who ventured within. Two of these inscriptions have been found. Four gates gave access on the N and S sides and one on the E. This last had doors of Corinthian bronze-work and may be the Beautiful Gate of Acts 3:2.

The first court inside (Women's Court) contained the chests for gifts towards the expenses of the services (Mk. 12:41–44). Men were allowed into the Court of Israel, raised above the Court of the Women, and at the time of the Feast of Tabernacles could enter the innermost (Priests') Court to circumambulate the altar. This was built of unhewn stone, 22 cubits away from the porch (*cf.* Mt. 23:35). The plan of the shrine copied Solomon's. The porch was 100 cubits wide and 100 cubits high. A doorway 20 cubits wide and 40 high gave entry, and one half that size led into the holy place. This was 40 cubits long and 20 cubits wide. A curtain divided the holy place from the inner sanctuary (the veil, Mt. 27:51; Mk. 15:38; *cf.* 2 Ch. 3:14). The inner sanctuary was 20 cubits square and, like the holy place, 40 cubits high. An empty room above the holy place and the inner sanctuary rose to the height of the porch, 100 cubits, thus making a level roof. Three storeys of chambers surrounded the N, S and W sides to a height of 40 cubits. Golden spikes were fixed on the roof to prevent birds from perching there.

The magnificent structure of cream stone and gold was barely finished (AD 64) before it was destroyed by the Roman soldiery (AD 70). The golden candelabrum, the table of show-bread and other objects were carried in triumph to Rome, as depicted on the Arch of Titus.

Top right: vault against S wall of the Temple Mount. This vault supported a street or terrace built against the outside of the wall. Roman forces under Titus destroyed these vaults by fire in AD 70.

Bottom right: blistered stonework of the wall where the vaults supporting an external terrace have been lost. The height and shape of the 'blistering' indicates a series of stepped vaults.

The Holy Land today

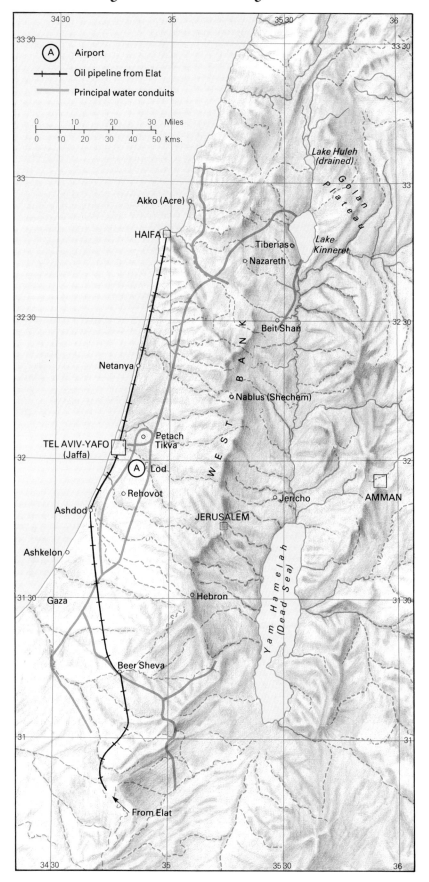

Airport

Oil pipeline from Elat

Principal water conduits

0 10 20 30 Miles

0 10 20 30 40 50 Kms.

Lake Huleh
(drained)

Golan Plateau

Akko (Acre)

HAIFA

Tiberias

Nazareth

Lake Kinneret

W E S T   B A N K

Beit Shan

Netanya

Nablus (Shechem)

TEL AVIV-YAFO
(Jaffa)

Petach Tikva

Lod

Rehovot

Jericho

AMMAN

Ashdod

JERUSALEM

Ashkelon

Yam Hamelah
(Dead Sea)

Gaza

Hebron

Beer Sheva

From Elat

Few areas of the world can have suffered so severely or so constantly from warfare and destruction as the Holy Land. Partly because of its strategic location on the coastal edge of the Fertile Crescent, and also precisely because it *is* a holy land for three great world religions, its history has been a record of violence: invasions and wars occurred throughout OT times and persisted in the days of the Maccabaean, Roman, Byzantine, Arab and Seljuk empires and under Crusader and Ottoman control. All of these, and more, were interspersed for good measure with periodic raids by the tribes of the E deserts driving towards the coast.

Repeated destruction led to the abandonment of settlements and the loss of forest and soil cover. Administrative neglect and the diversion of world economic attention away from the Mediterranean produced a situation in which, by the mid-nineteenth century, the country possessed not a single road, and its pastoral subsistence economy was little different from that which Abraham had known.

Among the factors which can be identified as ushering in a new era are the following:
1. a revival of interest in the land itself among Europeans, from 1860 onwards, with the Palestine Exploration Fund taking a lead;
2. the first Jewish settlements of the modern era on the coast in the 1870s; **3.** construction of the first railway (Gaza-Jerusalem), opened in 1892; **4.** urbanization of the central littoral and the growth of the new city of Tel Aviv (1922:15,000 inhabitants; 1983: urbanized area one million); **5.** opening of the modern port of Haifa in 1933; **6.** proclamation of the state of Israel, 1948.

Although this last development was born out of war and has generated a new era of conflict, the cumulative impacts on the landscape of the past half-century have been very striking. Briefly, they are the product of:

The spread of irrigation. The main change has been one of scale: from small-scale irrigation by well or runnel to major water transfers by aqueduct or pipe. Like California, the Holy Land has the problem that most of the water is in the N, while most of the irrigable land is in the S. The water supplies of Galilee are therefore critical, not only to Israel but also to Jordan, which has its own irrigation projects; the two countries must divide available resources between them. In Israel, where all water rights are owned by the state, transfer takes place over the full length of the country, from Galilee to the Negeb. Tel Aviv is supplied by the same means.

The Holy Land as it is today.

The commercialization of agriculture. The former subsistence economy is being steadily replaced by cash-crop production of fruits and vegetables, largely grown under irrigation. These compete in export markets not only in W Europe but also — in the case of Jordan's products — in the expanding markets of the Arab oil states.

Conservation and afforestation. To arrest the destructive process of erosion which has continued for so long, modern conservation methods have been introduced, as well as a revival and extension of the ancient practice of terracing hillsides. The planting of trees fixes bare slopes and produces wind breaks. It is too late to recover the soil losses of centuries, but it is at least possible to minimize them in the future.

The growth of industry. Difficult as this growth has been in an area whose resources of fuels and metals are negligible, it has been vital to the economic life of Israel, where so many immigrants have arrived from urban-industrial backgrounds in Europe. Lack of raw materials has in part been compensated by the skills these immigrants possess, and the growth of the urban core around Tel Aviv has been spectacular.

The colonization of empty areas. On Israel's proclamation day, in 1948, the Jewish population was about 650,000. Since then it has quadrupled. To accommodate this increase, Israel has established hundreds of rural settlements — the *Kibbutz* and the *moshav* — many of them in empty areas where long-deserted towns or villages have been revived. At the same time, large numbers of Arabs have fled or been displaced from existing settlements, and have either had to be resettled or have remained as refugees. Between nation and nation, cause and counter-cause, the distribution of population in the Holy Land has been profoundly altered since 1948.

*Irrigation pipe,
Quetara Kibbutz.*

The Holy Land today

Right: Modern Tel Aviv.

Far right: Jerusalem ancient and modern: the Lion Gate, the Old City and modern buildings beyond.

Below: Picking up peppers in a Kibbutz.

Time charts

1 MESOPOTAMIA

3rd-2nd millennia BC (main periods with selected reigns)
3100-2700 Uruk IV-Early Dynastic I Periods
2600-2370 3rd Early Dynastic Period
2370-2228 Old Akkadian (Agade) Period
   2306-2292 Maništusu
   2254-2230 Šar-kali-šarri
2113-1991 3rd Dynasty of Ur
   2113-2096 Ur-Nammu
   2037-2029 Šu-Sin
   2028-2004 Ibbi-Sin
1991-1786 Isin-Larsa Dynasties
   2017-1985 Išbi-Erra
   1934-1924 Lipit-Ištar
1894-1595 Old Babylonian Period (1st Dynasty of Babylon)
   1792-1750 Hammurabi
   1646-1626 Ammisaduqa
1605-1150 Kassite Period

1st millennium BC
Assyrian Empire
   883-859 Ashurnasirpal II
   858-824 Shalmaneser III
     (853 *Battle of Qarqar*)
   823-811 Shamshi-Adad
   810-783 Adad-nirari III
   782-773 Shalmaneser IV
   772-756 Ashurdan
   755-745 Ashurnirari V
   744-727 Tiglath-pileser III
   726-722 Shalmaneser V
   721-705 Sargon II
   704-681 Sennacherib
   680-669 Esarhaddon
   668-630 Ashurbanipal
   629-627 Ashuretililani
   626-612 Sinsharishkun
     (612 *Fall of Nineveh*)
   612-609 Ashuruballit
     (609 *Fall of Haran*)

Babylonian Empire
   626-605 Nabopolassar
   605-562 Nebuchadrezzar II
   562-560 Amēl-Marduk (Evil-merodach)
     (562 *Captive Jehoiachin favoured by Amēl-Marduk*)
   560-556 Neriglissar
   556   Labashi-Marduk
   556-539 Nabonidus, Belshazzar
     (*co-regents 549-539*)
     (539 *Fall of Babylon*)

Persian Empire
   539-530 Cyrus
   530-522 Cambyses
   522-486 Darius I
   486-465/4 Xerxes I (Ahasuerus)
   464-423 Artaxerxes I
   423-404 Darius II Nothus
   404-359 Artaxerxes II Mnemon
   359/8-338/7 Artaxerxes III Ochus
   338/7-336/5 Arses
   336/5-331 Darius III Codomanus
   331-323 Alexander of Macedon

2 EGYPT

3rd millennium BC
*c.*3100-2680 Archaic Period (Protodynastic): Dynasties 1-2
*c.*2680-2180 Old Kingdom or Pyramid Age: Dynasties 3-6 (*First great flowering of Egyptian culture*)
*c.*2180-2040 1st Intermediate Period: Dynasties 7-11

2nd millennium BC
*c.*2134-1786 Middle Kingdom: Dynasties 11-12 (*Second great age of Egyptian culture*)
*c.*1786-1540 2nd Intermediate Period: Dynasties 13-17 (*including the Hyksos*)
*c.*1552-1069 New Kingdom or Empire: Dynasties 18-20 (*Third great period in Egyptian civilization*)
   1552-1305 (or 1294) 18th Dynasty (selected reigns):
     1490-1437 (or 1479-1426) Tuthmosis III
     1390-1353 (or 1394-1357) Amenophis III
     1361-1345 (or 1365-1349) Amenophis IV/ Akhenaten
   1305-1198 (or 1294-1187) 19th Dynasty (selected reigns):
     1305-1304 (or 1294-1293) Rameses I
     1304-1290 (or 1293-1279) Sethos I
     1290-1224 (or 1279-1213) Rameses II
     1224-1214 (or 1213-1203) Merenptah
   1198-1069 (or 1187-1069) 20th Dynasty (*i.e.* Setnakht and Rameses III-XI)

1st millennium BC
*c.*1069-332 Late Period: Dynasties 21-31 (*Long period of decay interspersed with occasional brief periods of recovery*) (selected reigns):
   945-715 22nd Dynasty
     945-924 Shoshenq I (Shishak)
   716-664 25th Dynasty
     716-702 Shabako ('Shabaka')
     702-690 Shebitku ('Shabataka')
     690-664 Taharqa ('Tirhakah')
   664-525 26th Dynasty
     664-656 Tanwetamani ('Tanutamen')
     664-610 Psammeticus I
     610-595 Neco II
     595-589 Psammeticus II
     589-570 Apries (Hophra)
*c.*332-30 Hellenistic Period
   *c.*332-323 Alexander the Great
   323-285 Ptolemy I Soter
     (satrap 323-305/4, king 305/4-285)
   285-246 Ptolemy II Philadelphus
   246-221 Ptolemy III Euergetes
   221-205 Ptolemy IV Philopator
   205-180 Ptolemy V Epiphanes
   180-145 Ptolemy VI Philometor
   145   Ptolemy VII Neos Philopator
   145-116 Ptolemy VIII Euergetes II

....
51-30 Cleopatra VII
30-   Roman province

Later history

*c.*30 BC-AD 641 Roman and Byzantine Epochs
Egypt (Coptic) becomes part of Christendom.
This is followed by the Islamic period, lasting to the
present day.

3   SYRIA

Hellenistic Period

312-64 BC The Seleucids

312-281 Seleucus I Nikator
281-261 Antiochus I Soter
261-246 Antiochus II Theos
246-226 Seleucus II Kallinikos
226-223 Seleucus III Soter
223-187 Antiochus III the Great
187-175 Seleucus IV Philopator
175-164 Antiochus IV Epiphanes
164-161 Antiochus V Eupator
161-150 Demetrius I Soter
150-145 Alexander Balas
145-138 Demetrius II Nikator
145-142 Antiochus VI Epiphanes
142-138 Tryphon
138-129 Antiochus VII Sidetes
129-125 Demetrius II Nikator
128-123 Alexander II Zebinas
....

64-   Roman province

4   BIBLICAL HISTORY

From Abraham to Saul

(There are two possible sets of dates for this early period.
See pp.38–39.)

Higher chronology	Lower chronology	
*c.*2165-1990 BC	*c.*2000-1825 BC	Abraham
*c.*2065-1885	*c.*1900-1720	Isaac
*c.*2000-1860	*c.*1840-1700	Jacob
*c.*1910-1800	*c.*1750-1640	Joseph
*c.*1875	*c.*1700	Entry into Egypt
*c.*1450	*c.*1260	Exodus
*c.*1380-1050	*c.*1200-1050	Judges period

The Monarchy

1050 (or 1045)-931/930 BC The United Monarchy

1050 (or 1045)-1011/10 Saul
1011/10-971/70   David
971/70-931/30   Solomon

931/30-587 The Divided Monarchy

JUDAH	ISRAEL
931/30-913 Rehoboam	931/30-910/09
(925 *Sheshonq invades*	Jeroboam I
Palestine)	910/09-909/08 Nadab
913-911/10 Abijam	909/08-886/85 Baasha
911/10-870/69 Asa	886/85-885/84 Elah
870/69-848 Jehoshaphat	885/84 Zimri
(co-regent 873/72-)	885/84 Tibni
848-841 Jehoram	885/84-874/73 Omri
(co-regent from 853)	874/73-853 Ahab

Simplified diagram of the history of Israel from patriarchal times to the fall of Jerusalem in AD 70.

Time Charts

841 Ahaziah
841-835 Athaliah
835-796 Joash
796-767 Amaziah
767-740/39 Azariah
 (Uzziah) (co-regent
 from 791/90)
740/39-732/31 Jotham
 (co-regent from 750)
732/31-716/15 Ahaz
 (co-regent from
 744/43; senior
 partner from 735)
716/15-687/86 Hezekiah
687/86-642/41
 Manasseh (co-regent
 from 696/95
642/41-640/39 Amon
640/39-609 Josiah
609 Jehoahaz
609-597 Jehoiakim
(605 *Battle of
 Carchemish. Daniel
 and his friends are
 taken to Babylon*)
597 Jehoiachin
(597 *2 Adar
 (15/16 March)
 Jerusalem taken by
 Nebuchadrezzar II.
 Many Jews exiled
 including Jehoiachin
 and Ezekiel*)
597-587 Zedekiah
(587 *Fall of Jerusalem.
 More Jews into exile*)

853-852 Ahaziah
852-841 Joram
841-814/13 Jehu
814/13-798 Jehoahaz
798-782/81 Jehoash
782/81-753 Jeroboam II
 (co-regent from 793/92)
753-752 Zechariah
752 Shallum
752-742/41 Menahem
742/41-740/39 Pekahiah
740/39-732/31 Pekah
732/31-723/22 Hoshea
(722 *Fall of Samaria*)

Synopsis of main events affecting the Holy Land from the exile to the end of the 1st century AD

538 Zerubbabel, Sheshbazzar and others
 return to Jerusalem
537 Rebuilding of the Temple begun
520 Temple-building resumed
516 Temple completed 3 Adar (10 March)
458 Ezra goes to Jerusalem
445-433 Nehemiah at Jerusalem
332 Palestine comes under the control of
 Alexander the Great
323 Death of Alexander
301 Ptolemy I of Egypt gains control of
 Palestine
198 Palestine passes from Egyptian to
 Syrian rule until 63
170/69 Antiochus IV Epiphanes launches his
 first campaign against Egypt
168 Antiochus' second Egyptian campaign
167 Antiochus' persecution of the Jews
 begins; pagan sacrifice in Jerusalem
 Temple. Mattathias inspires revolt at Modin
167-40 Maccabees/Hasmonaeans dominate Judaea
164 End of persecutions; purification of the

Temple by Judas Maccabaeus
150 BC-AD 70 General period of the Dead Sea Scrolls
 143/2-135/4 Simon the last Maccabee
135/4-104 John Hyrcanus I, the first
 Hasmonaean
103-76 Alexander Jannaeus expands Jewish
 kingdom
63 Pompey establishes Roman protectorate
 over Hasmonaean princes
40 Herod the Great king of Judaea
?8/7 BC Birth of John the Baptist
 Birth of Jesus
?29 Baptism of Jesus
 Death of John the Baptist
30 (Passover) Jesus in Jerusalem (Jn. 2:13)
30/31 (Dec./Jan.) Jesus in Samaria (Jn. 4:1-42)
31 (Feast of Tabernacles) Jesus in Jerusalem
 (Jn. 5:1)
32 (Passover) Feeding of 5,000 (Jn. 6:4)
 (Feast of Tabernacles) Jesus in Jerusalem
 (Jn. 7:20
 (Feast of Dedication) Jesus in Jerusalem
 (Jn. 10:22)
33 (Passover) Crucifixion and Resurrection,
 Pentecost
34/35 Paul's conversion
37/38 Paul's first visit to Jerusalem
46/47 Paul's first missionary journey
48 Apostolic Council in Jerusalem
48-51 Paul's second missionary journey
50 Paul reaches Corinth
53 Paul's third missionary journey begins
54–57 Paul in Ephesus
57 Paul's departure for Troas
58 Paul meets Titus in Europe
58-59 Paul in Macedonia and Achaia (and Illyria?)
59 Paul returns to Jerusalem
59-61 Paul imprisoned in Caesarea
61 Paul appeals to Caesar and departs for Rome
62 He arrives in Rome
62-64 He is imprisoned in Rome
?62 Martyrdom of James, brother of Jesus
66 Outbreak of war with Rome
70 Fall of Jerusalem to Titus
74 Fall of Jewish zealots at Masada
81-96 Persecution of Christians by Domitian
c. 100 Death of John

Hasmonaean rulers 142-37 BC
143/2-135/4 Simon the Maccabee
135/4-104 John Hyrcanus I
104-103 Aristobulus I
103–76 Alexander Jannaeus
76-67 Salome Alexandra
67-63 Aristobulus II
(63 *Pompey establishes Roman
 protectorate*)
63-40 Hyrcanus II
40 Herod the Great
 appointed King of Judaea
40-37 Antigonus
37 Herod the Great assumed power

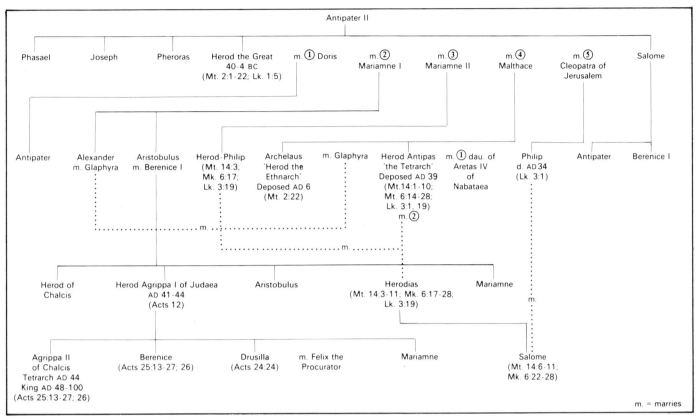

Simplified family tree of Herod the Great.

Herodian rulers
(Where dates are omitted the area reverted to direct Roman rule).

JUDAEA	GALILEE	ITURAEA *etc.*
37-4 BC King Herod the Great	37-4 BC King Herod the Great	22-4 BC King Herod the Great
4 BC - AD 6 Herod Archelaus, ethnarch	4 BC - AD 39 Herod-Antipas, tetrarch	4 BC - AD 34 Herod Philip, tetrarch
41-44 King Herod Agrippa I	39-44 King Herod Agrippa I	37-44 King Herod Agrippa I
	56/61-93*(?) (parts) King Herod Agrippa II	50-93(?) King Herod Agrippa II

* From AD 56 or 61 Agrippa II (d. AD 93?) ruled East Lower Galilee and South Peraea; whether he retained them after AD 70 is not known.

Roman governors
Between the rule of Archelaus and Herod Agrippa I:

6-9 AD	Coponius
9-12	M. Ambivius
12-15	Annius Rufus
15-26	Valerius Gratus
26-36	Pontius Pilate
36-37	Marullus
37-41	Herennius Capito

Between Herod Agrippa I and the Jewish Revolt:

44-46	Cuspius Fadus
46-48	Tiberius Alexander
48-52	Ventidius Cumanus
52-60	M. Antonius Felix
60-62	Porcius Festus
62-64	Clodius Albinus
64-66	Gessius Florus

5 ROMAN EMPIRE

Roman emperors (a selective contemporary list)

27 BC - AD 14	Augustus
14-37	Tiberius
37-41	Gaius (Caligula)
41-54	Claudius
54-68	Nero
69	The Year of the Four Emperors (Galba, Otho, Vitellius and Vespasian)
69-79	Vespasian
79-81	Titus
81-96	Domitian
96-98	Nerva
98-117	Trajan
117-138	Hadrian
138-161	Antoninus Pius
161-181	Marcus Aurelius

Further reading

FOR THE GENERAL READER THE FOLLOWING
BOOKS ARE SUGGESTED:

Old Testament
Y. Aharoni, *The Land of the Bible*, second edition (Burns
and Oates, 1979).
Denis Baly, *The Geography of the Bible* (Lutterworth, 1957).
C. Burney, *From Village to Empire: an introduction to Near
Eastern Archaeology* (Phaidon, 1977).
P. R. S. Moorey, *Biblical Lands* (Elsevier-Phaidon, 1975).
D. J. Wiseman (ed.), *Peoples of Old Testament Times*
(Oxford University Press, 1975).

New Testament
M. Cary and H. H. Scullard, *A History of Rome down to the
Reign of Constantine* (Macmillan, 1975).
E. Schürer, *The History of the Jewish People in the age of Jesus
Christ* (revised 1973 and 1979, eds. G. Vermes, F. Millar
and M. Black) (T. & T. Clark, 1973).
J. Wilkinson, *Jerusalem as Jesus knew it: Archaeology as
Evidence* (Thames and Hudson, 1978, reprinted with
corrections as *The Jerusalem Jesus knew*, 1982).
The Oxford Classical Dictionary, second edition (Oxford,
1972) has short accounts of all matters connected with
the Greeks and Romans.

FOR THOSE INTERESTED IN A MORE DETAILED
STUDY OF ARCHAEOLOGY:

Student Map Manual: Historical Geography of the Bible Lands
(Zondervan Publishing House, 1979).

Those unfamiliar with archaeological work are often
baffled in their attempts to keep up to date with new
excavations. It is worth pointing out that the English-
language journals *Biblical Archaeologist, Israel Exploration
Journal*, and *Palestine Exploration Quarterly* can be used
and understood by non-specialists; and each is the organ
of a society which anyone interested in archaeology can
join. Important bibliographies (from a card-index
established by N. Glueck) are published in *HUCA* (*Hebrew
Union College Annual*) for 1971 and 1981. Reports on
current work are made in *IEJ* and in the *Revue biblique* (in
French).

Acknowledgments

Acknowledgment of the sources of illustrations
The publishers have made every effort to trace the
copyright holders of illustrations in this book. Should any
have been inadvertently missed, copyright holders are
asked to contact the publishers.

Relief maps
Relief maps © Copyright George Philip and Sons Ltd and
Inter-Varsity Press appear on pages: 16, 19, 21, 28 (2), 29,
33, 35, 36, 40, 43, 44, 45, 46, 47, 49, 50, 51, 52, 55, 67, 71,
72, 74, 75, 80, 81 (2), 82, 85, 88, 89, 90, 91 and 95.

Contour maps © Copyright Djambatan b.v.,
Cartographers, The Hague, Holland, pages 9 and 87.

End-papers: from the archive of the Palestine Exploration
Fund.

The six archaeological sites maps appearing on pp.30, 38,
53, 54, 78 and 79 are based on information from the
Student Map Manual, published by Zondervan Publishing
House (1979).

Diagrams, charts, illustrations and plans
All diagrams, charts, line drawings, colour illustrations
and town plans have been specially prepared for Inter-
Varsity Press, some of them for *The Illustrated Bible
Dictionary* (1980). The publishers are glad to acknowledge
their indebtedness to sources indicated:

MODEL OF PART OF THE HOLY LAND, p.8
Supplied by the Palestine Exploration Fund.

SECTION OF THE DEAD SEA, p.21
Based on information given in E. Orni and E. Efrat,
Geography of Israel (Israel Programme for Scientific
Translations, 1966), p.88.

SECTION THROUGH A TELL, p.25
Based on A. R. Millard, *The Bible BC* (IVP, 1977), p.10.

PLAN OF TEL BEERSHEBA, p.26
After Y. Aharoni, 'The Beersheba Excavations' in *Tel Aviv*
2 (1975), p.148.

RECONSTRUCTION OF THE QUMRAN SETTLEMENT,
pp.60-61 and jacket of the British edition of *New Bible
Atlas*.
Based on a model in the Pittsburgh Theological Seminary
and set against a photograph of the surrounding terrain
by Rex Nicholls.

PLAN OF THE QUMRAN SETTLEMENT, p.62
Based on R. de Vaux, *Archaeology and the Dead Sea Scrolls*
(Oxford University Press, 1973), pl.39.

PLAN OF THE MASADA FORTRESS, p.68
Based on Y. Yadin, *The Excavation of Masada, 1963-4,
Preliminary Report* (Israel Exploration Society, 1965).

GREEK NEW TESTAMENT MANUSCRIPTS, p.76
From Victor Martin, *Papyrus Bodmer II* (Evangile de Jean chap.1-14) (Bibliotheca Bodmeriana, 1961) pl.25-26 and p.27.

EARLY CHURCH CONGREGATIONS, p.83
After F. van der Meer and C. Mohrmann, *Atlas of the Early Christian World* (Nelson-Elsevier, 1953), map 1.

ATHENS, p.96
Based on ACA, p.155.

CORINTH, p.97
After ACA, p.155.

GROWTH OF JERUSALEM, pp.102-104
Based on Walter de Gruyter (ed.), *Atlas of Jerusalem*, maps 3:1, 3:2 and 3:6 (Jewish History Publications, 1973).

HEROD'S TEMPLE, p.109
Based on Y. Yadin (ed.), *Jerusalem Revealed* (Israel Exploration Society and Yale University Press, 1976), p.27.

HEROD'S FAMILY, p.119
Based on S. Perowne, *The Later Herods* (Hodder and Stoughton, 1958), table 1.

HERODIAN RULERS and ROMAN GOVERNORS, p.119
Based on *Oxford Bible Atlas*, second edition, 1974, pp.35 and 44.

Photographs

The photographs in the *New Bible Atlas* are reproduced by permission of the following persons or agencies:

John J. Bimson, p.37
British Museum, p.30
Maurice Chuzeville/Louvre Museum, p.48
Ken Garfield, p.8
Sonia Halliday/Laura Lushington Photographs, pp.20, 32, 34, 61, 69 (bottom), 105, 113, 114 (2) and 115
Michael Holford, p.96
John P. Kane, pp.110 (3) and 111 (2)
Middle East Photographic Archive (MEPhA), pp.22 and 106
Alan R. Millard, p.97
Nigel Press Associates Ltd., pp.12-13
Robert Pitt, p.74
Popperfoto Photographic Agency, p.18
Tel Aviv University, p.27
John C. Trever, p.63
Donald J. Wiseman, p.93 (2)
Y. Yadin, Weidenfeld and Nicolson Archives, p.69 (top)

Additional text material

The bulk of the text of the *New Bible Atlas* was written by the contributing and consulting editors specially for this work. In addition a few articles from *The Illustrated Bible Dictionary* (1980) have been used as source material and we are grateful to the following authors for their consent to our using their work in this way:

HEROD THE GREAT, p.67
The late F. F. Bruce, M.A., D.D., F.B.A., formerly Rylands Professor of Biblical Criticism and Exegesis in the University of Manchester.

PAUL'S 'MISSIONARY JOURNEYS', pp.80-81
E. E. Ellis, Ph.D., Research Professor of New Testament Literature, New Brunswick Theological Seminary, New Jersey.

ASIA MINOR: THE SEVEN CHURCHES (in part), pp. 82-83
E. M. B. Green, M.A., B.D., Professor of Evangelism, Regent College, Vancouver, BC, Canada.

ASIA MINOR: THE SEVEN CHURCHES, pp.82-83
The late C. H. Hemer, M.A., Ph.D., formerly Research Fellow, Tyndale House, Cambridge.

PALESTINE: CLIMATE, p.14
: PRINCIPAL WATER-COURSES, p.16
THE NEGEB, pp.22-23
J. M. Houston, M.A., B.Sc., D.Phil., Chancellor of Regent College, Vancouver, BC.

THE TEMPLES OF SOLOMON AND HEROD, pp. 108-111
A. R. Millard, M.A., M.Phil., F.S.A., Rankin Reader in Hebrew and Ancient Semitic Languages, University of Liverpool.

JERUSALEM, pp.106–107
D. F. Payne, B.A., M.A., Academic Registrar, London Bible College.

ASIA MINOR: THE SEVEN CHURCHES (in part), pp.82-83
M. J. S. Rudwick, M.A., Ph.D., Sc.D., formerly Professor of History of Science, The Free University, Amsterdam.

THE TETRARCHS, p.70
D. H. Wheaton, M.A., B.D., Vicar of Christ Church, Ware; Canon of St Albans Cathedral.

Design and typesetting

Swanston Graphics Limited
Design: Irene Bates and Tony Hoyle with Andrea Fairbrass, Anne Hall, Phyllis Hoyle, James Mills-Hicks, Rex Nicholls, Ivan Sendall and Malcolm Swanston
Typesetting: Andrew Bright and Jeanne Radford

Editorial and production

Inter-Varsity Press
Editorial: Derek Wood with Katy Coutts, Marie Cross and Angela Middleton
Production: Michael Sims

Index

Index

Index

Index